HOW IT WAS

Memories of Growing Up in the 1930s,
'40s and '50s

Howard Temperley

authorHOUSE®

AuthorHouse™ UK Ltd.
500 Avebury Boulevard
Central Milton Keynes, MK9 2BE
www.authorhouse.co.uk
Phone: 08001974150

First published by AuthorHouse   9/30/2010

ISBN: 978-1-4520-7087-2 (sc)
ISBN: 978-1-4520-7086-5 (hc)

This book is printed on acid-free paper.

To my grandchildren.

I hope that they will get as
much pleasure from exploring
their worlds as I did from
exploring mine.

Contents

1: PIT HEAPS AND LEGENDS

AT THE FIRST sight of me my father fled into the street. Knowing little about babies and nothing whatever about childbirth he had been unprepared for the sight that confronted him. Mine had been a difficult birth ending in a forceps delivery. Tired of hanging around he had gone to work as usual so that by the time he got back to the nursing home it was all over, my mother was asleep and there was I being held up for his inspection. He'd been warned that I might look a little bruised. What alarmed him, however, was not that there were bruises, but that my head looked unlike that of any human being he had ever set eyes on. It was pear-shaped. The features below, by his account, looked much like those of any other new-born baby, which is to say a bit squashed and bleary-eyed, but what made it truly amazing was that the cranium, in fact everything from the eyebrows upward, tapered to a point like a dunce's cap. His first-born, he concluded, was an idiot.

Naturally the nurses did not dare tell him that. How could they say: "Here's your son, a bouncing boy, weighs eight-and-a-half pounds, only unfortunately he is an idiot." They wouldn't have told my mother either. The truth would have to come from a higher authority. Walking the streets, he realized that sooner or later it would have to be confronted. Stopping at a telephone kiosk, he pushed two-pence into the slot, dialled the number, pressed button A, and asked to speak to Dr Nichols.

"He is normal isn't he?" Father quavered.

"Of course not," was the robust reply.

I had given him, Father would later say, the worst night of his life.

The next day it was all sorted out. Babies, he was told, often got their heads squeezed without it doing their brains any harm. Wait a week or two and I would begin to look more normal. In his retelling of the tale Father always insisted that it was Dr Nichols who had misheard. Mother, the more level headed of the two, suspected otherwise. Father, as she used to say, was a "worrier." So it turned out that I was not an idiot, at least not the kind of idiot that was initially supposed.

No comets or eruptions heralded my arrival. In so far as 16 November 1932 is a date to be remembered it is on account of its being in the middle of the very worst month of the very worst year of the Great Depression. It was the week after Roosevelt was elected President of the United States and the week before Hitler was first offered the Chancellorship of Germany. Twenty per cent of the world's industrial workforce was unemployed. Japan, in defiance of League of Nations, had begun carving out an empire for itself in the Far East. Things were coming apart

Sunderland had been particularly hard hit. Even at the best of times it had never been a place of beauty. Industry was its speciality. With its cobbled back streets and rows of back-to-back houses it was a place that few went out of their way to visit or chose to linger longer than circumstances required. Two centuries earlier it had been little more than a fishing village at the mouth of the Wear. But then had come the industrial revolution and with it the growing demand for coal and shipping, drawing in workers from as far away as Ireland and turning it into a boom town. In its heyday it had had been a place of Promethean energy, the North East's second city, turning out more ships than the Clyde and exporting more coal than the Tyne. But that was in the past. Now, with half its workforce unemployed, its shipyards idle and its coal mines nearing the end of their days it was a town largely bereft of purpose, a workshop without work.

Hitherto my parents had managed better than most. Since their marriage eight years earlier they had lived at 31 Azalea Terrace, a spacious Victorian town house on a tree-lined street in what up to then had been a solid middle-class neighbourhood. But houses were being bought up to be converted into flats and the area was going down. We were among the last to flee. I remember it only as the slum it later became – whole families living in a single room, children without shoes, toddlers without pants, litter everywhere. It was bombed in the war and what was left got into such a bad state that eventually it all had to be torn down.

So the only family home I remember is 3 Braeside, a small three-bedroom semi on the southern edge of town, one of millions built in slightly varying shapes and sizes during the inter-war years. For my parents it was something of a come-down. Nevertheless, anxious to preserve middle-class proprieties only one of our two downstairs living rooms was put to regular use, the other being kept for "best," which is to say for when we had visitors, but as we rarely had visitors it remained virtually unused. What we ought to have done was run the two rooms together, as some of our neighbours had done, but that would have required calling in builders and running up higher heating bills – in other words expense, always a sensitive topic so far as my father was concerned. Never having had any money to speak of he was naturally cautious about using what little he had, his only extravagance, as I have belatedly come to realise, being his willingness to invest in his children's education. So almost our entire family life was spent in one small room where we ate, listened to the wireless, read books, pursued our various hobbies, and, in winter, huddled around the fire to keep warm.

Nowadays, when practically everyone lays claim to being middle class, it's hard to say what middle-classness amounts to, but in the 1930s we must have been about as solidly middle class as it was possible to be, at least by Sunderland standards. In short we lived in a style that would nowadays be associated with considerable poverty. Like the other housewives of the neighbourhood my mother spent a good part of every day shopping, plodding from grocer to baker to butcher, buying a bunch of carrots here, a packet of rice there and picking up a packet of 20 Players along the way. J B Priestley in his 1933 *English Journey* deplored the proliferation of small shops and the poor quality of the produce they offered. What England needed, he said, were "food warehouses," properly managed establishments where the produce would be fresh and shoppers would be saved the traipsing about. Eventually we would get them in the form of supermarkets, but not for another half century, too late for my mother and the women of her generation.

Domestic central heating was then unknown, as were refrigerators, dish washers, clothes washers, food processors and practically every other gadget found in the modern kitchen. A few people had telephones, usually because of some particular need, as in the case of midwives and ships' officers, a number of whom lived nearby. None of us, at least in our immediate neighbourhood, was grand enough to own a motor car. Doctors had cars for obvious reasons, as did some lawyers, businessmen and others who used them for professional purposes, as in the case of my Uncle Walter, a marine engineer. Cousin Fred had a car by virtue of owning a garage and was spoken of within the family as being "a good driver" much as one might speak today of someone who had taken up hang gliding, mountaineering, or some other pastime regarded as hazardous and requiring no small measure of skill and determination.

It was a time when policemen still walked the streets, milk was delivered in bottles, tea came loose, men whistled as they worked, fire engines were drawn by horses and trolley buses were thought ultra modern. Men wore shirts with detachable collars and seldom ventured out of doors without a hat, which they doffed on encountering those of their acquaintance. Generally speaking the type of hat they wore denoted the class to which they belonged. Working men made do with flat caps. Middle-class men like my father owned a variety of hats: a bowler for going to work; a trilby for going out in the evening and a flat cap for walks in the country. Grander folk, like the governors of my school, owned top hats, which they wore for formal occasions such as school speech days, ship launchings or when appearing on political platforms.

Maids wore frilly lace caps. We had a maid, Gladys, who slept in the small room at the top of the stairs. She came from Silksworth, the pit village up the road. Mining being men's work there was not much for unmarried women to do there, so living in a respectable home in return for bed, board and ten shillings a week was reckoned better than working in a pickle factory or clipping tickets on the trams. In fact Gladys was more of a nanny than a maid. Although she helped with the dusting and cleaning, her main job was looking after me, and, in due course, my younger brother Alan.

Pit Village

5

So middle-class life Sunderland-style was not quite as Hollywood would have pictured it. No Mrs. Minivers – or Mrs Dalloways for that matter – lived down our way. Yet compared to the unemployed living on 29s 3d a week dole money, scavenging on the slag heaps, hawking coal from door to door, walking their whippets, or simply watching the boats going in and out of the harbour there was no escaping the fact that we were privileged. We might not be rich enough to own a car but at least we were not malnourished, which was more than could be said for a good slice of the North East's population.

Most days Gladys would take me to the fire station to feed sugar lumps to the horses or to Barnes Park to feed bread to the ducks. My very earliest memory is of the time she took me to Backhouse Park to see King George V and Queen Mary. It must have been a long walk, for Backhouse Park is on the far side of town. All I can remember is that I was in a push chair and we were on a grassy knoll looking down on a road lined with schoolchildren clutching tiny Union Jacks. Gladys bought me a ha'penny one to wave when the King came.

The first we knew of his coming was when we heard a distant drumming that slowly grew louder until the band came marching over the brow of the hill and we got the full Oompah-Oompah. The bandsmen, led by a man with a baton, wore smart uniforms and carried shiny instruments. Perhaps it was because I had expected it to be a solemn occasion, the King being so important, that I could not believe my ears when, in pace with the marching, I heard someone in the band blowing enormous raspberries, raspberries of such joyous brazen irreverence as I had never heard or could have imagined. I looked around not daring to laugh, but no one else seemed to think it as funny as I did. However they were all excited and soon they were waving their flags, so I laughed and jumped up and down and waved my flag too. The King and Queen were in the biggest car. He had a beard and looked grave, but the Queen, who wore elbow-length gloves and a large hat, smiled and waved. After they had gone Gladys took me down to talk to the bandsmen who, it turned out, were friends of hers. As I had never imagined her having any life other than the one she led at 3 Braeside I wondered how she came to know them. They had unbuttoned their tunics and were putting their instruments in cases. She took me over to meet the man with the brass horn that blew the raspberries.

Because she never got angry however much of a mess I got into, and partly no doubt because she was younger and prettier, I preferred Gladys to Mother. Mother was the disciplinarian. She kept Father's old army swagger cane on a shelf in the hall and threatened to use it on me if I was naughty, although she never did. So when I needed cleaning up it would be Mother who would reprimand me but Gladys who would strip me off, boil up a kettle and sponge me down, as on the occasion a neighbour took me to the Roker Illuminations and I messed myself in he tram on the way back.

My most dramatic misadventure, however, was when I fell into the river and the postman brought me home. Mostly it wasn't much of a river, a muddy stream really. Perhaps it had rained the night before. Anyway, trying to leap across, one foot went in and came up without a shoe. I'd been scolded by Mother for coming home with dirty shoes. To arrive home with one shoe missing didn't bear thinking about. So I'd waded in to retrieve it and was struggling against the current when a hand came from nowhere, grabbed me and hauled me out.

When we first moved into Braeside there was still building going on all around. Gladys used to take the builders mugs of tea and I'd stay behind to bring the mugs back. After a while they got used to having me around and let me build sandcastles on their sand heap. "Watch out for the little bugger" they'd shout when a lorry came to deliver a new load or if I was in danger of having a brick dropped on my head. It seemed like a term of affection, so one day I called Gladys that, at which she wagged her finger and told me it was not a proper word to use. So I tried it out on Mother, from whom I got a sterner response. I had discovered the magical power of words! When Father returned home I was told to repeat what I had said.

"Little bucket," I proudly announced, but instead of its producing the effect I'd expected there were gales of laughter. Was I sure those were the words I had used?

"Yes."

More laughter. They couldn't get over it for days. They told the neighbours and the neighbours laughed too. For the life of me I couldn't work out what had gone wrong, nor would they tell me however much I pleaded.

The only regular visitors to 3 Braeside were Aunt Ethel and my cousin Elizabeth. Ethel was Mother's older sister. Both were heavy smokers. After meals there would be a throwing of cigarettes back and forth, each claiming it was her turn to offer. Meanwhile, Father, at the head of the table, would be lighting up his pipe. From breakfast until bedtime, domestic life at 3 Braeside was conducted in an agreeable cloud of pipe and cigarette smoke.

I did not look forward to my cousin's visits. Elizabeth was six months older than me and stronger. She was for ever being held up to me as an example of good behaviour. I didn't mind her being a goody-goody; what I objected to was that she used to beat me up. It was not just a matter of spontaneous squabbling over toys, although mostly it began that way. Why our mothers, instead of separating us, urged us on is hard to explain. My parents had waited eight years for me to arrive and Aunt Ethel and Uncle Walter had waited 12 for Elizabeth, so perhaps there was some element of sisterly rivalry involved. Whatever the explanation it meant that my first encounters with a contemporary of the opposite sex involved my being physically overpowered and half suffocated. I recall, too, Mother and Ethel being remarkably coy about putting us in the bath together. What they expected to happen I can't imagine. Whether at that age I noticed in what specifics Elizabeth and I differed I do not recall. Had she had cloven hooves or tiny angel's wings I doubt it would have struck me as being especially out of the ordinary. Later, when I was told that a sister was expected and Alan turned up I was puzzled as to why they didn't make the best of it and just dress him up as a girl and maybe that was somehow what he would become.

In a world where everything was strange one thing seemed as strange as another. Nor did people's explanations help. They told me sandwiches were called sandwiches because they had sand in them, which, because we mostly ate them on the beach, they generally did have. They said that if they didn't have sand in them they weren't proper sandwiches, so I should stop complaining and eat them up, because if I were a little Chinese boy I wouldn't have any sandwiches with or without sand, or, indeed, anything to eat at all, that being the way things were in China. It was all very puzzling.

Nevertheless, I soon became aware that there were certain matters into which it did not do to enquire too closely. It started one day while I was watching Mother dressing and she happened to expose her breasts. Having never had occasion to notice them before – Alan and I were bottle-fed

usually yielded enough crabs to fill three or four barrels. The Farnes were my first introduction to a world that existed quite independently of human beings, an experience that stirred my imagination even more than my visits to Hulne Park and Father's other former haunts. We would set off shortly after dawn, approaching the islands in an early-morning mist through which guillemots and puffins zoomed like winged projectiles. Grey seals, in the manner of portly gentlemen, would pop up to watch our passage. Then there were the terns fragile, light as air, and the more heavily built gannets that would hover and dive. On the way back to harbour the gulls would snatch from the air the fish heads and other scraps I threw them. Much as I loved Alnwick, I loved the Farnes more in that they offered a glimpse of a pristine world that had existed long before our time, a place of incessant activity where birds and animals went about their business much as they must have done before stone-age man and his successors happened by and began making a mess of things.

Our 1938 holiday in Beadnell was memorable for another reason in that Father borrowed a 4.10 shotgun and took me rabbit-shooting along the links. I doubt he had ever been much of a shot, fly fishing being more in his line. Every time he missed he'd curse in a way that I'd never heard him do before – and very likely he hadn't done since boyhood. Finally, with a triumphant "Ay, that-un's deed," he bowled one over.

Looking back I suspect it was a pivotal moment. If I had to say when my fascination with guns began I would have to say it was with his bowling over of that rabbit. Had he taken me trout fishing my life over the next decade might have been quite different. He *did* take me cod fishing, but that was like hauling up sacks of coal. What you could do with a gun was magical. You could stop a fast-running rabbit with a gun. You could pluck fast-flying birds out of the air with a gun. Catapults, slingshots, and bows and arrows were OK, but guns were better.

Thus were born two passions, one for shooting, the other for preserving nature, that were to dominate my early years. It did not occur to me then, nor did it until long after, that the two might conflict.

Back in Sunderland the talk of war percolated down even to Bev's and my level. Once, on the walk home from school, we thought it must have broken out for the sky was scribbled over with white contrails. Either it was war or the Martians had arrived. We ran all the way to Braeside, hammering on the door until Mother opened it, only to be told that they were vapour trails and nothing to worry about. It was just the Hurricanes from Usworth practising. She did not say what it was they were practising for.

2: AT THE EDGE OF THE STORM: 1939-45

IT WAS NOT UNTIL I reached the top of the street and saw Uncle Walter's Ford at the gate that I realised something unusual was happening. I'd meandered home from school in my usual desultory way. Now Gladys was catching me by the elbow and rushing me into the house. Bags were packed and standing in the hallway. Aunt Ethel and Elizabeth had turned up. War, I was told, had been declared. Father and Gladys would be staying, but Mother, Aunt Ethel, Elizabeth, Alan and I were leaving and would be away for some time. Plainly everyone was in a panic.

So off we went over the Scots border to Allanton, a tiny village in Berwickshire. By the time we got there it was dark. Our landlady, oil lamp in hand, greeted us in broad Scots. It was the first time I'd been in a house without electricity. The floors were stone flagged; there was an open fire, a blackened kettle on a hob and a cat asleep on a rag carpet. We children were hurried out to the loo, a smelly shed out back among the cabbages and Brussels sprouts before being despatched upstairs to bed. Up the wooden stairs we clomped, the landlady's oil lamp casting elongated shadows. Life in Allenton was going to be different.

Our flight had been more precipitate than most but others were also on the move. The next morning, as we sat in our landlady's front parlour eating fresh-baked buns from the bakery down the road, a man wearing an air-raid warden's armband popped in to show us the bell, a big brass affair he would ring to warn us of air raids. Presently a sizeable party of school children and teachers bearing gas masks and suitcases approached with the weary air of refugees fleeing an advancing army.

As they drew level with our window, faint but unmistakable, came the sound of the warden's bell. "Air raid," someone shouted. "Take cover," someone else shouted. Pandemonium ensued. Teachers and children swarmed into the house. A teacher fainted and was laid out flat in the stone-flagged hallway. While efforts were being made to revive her, the warden, looking sheepish, popped in to say he had only rung the bell to see if the sound carried.

That was the only moment of real excitement we experienced during the whole of our stay. On closer acquaintance Allanton turned out to be not so much a village as two straggling rows of houses sprung up for no apparent reason along the main road linking Coldstream and Eyemouth. Apart from the bakery, an inn and a post office that sold groceries, hardware and fishing tackle, that was about all there was. Allanton's only claim to fame was its proximity to two notable fishing rivers, the Whiteadder and Blackadder. Mounted in glass cases on the walls of the inn's foyer were surly looking salmon plucked from their waters.

Even trout were big game by our standards. Minnows and stickleback were more our line. Most afternoons we went down to the riverbank where Elizabeth and I busied ourselves catching them in a net while Alan slept in his push chair and Mother and Ethel sat knitting. Mornings and evenings I spent among the ruins of Blackadder Hall, now much overgrown, firing my catapult at rabbits, achieving many near misses but never actually managing to hit one. After a while, even that palled.

Occasionally Father and Uncle Walter paid us a visit. The journey was a good hundred miles. As banks opened on Saturday mornings and Walter, a marine engineer, was being kept furiously busy thanks to the demands of wartime, their stay with us was necessarily brief. We bought snares from the post office, which Father showed me how to set, but I never caught any rabbits. If there were local children, as presumably there were, Elizabeth and I had no contact with them. As the weeks passed, relations with our landlady worsened. With winter now approaching, going on like this was out of the question.

So, after a couple of months, like other families, we returned home to find that nothing much was happening there either. Schools were still closed. Enterprising local ladies had begun offering lessons, converting their drawing rooms into classrooms. I attended one such, arriving each day clutching one-and-sixpence. Unlike my regular school it contained children of all ages and operated only in the mornings. My personal task consisted of filling exercise books marked with lines a quarter of an inch and an inch apart in such a way that that the small letters of the words I copied touched the lower line and the tall letters the upper. Having lately learned that the early kings of England were illiterate, a stalwart bunch to judge from the battle scenes in my *Illustrated History of England*, I became increasingly doubtful as to the usefulness of the exercise. Eventually I punched another boy, a letter was written to my parents, and I ceased attending. As Christmas approached it began to seem as if the summer holidays would go on for ever.

Up to that time no one had any clear idea of what the effect of bombing would be. Nevertheless, it was possible to imagine casualties running into the millions, whole cities devastated and populations fleeing into the nearby countryside. Bev and I rather looked forward to it, never imagining that we might be the ones killed. So when the real thing actually occurred it proved something of a let-down. My first experience – it must have been early in 1940 – was on a Saturday morning. I was in town shopping with Father when there was a loud bang from Monkwearmouth across the river. This time there was no panic. Along with a crowd of other sightseers, we surged across the bridge to find out what had happened. Disappointingly, very little had. The bomb, aimed with unusual accuracy, had passed through a railway bridge and exploded harmlessly on the road below leaving a rather small crater.

More typical of those early sneak raids was one that occurred a few weeks later. I was visiting my Aunt Kate in Herrington a couple of miles out of town. It was a sunny afternoon and I was in the garden catching bees in a jam jar when there was the sound of a low-flying aircraft, as was not unusual, for Usworth aerodrome, home to a squadron of Hurricanes, was nearby. This, however, was not a Hurricane but a Messerschmitt 109, boldly marked with swastikas and black crosses, and there, sitting upright in his cockpit and clearly visible as he banked low over the house, was a real live German. As I watched he flew towards Silksworth Colliery, its enormous presence dominating the hilltop opposite, a target so large one would have thought it impossible to miss.

Nevertheless, the pilot released his bomb too soon, leaving a tiny crater in a cow pasture a good half mile short that we later went down to inspect. The cows appeared unharmed.

Those early sneak raids were presumably intended to probe our defences. The night raids that came later were a very different matter. Crouching in our shelter we could hear the planes overhead and feel the house shudder as the bombs fell. I recall the excitement of getting up early on bright sunny mornings to collect the shiny new-laid fragments of shell and bomb casing that littered the streets, all gnarled and twisted by the force of the high explosive they had contained,. Schools had by that time opened and along the way there would be houses sliced in half, their bedsteads, mirrors, and contrasting wallpapers indecently exposed to public view. When word reached us of a crashed plane Bev and I would bicycle over to inspect the wreckage and in the hope of being able to sneak through the police cordon and break off pieces to add to our souvenir collections. Like stamp collectors, we would swap our finds with other boys at school.

Daylight raids soon petered out, although I do remember one, probably in the autumn of 1940. The target must have been somewhere inland, for the planes, a dozen or so in formation, were high and headed back towards the North Sea and Germany. We stood in the garden watching the puffs of bursting ack-ack shells while the planes flew serenely onward.

"Never mind," a neighbour said as they disappeared over the rooftops, "the Navy will get 'em."

This was reassuring. Everyone knew we had the finest navy in the world. Even so, I could not help wondering why sailors, presumably firing from pitching decks, would manage so much better than our land-based gunners. However, it was said with such pride that it seemed unpatriotic to ask.

Yet the situation was plainly grim. Father reported that Jewish customers were changing their names. In the expectation that the bombing would get worse, or that the country would be invaded, a distinct albeit unmentionable possibility, some parents were sending their children to havens overseas. We had relatives in Montreal, a childless couple who said they would be delighted to have me. Our vicar's two sons, also bound for Montreal, came around to be introduced. They, too, would be sailing on the *City of Benares*, although on the voyage before mine. Four days and 600 miles out to sea they were torpedoed and both were lost along with most of the other children.

In consequence of this disaster it was decided that, rather than sending them out onto the high seas, it would be safer to keep children at home. Nevertheless, life in Sunderland was becoming distinctly dangerous. Collecting pieces of shrapnel might be fun, but a neighbour just up the road was struck dead on his own doorstep by just such a piece as I was picking up. Much of the damage to property was caused by incendiary bombs, cylinders not much larger than spray cans, the burned-out remains of which littered the town. Father took me down to see the two major department stores burning, sending up huge columns of smoke visible for miles around. As we watched there would be fresh cascades of flame and sparks as yet another floor collapsed. More to be feared than the incendiaries, however, were the high explosive bombs, most of all parachute bombs like the one that hit Victoria Hall and wiped out the whole surrounding area leaving nothing but the stumps of chimneys and a pattern of roads to show where houses had once been.

Once a week my father would depart at nightfall with a flask of coffee to spend the night on the roof of the bank, stirrup pump and bucket at the ready, in order to deal with any incendiary bombs that might come its way. Our local ARP wardens, similarly armed, would gather nightly in one or another neighbouring house while the women of the neighbourhood, plainly enjoying themselves no end, shuttled back and forth with coffee and sandwiches, the war having created a spirit of neighbourliness that had never existed before.

Most people had Anderson shelters, underground bunkers some six feet deep, dug in their gardens and roofed over with bent corrugated iron and soil. Although cheap to construct in terms of the materials used digging a hole of the size required took a lot of effort. Richer folk, like my cousin Fred up in Herrington, built stalwart brick shelters, windowless structures with iron doors that looked like mausoleums. Early in the bombing I was sent out there for safety. Being a heavy sleeper I failed to wake the first time I was carried to the shelter and as there were commonly several alarms a night I was left there to sleep while the rest trooped off to bed. Waking up some time later and wishing to go to the toilet I had no idea where I was, it being pitch dark. Groping around I could feel nothing but brick and iron. How long I was left like that I do not remember, nor do I recall whether I screamed or lay in terrified silence. What I do recall is its being already daylight when they finally released me and their apologising profusely to my parents later the same day.

Our own shelter was an idiosyncratic affair. Always on the look out for bargains, Father had spotted an advertisement for an interior shelter that was both inexpensive and easy to erect. It was, moreover, based on a principle the truth of which he had had ample opportunity to observe while serving in France in the Great War, namely that the sturdiest feature of every house is its chimney. A man duly arrived and in no time at all had moulded us a cosy lean-to cave made out of what looked like rabbit wire and plaster right next to the fireplace in our tiny living room. Although flimsy in appearance he assured us it would bear the full weight of a collapsing house. So there we cowered night after night while mayhem reigned outside.

The notion of sending me to Canada having fallen through, it was decided to send me to the Newcastle Royal Grammar School. As with our own precipitate flight to Berwickshire, the RGS had moved across the Pennines to Penrith, a small market town in an area principally devoted to the raising of sheep and so regarded as unlikely to attract the attention of

German bombers. Thus what had been a day school had transformed itself into an odd sort of boarding school in which the boys, instead of boarding in the school, lived in the town and the countryside round about.

In spite of its having been there for two years, at the time of my arrival living arrangements were still pretty makeshift. Half the boys lived with local families, the rest in old vicarages and other large houses requisitioned for use as hostels, each run by a housekeeper and supervised by one or more masters. So far as instruction was concerned, the RGS shared facilities with Penrith Grammar School on a half day basis, otherwise relying on the town's church halls and assembly rooms. Those of us in the Junior School had most of our classes in Christ Church Parish Rooms, a stone's throw from Woodland House the junior hostel where most of my classmates lived.

Had I gone to Woodland House I would have been in the capable hands of the two Miss Kydds, an amiable and competent couple, as I would later discover when I briefly lodged with them during a scarlet fever scare. Had I gone to a Penrith family things would have been different again. But for reasons never fully explained I was placed, aged eight, in a hostel designed for boys aged 11 to 18. Presumably, like so many things in wartime, it was a matter of availability. Whatever the cause, it would affect my life in important and unforeseen ways, not only at the time but for many years thereafter.

On the eve of my departure, worried about how I would cope, Father gave me a lecture. Reader of stirring tales that he was, he had a high regard for manliness. I was not to pick fights but I needed to be prepared to stand up for myself. Above all, I was not to be a cry baby and go complaining to the authorities when things went wrong. It never did to give in to bullies. Mother, more concerned about my physical welfare, thoughtfully packed a large jar of malt in my trunk. Bless them, they meant well.

So there we all were in Newcastle Central Station that morning in early September 1941, our mothers smartly turned out for the occasion, we in our blue caps and blazers. Last hugs and kisses were exchanged and off we went across the Pennines to such fates as awaited us. In my case this meant being put on a bus for Beaumont, on Graham Street, halfway up Beacon Hill, where, having lugged our trunks upstairs, we were put to work peeling potatoes, mine somehow disappearing in the act of peeling.

Later that evening I made a disturbing discovery – my jar of malt had shattered. I closed the lid of my trunk and said nothing. The following evening I suffered a second misfortune. On the waste land behind Beaumont there was a sten-gun firing range. Tucker Anderson, the master in charge of Beaumont, warned us strictly not to go there. But what possible danger could there be when no one was firing? Besides, all that separated the Beaumont garden from the waste ground was a straggly barbed wire fence. The wire broke as I climbed over, cutting a deep wound in my thigh. Fortunately it was covered by my trousers. Again, I kept quiet.

This second misadventure was more immediately inconvenient than the first in that it meant that I couldn't have a bath. Beaumont had only one bathtub and a meagre supply of hot water for the thirty or so boys living there, an arrangement that necessitated our being bathed in groups of eight or ten at a time, so my absence was never noticed. After a while another complication arose in that my wound turned septic and I developed a large lump in my groin. However, I had a penknife and a handkerchief and when no one was looking I would lock myself in the toilet or creep away under the bushes and clean out the pus. Thus, from the very start, I had a secret unknown even to my roommates. After three or four weeks my wound began to heal and the swelling in my groin went down. More alarming was what was happening inside my trunk. When no one was around I would peek in it from time to time only to find that the original sticky mass had acquired a furry mouse-like mould that in time gradually transformed itself into an all-encompassing fungal growth.

And so the weeks passed with me still wearing the clothes that I had worn when my mother had bravely waved me off at Newcastle station. I could not tell the time, but that didn't seem to matter because our days followed a regular pattern. And always there was the horror of what was happening inside my trunk. What eventually brought my situation to light was the preparation of laundry bills for us to take home at half term and the housekeeper's belated discovery that the only article I had sent to be laundered was the handkerchief I had used in the course of my surgical operations. I still recall the heavy tread of the posse that followed me upstairs, the dragging out of the trunk and the intake of breath that followed the flinging open of its lid.

That it had taken eight weeks for my situation to come to light reflected the makeshift nature of the arrangements. Doubtless there were others who experienced far worse misfortunes. The particular circumstances responsible for mine, however, are worth describing because they explain much else that happened, both then and later.

Besides running Beaumont, a full-time job in itself, Tucker Anderson was responsible for billeting the entire school, and so to a considerable degree for the welfare, of some 450 evacuees. In performing these duties he expended not only immense energy, but, as his biographer would later reveal, a fair amount of his own money. Humble, patient, an antique bicycle his only means of transport, he positively radiated goodness, a quality that before the war had made him a formidable figure on the local political scene by way of organising food relief for the beleaguered Spanish Republicans, promoting the League of Nations and heading up various other good causes of a Christian pacifist persuasion.

Presumably it served him equally well in his dealings with the families with whom RGS boys were billeted. How could one refuse a request from one so patently self-sacrificing? Colleagues, it is said, lived in fear of his kindly hand descending on their shoulders. These qualities, however, proved less effective in his dealings with those of us who came under his immediate command, not because we failed to recognise his manifest saintliness but because we had yet to develop consciences of the kind needed for it to have much effect on our behaviour. Young savages that we were, there was simply no way that any single individual, however endowed, could have kept an eye on us while performing all the duties he had undertaken.

TUCKER ANDERSON

"Now boys," he would say confronted with yet another scene of pandemonium, "this isn't good enough!"

He would have managed better had Ma Wood, the Matron, played a more active role. To give her her due, on discovering my plight she lost no time in getting me sufficiently cleaned up to be sent home. Even so, it was plain to my parents, surveying me and my belongings, that all was not well and a letter was duly written.

Anxious not to be returned to Penrith I employed the half-term trying to break my arm. A year earlier I had done so with casual ease by simply by tripping over. I even ran and tried falling on the self-same spot, but to no avail. Tying my arm behind my back and jumping off a fence simply wrenched my shoulder. I told my parents that the boys at Beaumont swore and they laughed at me. I wasn't going to get out of things that easily.

Following my return to Beaumont, Tucker Anderson wrote assuring them that I had arrived safely and that he would see I took my malt and cod liver oil pills. Agnes Kydd, my form teacher, wrote almost weekly accounts of my various mishaps – a can of oil had leaked in my pocket, my tie was beyond repair, I needed a new pair of shoes for which both coupons and money would be required.

Yet, in spite of this additional care, it remained a time of misery. Every minor scratch turned septic. Having picked at my cuticles, my nails inflated with pus and one after another had to be frozen and excised at the base. My letters home, lovingly preserved by Mother in a box tied with ribbon, invariably mentioned the rate at which different nails were growing, not because it was a subject that especially preoccupied me but because I regarded letter writing as a chore and that was a way of filling space.

"Dear Mammy," I wrote. "I am very well and my thumb nails have come of when I took my bandages of my nails fell out."

Worst of all was my aching homesickness. Even had I wanted, I lacked the words to describe it. Dragging myself back and forth to Beaumont I thought of the family gathered around the fire, Mother darning socks, Father listening to the wireless, Alan on the floor with his toys, Gladys busy in the kitchen, all of which would actually be happening at that very moment only sixty miles away. Even today, the perky songs of the period – *Run Rabbit, Hey Little Hen, Amapola, Wish Me Luck* – turn my heart to lead. The only one that spoke to my condition was *Show Me the Way to Go Home*.

One thing I didn't tell my parents about was the bullying. Knowing how squeamish they were regarding sexual matters how could I describe what went on – that debagging involved more than simply depriving people of their trousers? Mostly it affected those around the age of puberty although it happened in my dormitory too. As I have since observed with flocks of birds, those picked on were the weak and timorous. By way of proving that I was neither, I took to performing acts of lunatic bravery, climbing trees, jumping out of high windows, and for a dare sticking a teaspoon into a broken lighting fixture in the Christ Church Parish Rooms toilet. This last did not strike me dead as we had been warned it would but left me disinclined to repeat the experiment.

On the whole, however, Father's advice about standing up for myself served me well. On arriving at Beaumont – in fact, that very first evening – having been cooped up in railway carriages all day there had been wrestling matches on the lawn into which I had entered with such gusto that someone had christened me "The Fighting Temeraire." What that was I'd no idea but it sounded better than names like "Pee-bed" and "Piffer" that were given to others. Shortened to "Temer," it stuck with me the rest of my time at Penrith. In short, I became the hostel's nipper, eager to join in any mischief that was going and not above initiating some of my own when the opportunity offered.

Back home for Christmas a letter arrived to say that there was a vacancy at Woodland House and that I could be transferred there. But by then it was too late. Being put in a hostel designed specifically for Junior School boys looked to me like a demotion, so I refused.

I returned to Penrith the following January to find that we had all been transferred to a new hostel, Hazel Bank, out on the Ullswater road. Life there proved very different from that at Beaumont. Being two miles out of Penrith getting to classes involved eight miles of travelling back and forth each day. In the mornings we either walked or bicycled; in the afternoons buses were laid on. We waited for these by the bridge over the railway. Letters describing these routines sometimes contained disquieting tidings:

> Dear Mammy, Yesterday I went to wate for the bus and then when we were having tea three police men came marching up the path after tea I herd that they wanted me and one or two others and put our names down a train had arrived in Penrith with broken windows someone was hert. I am quaight all right my nails are nearly almost grown.

In fact I was not one of those who had thrown stones at the train's windows, although I was guilty of other misdemeanours, such as trying to drop stones down trains' funnels. On the way to and from school in the mornings we found the white ceramic insulators on telegraph poles made excellent targets for our catapults, shattering most satisfactorily whenever one of us scored a direct hit.

Riding home on the bus in the evening was always a jolly experience so much so that we would often burst into song, although what we sang depended very much on who was riding with us. If it was Tucker Anderson or someone else in authority it might be *The Blaydon Races* or *The Great American Railway*, but if we were on our own *The Ball of Kerrymuir* or *The Good Ship Venus* were more likely. There were also topical songs, such as, sung to the tune of *Colonel Bogey*:

> Hitler, has only got one ball,
> Goering, has two but very small,
> Himmler, is somewhat similar
> But poor old Goebbels, has no balls, at awwwll!

We also sang about the foibles particular masters, this to the tune of *The Battle Hymn of the Republic*:

> We'll tell Spitty Williams that he's twenty seconds late
> We'll tell Spitty Williams that he's twenty seconds late
> We'll tell Spitty Williams that he's twenty seconds late
> When the Red Revolution comes.

Although my nails were on the mend I began having trouble with my teeth, presumably because I never brushed them, the result being that over the next two or three years some eight or nine had to be pulled out. Appalling though this now appears it was not considered out of the ordinary at the time. My parents and most of my adult relatives had lost all their teeth at relatively early ages. I had always had poor teeth as compared with Alan, it being frequently remarked that I would look better once I got false ones. In the event modern dentistry arrived, although only just in time, to save me from having to do so.

It is plain from the letters they wrote to my parents, also preserved in the box with the ribbon, that those responsible for my welfare in Penrith were doing their best to cope, a task made all the more difficult in my case by the fact that my tribulations were largely of my own making. My chosen role model at that time was Wilson (he appeared not to have a Christian name), accounts of whose adventures appeared weekly in *The Wizard*. Many years later I came across an article about their anonymous author who, it turns out, was responsible for numerous other comic book heroes whose adventures I also followed. ("The Pen-pushing Puncher from Poison Creek" was another.) None of them, however, compared with Wilson. It was not just that he was a hero – they were all heroes – but because he was a hero with whom I could readily identify.

Born in 1795, he had started out as the village weakling, scoffed at and humiliated by the local toughs. Unwilling to put up with this, he had run away from home determined to develop his physique. Thanks to the Spartan life he led and by continual practice high up in the Pennines he had duly returned to his village and triumphed over the local bullies. But, hero that he was, it was not public acclaim that he sought but personal satisfaction; so rather than staying to be congratulated he had returned to his mountain fastness to prepare for his subsequent achievements as sprinter, marathon runner, pole-vaulter, weight putter, gymnast, wrestler, and so forth, assiduously training for each event, often for years at a time. Unlike Superman and other comic book characters he did not possess x-ray eyes, a bullet-proof skin, powers of levitation or other supernatural attributes of the kind that gave them an advantage over their opponents. He was just an ordinary human being who by his will power demonstrated, time and again, that there were no limits to what could be achieved by sheer grit and determination. It stood to reason. For a century, thanks to ever more strenuous training, athletic performances had been improving. If strenuous training programmes were good, even more strenuous training programmes must be better. What Wilson had done was to improve his physique so far beyond what was supposed to be humanly possible *that he never grew any older!* It was the whole jogging mystique! That was how records were broken, and that was how Wilson wiped the smiles off the faces of the Nazi leaders at the 1936 Berlin Olympics.

Whether or not he brushed his teeth we were never told. Apart from his training schedules (he nearly came to grief racing Stephenson's *Rocket*), little was said about his daily life other than that he lived in a cave, slept on a stone slab, wore a woollen leotard and barbecued hares that he was able to out-run thanks to his long loping stride. This last I attempted, but found my stride insufficiently long and loping, besides which walls and hedges got in the way. On the other hand, I found no difficulty in abandoning tooth brushing, hand scrubbing and other practices I associated with conventional living.

Thrown as I was into lonely self-reliance, it's easy to see why Wilson became my idol. Geographical circumstances also contributed. Penrith was in a valley with the Pennines on one side and the Lake District fells on the other. I'd never before so much as seen a mountain; now they were all around me. I recall the magical moment – it must have been halfway through that first miserable term – when I looked up and saw Cross Fell covered in snow. I dreamed of running away and like Wilson living in a cave or deserted shepherd's cottage. If he managed to survive wearing nothing more than a leotard, I'd presumably find a way of getting by too.

Whether such romantic notions occurred to others I do not know. I doubt they would have seized my imagination had the ground not already been well-prepared by Father's accounts of travel and adventure. Smelling agreeably of Wills' Cut Golden Blend and with me perched on the corner of his chair he had read me Jack London's *The Call of the Wild*, the story of a sledge dog on the Klondike that became the leader of a wolf pack. It caught my imagination for much the same reason that Wilson did and made me regret not having been evacuated to Canada. But as things turned out I *did* find a sort of Wild West, only it wasn't across the Atlantic.

If supervision had been lax at Beaumont, at Hazel Bank it was practically non-existent. The approach was up a long gravelled drive flanked by firs and rhododendrons. The house itself, an ivy-covered late-Victorian mansion complete with Gothic tower and battlements, faced onto a wide lawn where in former times tea parties had doubtless been held and croquet played. On one side, concealed behind a high hedge, was the conservatory and kitchen garden, on the other, the coach house and orchard. Beyond lay the outhouses and servants' cottages. Set in handsome wooded grounds and surrounded by a tall stone wall it had obviously belonged to a family of considerable wealth. Cold, empty and echoing though now was, Hazel Bank conjured up a vision of life on a far grander scale than that with which most of us were familiar.

Being in Yanwath meant we were within an easy bike ride of the Lakeland fells. Of more immediate interest, however, was our being on the edge of a vast military training ground, emptied of civilians and extending virtually from our doorstep to Barton Fell. What had previously been a well-tended patchwork of meadow and woodland had been transformed into a war-torn landscape, scarred by tank tracks and dotted with tented encampments. Although the roads leading to it were all strictly guarded, once we had gained entry, as we could do by cutting across the fields, we found we could wander pretty much at will. The soldiers we encountered didn't seem to mind our presence. Halfway between Yanwath and Askham was a vast fuel dump, a mini city constructed entirely out of jerry cans.

The command headquarters, Lowther Castle, was everything a castle was supposed to be, all towers, turrets and Gothic arches – in fact just the kind of story-book castle from which one could imagine knights sallying forth and princesses being rescued. In fact it was not a real castle at all but an early nineteenth-century extravaganza designed by the young Robert Smirke who, albeit in more sober spirit, would later design the British Museum. At the time he was working on Lowther Castle he was also busily redesigning Covent Garden Theatre and something of the same theatrical exuberance imbues both projects. Over the years many famous guests, the Kaiser included, had stayed there. From its oriental gardens, now neglected and overgrown, we watched the staff cars coming and going in the hope of catching a glimpse of General Patton and his legendary pearl-handled revolvers.

But Lowther Castle was only one of the area's many wonders. The local farmhouse was not simply any old farmhouse but the best-preserved late-medieval fortified manor house in England, one of the few to have survived the centuries of border warfare. Wordsworth had stayed there and on occasion helped its owner, his Quaker friend Thomas Wilkinson, dig the garden, an experience he had written some lines to commemorate.

YANWATH HALL AND FARM

Naturally I knew none of this. All I knew was that it was an old building with thick walls, low beams, sheepdogs and rows of muddy boots thus being what to my way of thinking a proper farmhouse ought to be. Similarly, Yanwath's seventeenth-century Gate Inn was exactly what a village inn ought to be. In fact everything around Hazel Bank – the fields, stone walls, woods, the Eamont River, the whole landscape together with the buildings and people it contained – were what, to my way of thinking, England *ought* to be.

Mindful of my misadventures at Beaumont, Tucker Anderson wrote reassuring my parents that all was now well:

> I am much struck by his love of the country and all that moves in it. He was quite right when he insisted in coming out to Hazel Bank. All his spare time, winter and summer alike, is spent out of doors exploring. He never finds life in the country dull and that is a great asset for a boy of his age to possess. For a boy of his age – he is our only junior at Hazel Bank – he manages his own affairs, his money, his clothes, his bedding, etc. with a minimum of help from outside. I shall be sorry to see less of him when we get to Newcastle and should like to assure you that so far as I can see he is developing along very good lines and should be a source of great pride to you in the years to come.

Needless to say, much went on that Tucker did not know about. Older boys had homework; we younger ones did not, or if we did I can't recall spending time on it. Ill-prepared though I was in other respects, I did know how to snare and gut rabbits. However, my first effort, at snaring, to judge by the missing peg and circle of trampled ground, had snared a cow. I expected terrible repercussions, but nothing happened. After that I had more luck. I would gut the rabbits on the spot, wrap them in newspaper to keep the blood off my exercise books, stuff them into the old army haversack I used as a satchel, and sell them to one or other of the butcher's shops in Penrith. Being meat off the ration rabbits were in great demand. As I explained to my mother at the outset, it was not merely an adventure but a commercial enterprise.

> Dear Mammy, I am very well and I have been getting a lot of money with rabbets I got a small one and got one and two pence for it I got a big one and tried to gut it and made a mess of it and so got no money. I have got my eye on a spring trap. I am relying on the snares to get me the money for it.

Tucker Anderson caught me with my first gin trap and being a humane man confiscated it. After that I was careful not to bring traps anywhere near Hazel Bank.

In time two other boys, both some years older than me, Rex Tate and Fungus Young (the Fungus was a corruption of Young, by way of Youngy and Fungi), joined in my bushwhacking expeditions, collecting moorhen's eggs which we boiled and ate, young woodpigeons which we plucked and gave to the woman at the pub to cook for us and hedgehogs which we sought (unsuccessfully) to cook Gipsy-fashion wrapped in clay. On one such expedition a rabbit in a trap alerted us to the fact that another trapper was at work. We took not only the rabbit but half a dozen of his traps as well.

The countryside was full of wonders – orchards heavily laden with apples, hedgerows full of blackberries, glossy-black flying beetles, house-martins feeding their clamorous young in mud nests under the eves, bats that emerged at dusk, clumps of brightly-coloured toadstools that sprang up overnight and brief glimpses of foxes, stoats, and weasels. Down by the river there were herons, moorhens and brightly coloured dragon flies. I recall, too, bicycle trips to a nesting colony of black-headed gulls where we collected eggs by the bucketful and got one of Ma Wood's scullions to hard-boil for us. With the standard egg ration down to one a week this was unaccustomed plenty, so I mailed a shoe box full, some hard-boiled, others fresh, to my mother, who duly wrote thanking me for my thoughtfulness but saying that sending eggs by mail was not a good idea and please not to send any more.

Across the railway there was a meadow where two barn owls hunted. I would go out at night and watch them, ghostly white apparitions patrolling to and fro, occasionally plunging into the long grass and after an interval taking off again. At one end of the meadow there was a barn stacked with bales of straw where the Irwin twins and I made a hideout. We were there one day when men arrived with horses and carts to take the straw away. When eventually we were discovered they shouted up:

"Hey, lads, you got any girls up there?"

We hung around and as they got towards the bottom the ground around our feet began seething with mice. There were tiny new-born pink ones that we put in our pockets with the vague notion of raising them as pets. After a while we began scooping up the bigger ones and putting them in sacks. Laden with these trophies we went back to Hazel Bank and up to our bedroom where we found empty suitcases to put them in, some inevitably escaping in the process. Then we went downstairs and boasted about all the mice we'd caught. Thereupon everyone wanted to see them; so we opened the suitcases and all except the baby ones jumped out and began running around the hallway and into other rooms.

The pandemonium alerted some of the seniors. We'd been bloody fools and the mice would have to be got rid of. This wasn't easy as they were now all over the place, moving so quickly that there was no hope of catching them by hand. The only solution was to chase them under beds where they could be squashed against the wall with suitcases. This, we claimed was cruel. But now the whole hostel had turned against us, not only requiring that we flush the pink babies down the toilet along with the corpses but that we crawl under beds and wipe off the splats of blood and intestine we'd left on skirting boards.

Nor was that the end of the matter, for soon there was a plague of mice. They could be heard scuttling about at night along the skirting boards and in the ceiling. Those who had difficulty sleeping blamed us for their misery. Mice got into Ma Wood's larder too. She, as usual, knew nothing of all this. Doubtless there had been mice around before – it would have been strange in a house like that if there had not been – but now, whenever there was any sign of them it was the twins and I who were blamed.

I was with the Irwin twins on another memorable occasion. We were peddling back from Penrith and had got as far as Eamont Bridge when I spotted two collies. One was trotting along happily while the other, which seemed to be attached to it, was being pulled along sideways and didn't look happy at all. This plainly called for my intervention, so I leaned my bicycle against the farm gate and went over and patted them. Finding them friendly, I tried in a gingerly sort of way pulling them apart. Again, they didn't seem to mind, although it didn't seem to do any good. As to how they had got themselves in that position I had no clear idea, but the Irwins, who were older and plainly did have, were laughing their heads off.

This made me all the more determined not to give up, so holding the one on four legs by the collar I opened the gate, led them across the farmyard and banged on the farm door, which presently opened to reveal a woman in an apron.

"Excuse me," I said, "I found these dogs in the road and they seem to be having some sort of difficulty."

She stood for what seemed an interminable time looking at me until a much larger figure in clogs and corduroy trousers loomed up from behind her.

"Excuse me," I began again rather waveringly, "I was just passing and I thought that perhaps if these were your dogs…"

He stood, arms akimbo, taking me in, before delivering himself of: "Dinna worry tha'sell. They'll coom apart after a bit," adding for good measure, "Aye, lad, and see it never 'appens to thee."

Back at Hazel Bank, the Irwins retold the story until I was sick of it. There were three Irwins: the twins, Eric and Ian, who were two years older than me, and Pat, who was older again. Their father, whom I would later meet in tragic circumstances, owned a farm in Ponteland, just outside Newcastle. He was a famous shot and owned a considerable armoury of weapons to which his sons had access, although it was presumably without his permission that Pat brought a .22 rifle to Penrith. Perhaps it had simply been thrown away as the barrel and trigger mechanism were coming away from the stock. There was no shortage of ammunition, which Pat stole from the School Cadet Corps. We took it with us on our bushwhacking expeditions, but because the barrel had to be aligned independently of the stock it was so inaccurate as to be virtually useless, even for shooting rabbits.

Of classroom instruction I have only the haziest of memories. Although I spent five days a week labouring with inky fingers at my tiny desk in

Christ Church Parish Rooms, my mind was mostly elsewhere. I recall spending whole days in contemplation of the lethal shot from my catapult with which I would despatch a particular rabbit that had taken to basking in the sun under a gorse bush I passed on my way back to Hazel Bank. All day I would ponder the nice question of how close I dared approach before firing, for if I approached too close, as I did on a number of occasions, the rabbit would be up and away before I'd had a chance to fire. Eventually the rabbit must have wearied of having its rest disturbed and found somewhere else to sun itself. That pretty much sums up my experience of catapulting stones at rabbits, although I did once manage to hit a pigeon with a long curving shot that brought it plummeting from its branch dead as a doornail.

Such were the attractions of the countryside that I came to regard what went on in Penrith itself, including what went on in class, as peripheral to what that went on in Hazel Bank itself and in the hills and woods around, which had become, so far as I was concerned, one vast adventure playground. And adventures there were in plenty, as on the day an ammunition lorry blew up scattering shells in all directions. I managed to retrieve one, which we spent hours trying to take apart. Eventually we gave up and buried it in Hazel Bank grounds, where presumably it still is.

The older boys, who had their own common room, led largely separate lives. As several later won scholarships to Oxford and Cambridge I can only assume their experiences were very different from mine. Nevertheless, there were times when we would compete, as in catching hold of the tailboards of trucks on the long haul up from Eamont Bridge and riding in their slipstream all the way into Penrith. It was a revelation when one who was exceptionally good at this and enjoyed a reputation for fearlessness on that account panicked on the slopes of Helvellyn and had to be escorted back to Patterdale.

ϡ ϡ

As in all closed communities life in Hazel Bank had its own dynamism. Rumours abounded. In the case of those of us not yet in our teens, there was virtually no limit to what we could be persuaded to believe. Like our crazes of the moment – squirting water pistols, firing paper pellets with elastic bands, throwing knives and flying balsa wood glider planes – rumours flourished and died. One was the old canard about Russians having been seen landing in Scotland; another that after the war the government intended wheeling Hitler around, Roman-fashion in a cage for us all to gawp at. Some stories died swiftly, as when word went around that there was to be a major battle with the Penrith boys, who used to taunt us by calling us "bloody bluebottles" on account of our blue caps and blazers. We duly bicycled into town ready for combat only to find that no one had told the Penrith boys. Some rumours, however, acquired a life of their own. One concerned Ma Wood's cat.

Ma Wood was a doctor's widow. From what she let drop she had previously led a rather privileged life, so being in charge of some 50 unruly boys was not the kind of thing she was used to. Occasionally she would give orders to the cook, Mrs Brown, and the two local scullions who helped out with the cooking. Mostly, though, she spent her time, her cat on her lap, warming herself in front of the kitchen range. This, as she was wont to tell us, was her contribution to the war effort.

During the winter months the kitchen was the only warm place in Hazel Bank, but unless we were engaged in some recognised task, like peeling potatoes or unloading the grocer's van, it was out of bounds to boys. There were, however, occasions, such as after dinner on Sunday evenings, when we younger ones would be allowed to sit warming ourselves around the range while she, her cat purring contentedly in her lap, regaled us with stories of her life before the war,.

"You know, boys," she would say. "You aren't the only ones who miss your homes. My Tim here misses his home too. Don't you Tim?"

Who first raised the notion that she was feeding her cat on our tinned salmon I never knew, probably because it began in the middle-school dormitory. Soon, however, it began cropping up in the rambling bed-time discussions we had after lights out. Mostly these were about sex, how much adults earned (about £800), the horrors of life in private billets (where strange perversions were practised), and in other hostels (where even stranger perversions were practised). What was remarkable was not that the cat story started but how quickly it became a matter of consuming interest. Unlike most of the other topics we discussed it should have been open to verification. Once lights were out a succession of volunteers, of whom I was one, crept down the maid's stairs to examine the cat's bowl. Although we found no actual salmon in it we agreed that it had a distinctly fishy smell. More compelling was the testimony of those who had carried in groceries and who reported having seen far more tinned salmon being delivered than could be accounted for by the amounts appearing on our plates.

So what had started out as a mere speculation came in time to be accepted as established fact and cause for righteous indignation. Salmon had become the ultimate wartime luxury. To acquire a single tin required the sacrifice of a whole week's supply of ration book points. By what authority, then, did Ma Wood feed our rations to her cat? Tinned salmon came from America; sailors risked their lives getting it to us. Surely there must be wartime regulations forbidding the feeding of animals on rations intended for humans. Criminal or not, it was plainly unpatriotic.

Then, at dinner one Friday evening, came the whispered news that the cat had been captured by Jones and Anderson, two of the middle-school boys, and was in the coach house. When Hazel Bank had been requisitioned its owners had locked away their treasures in the coach house, a veritable Aladdin's cave to which we had gained entrance by climbing over the adjoining stable roof. It contained an actual coach, elaborately painted; a couple of cars laid up on blocks; innumerable mirrors, pictures, and ornaments; various pieces of furniture, including bedsteads, tables and a roll-top desk in the drawers of which we found no end of treasures, including a box of cigars, much dried-out, which we had made ourselves sick by smoking.

When six or seven of us scrambled in the following morning, sure enough, there was Tim in a sack hanging from a beam. But what were we to do with him? Various possibilities were mooted. The idea of throwing him off the viaduct seemed preferable to simply beating him to death where he hung, that being the other suggestion. Even if we could bring ourselves to beat him to death we would still have to get rid of the body. And what was so bad about throwing a cat into a river, albeit from a great height? That, at least was the view of Jones and Anderson, who, as the cat's captors, claimed right of possession. It was a proposal that appealed to the rest of us. Not only did it mean disposing of Tim in style that would provide a spectacle worth seeing but it also left open the possibility of his surviving by floating downstream and finding himself a new home. It was also the case that Jones and Anderson would be taking a bit of a risk themselves, for they would have to run up onto the main London to Glasgow line around the bend of which trains came at great speed and without warning. We often went up on the line to flatten pennies, but venturing out onto the viaduct was another matter.

So off our little lynch mob set, Jones and Anderson leading the way, holding the sack by either end, the rest of us following trailed by another boy lately arrived at Hazel Bank and said to be of a religious persuasion, who kept wailing, "Why pick on the poor cat? It's done you no harm." From time to time we paused to rest and throw stones at him so that after a while he wandered off. Arrived at the edge of the Eamont gorge, we sat awaiting the spectacle while Jones and Anderson hauled the sack up the embankment and ran out onto the viaduct. But then there was a hitch. We saw them leaning over the railings and shaking the sack but no cat fell. Presently Anderson came running back for a stick and after more prodding and shaking the cat did fall, not into the main current but into the shallows on the far bank. We saw it bounce, lie still, begin floating gently downstream, then, very slowly raising itself, we saw it crawl across the shore and disappear into a bed of nettles.

Meanwhile the pair from the viaduct were running back, wild eyed, scrambling down the embankment thinking they heard a train coming. On being told that Tim was somewhere in the nettles on the far bank they changed tack. Instead of its being the monster consumer of our rations it became a poor injured thing that needed putting out of its misery. Disinclined to risk the viaduct, we went downstream half a mile to a place shallow enough for us to take off our shoes and stockings and wade over. When, however, we got back to where Tim had disappeared there was no sign of him.

What became of him we never discovered. For a while I lived in fear that someone would give us away, but no one ever did. Every now and then Ma Wood would go out into the courtyard and call. For weeks she clung to the belief that he was making his way back over the Pennines to Newcastle and that she would receive a letter saying he had arrived, but no such letter ever came. Meanwhile, as we sat stony-faced listening to her monologues of a Sunday evening as she would console herself with the thought that cats had a marvellous way of surviving.

The same two boys were presumably involved in another episode that might have ended even more tragically. For reasons I do not recall – the wrong kind of accent, the wrong kind of boots – a third boy became the object of merciless bullying, not simply by them but by the entire middle dormitory. I remember peeking around the door and seeing him naked, streaked with brown boot polish, and screaming like a pig as he was pushed back and forth by other boys. I also recall word going around at breakfast one morning that he had gone off at dawn, waving a bottle and saying he intended to break it, cut a vein and thereby do away with himself. We had heard tall stories before, but when he failed to turn up for lunch or tea excitement spread and little groups of us went off to scour nearby hedges and ditches in search of a body. By dinner time excitement had reached fever pitch. Perhaps he had jumped in the river, gone back to Newcastle. His body might be lying anywhere.

Then, shortly before bedtime, as we were gathered on the lawn discussing which veins we would have chosen to cut had we been intent on doing away with ourselves he came strolling jauntily up the drive looking distinctly pleased with himself. It turned out that he had gone out beyond Lowther Castle to the tank firing range on Barton Fell where some soldiers had befriended him, shared their rations and given him rides on their tanks. This was further than any of us had been. While he was there he had seen no end of marvels, including tanks mounted with huge searchlights, which explained why the sky in that direction lit up at night. He had come back with a pocket full of sweets and chewing gum which, with remarkably generosity, he shared with the rest of us.

෨ ෨

Around the spring of 1944, the tanks began departing, taking off the corner of Yanwath's seventeenth-century Gate Inn as they went. We'd hear the rumble of their convoys passing in the night. Bicycling into Penrith the following morning the roads would be bespattered with chunks of mud and churned up at the edges by tank tracks.

Then, suddenly, the whole area they had occupied, hitherto the scene of incessant military activity, was empty not only of the army but of people of any sort. With the sentries gone, we could walk up the main road to Askham through a ravaged landscape of broken walls and shattered barns – looking, in fact, much like the photographs of France and Germany featured not long afterwards in the *Picture Post*, only instead of there being shabby French and German refugees lining the roadsides there was nobody.

Another sign that times were changing was the arrival of the Americans. Their equipment was much more impressive than ours. Southward bound convoys of enormous trucks, driven by black drivers and slung about with towing cables and spare tyres, roared through Penrith. Meanwhile, little groups of sad-looking Italians had begun appearing on local farms, talking to us in broken English and showing us pictures of their families and girlfriends.

By the early summer of 1944 we, too, were preparing to leave. Unlike my first year, a time of desperate loneliness, I had now fully adjusted to living away from home. Transformed into a sort of bush boy I was tough as whipcord. On our last evening Fungus, Rex and I gathered up our traps and left them on the same warren from which we had stolen them some two years earlier.

Our return to Newcastle was free of the drama associated with the School's original flight, or for that matter with the excitement that had accompanied our earlier returns when we had craned our necks out of the train windows to see the columns of black smoke rising from burning buildings. We had long since ceased carrying gas masks. The barrage balloons, too, had gone. We and the Yanks now controlled the air.

Back in Sunderland life was returning to normal. We still had to black out our windows at night but air raid wardens no longer came knocking if they saw a chink of light. In fact air raid wardens were no longer much in evidence. Captain Whitfield from across the road brought tales of doodlebugs falling on London and of some other kind of rocket, more mysterious and terrifying, that arrived without warning. However nothing of the sort was happening up our way and with the newspapers full of maps with arrows showing our forces pushing further and further east it seemed unlikely that it would. The shelter in which we had huddled night after night was thus now redundant. As we all realised, it was a symbolic moment when Father brought in the coal hammer, laid newspapers across the floor, rolled up his sleeves, and as Mother, Alan and I stood watching, dealt it a sharp blow, whereupon the entire structure sagged. A couple more blows and it disintegrated entirely. He wrapped the remains in the newspaper and looking distinctly sheepish carried them out for the bin men to take away.

We had been lucky in more ways than one. A vast cruelty had swept the world, the full effects of which were only now becoming apparent. Every day the papers were full of pictures of bodies – bodies strewn over battlefields, hanging from telegraph poles, being bull-dozed into pits. We had escaped the worst of it – the fear of the midnight knock, the deportations, the gas chambers – although we had had our casualties too. The body of my Uncle Bert, Aunt

Laura's husband, had been washed up near the Kyle of Durness after his ship had broken up in high seas. Uncle Walter, a marine engineer largely unemployed during the Depression and massively overworked subsequently, had collapsed with a perforated ulcer and died in the course of a botched-up operation. As neither had perished as a direct result of enemy action Laura and Ethel did not qualify for war widows' pensions and were to spend the rest of their lives in dire poverty. Uncle Gordon, Mother's brother, received a leg wound in Italy and was flown back to recuperate in Sunderland's Backhouse Hall, lately converted into a temporary hospital. Mother would visit him in the afternoon and Father and I in the evening. He'd been a tank gunner with the 8th Army and fought his way from El Alamein until, in a vineyard on the outskirts of Rome, a mortar round had come in while he had been brewing up a pot of tea. He couldn't, he said, have wished for a cushier wound. The German had done him a favour. It hadn't even hurt much. I asked him if he had shot any Germans. He said he couldn't tell as they had simply been dim shapes looming up out of the dust and smoke, but he certainly hoped so.

It would be presumptuous to compare my experiences to those of returning veterans like Gordon. All the same, the war had dislocated my life in ways not altogether dissimilar and at an age when my character was far from being fully moulded. Some of its effects were good. It took me to places I would not otherwise have visited and gave me experiences that I would not otherwise have had. It also allowed me the freedom to behave in ways that in normal times would never have been permitted and accustomed me to getting along with boys older than myself. Above all, it had toughened me up and to that extent made me better prepared to face life's vicissitudes. Conversely, it made me intolerant of weakness, neglectful of others' feelings. In short, I had coped as well as might be but at some emotional cost, becoming harder, more guarded, less willing to express, perhaps even to feel, spontaneous emotions. Mammy and Daddy became Mother and Father. There was an academic price to be paid too. I never learned my tables and cannot to this day readily tell you the product of 8 x 9. But the most troubling effect of the years spent running wild in the Lake District was to make it difficult for me to settle down to the humdrum routines of post-war life in the urban North East. As was the experience of many others, the war's ending meant having to acquire a new identity, and that, as I was to discover, would not be easy.

3: SHADES OF THE PRISON HOUSE: 1945-47

DURING THOSE LONG war years Vera Lynn's voice had rung out clear as a bell.

> It's a lovely day tomorrow, tomorrow is a lovely day,
> Come and feast your tear dimmed eyes on tomorrow's clear blue skies
> If today your heart is weary, if every little thing looks grey
> Just forget your troubles and learn to say, tomorrow is a lovely day.

But when tomorrow came it wasn't a lovely day. Most little things still looked pretty grey, at least to me. I'd hoped that once the war was over things would go back more or less to where they had been before, but they didn't. Gladys had left early in the war. She had sent us a photograph of herself looking very smart in her RAF uniform but that was all we ever heard from her. Basil Dixon from across the road, who used to let me fire his air pistol, had gone to sea at fourteen as a cabin boy and on his first voyage had been drowned in the icy waters off Murmansk. The Whitfield boys did come back from Bishop Auckland but as young men with deep voices, more concerned with getting into college than messing about with me.

Things weren't too cheery for other people either. The Americans who had helped us win the war were proving less generous than formerly. There seemed to be less than ever in the shops and the queues for what little there was had grown even longer. When bread and potato rationing were introduced, something we had never experienced even at the height of the submarine blockade, it became clear that, materially speaking, things were actually getting worse. We children always got enough to eat, but it gradually dawned on me that Mother was starving herself for our benefit, something she had never done before.

Nevertheless, Father's allotment helped keep us supplied with vegetables and thanks to his position at the Bank local farmers sold us the occasional dozen black-market eggs. What banking favours they got in return I never thought to ask, although, knowing Father, I doubt there was any cutting of corners. We certainly paid for the eggs, as I know because he and I used to walk out to the farms to collect them. All the same, these were illegal transactions to be concealed not only from the vigilant authorities but from prying neighbours who might report us to them. Rather than a carrier bag, Father would take a coat with pockets large enough to accommodate egg boxes. One year, again thanks to his banking influence, we acquired for Christmas dinner what I suspect must have been the oldest goose in England. To increase its tenderness we let it hang for a week before we plucked it. Nevertheless, it proved to have had a skin like leather. Aunt Ethel and Elizabeth had come over for the occasion. While we sat expectantly, Father first tried slicing it, then stabbing it, but to no good effect. Finally, giving up in exasperation, he bore it on the end of his carving fork to the fire. At first it burned slowly, then, as the fat began to run, the flames increased alarmingly, until, with a great whoosh, the chimney caught fire.

"You know, Fred," Aunt Ethel said to Father afterwards, "it's the first time I've felt really warm this Christmas."

༺ ༻

The School's return to Newcastle coincided with my moving into the Middle School. Sometime in the summer of 1944 I had taken what in retrospect I realised must have been the 11-plus exam or its RGS equivalent. By getting into the RGS through the Junior School I had avoided the ferocious competition that would henceforward govern grammar school entry and in due course prevent my brother Alan getting into the RGS. I'd got in the easy way. Whether I would have got in the hard way is doubtful, but as my poor performance was arguably the School's fault they could hardly throw me out.

So it was like starting school all over again. At Penrith I had felt I was a somebody; now I was just another new boy. No one called me "Temer" any more. No longer did I enjoy the kudos of being a Junior living in a Senior Hostel. It was as if the years at Penrith had never happened.

Like most in my year from Penrith I had been assigned to the B stream. Even there, however, we found ourselves outnumbered by well-scrubbed newcomers in brand new uniforms carrying shiny leather satchels full of rulers, pens, pencils and geometrical instruments. Some of those in the A stream even had the effrontery to adopt superior airs. At Hazel Bank I had worn hobnail boots and gone bare-legged; now I wore shoes, a regulation tie and grey socks held up by an elastic garter just below the knee. Fungus Young and others to whom I had been close had left the School. Fungus wrote about his rabbit shooting and other country pursuits but as I had no equivalent adventures to report our correspondence soon lapsed. The Irwins were still around, but being in years senior to mine I saw little of them.

To make my mark I resorted, as usual, to showing off. In cricket I gained a reputation as a fast bowler, in rugby as a wing three-quarter, in boxing I knocked people out. When the ground was too hard for games and we were sent to run around the old Isolation Hospital on the Town Moor I was always back first. But sport was only a small part of the curriculum and being confined all day to the school grounds the opportunities for devilry were limited.

As Wordsworth wrote, looking back on his Lake District youth, "Shades of the prison-house begin to close upon the growing boy." They certainly seemed to be closing in on me. Instead of having trees to climb and countryside to explore I found myself transformed into that dreariest of all beings – an urban commuter. No one else from Sunderland went to the RGS. Instead of walking through fields I found myself hanging about on station platforms among piles of mail bags and crates of fish. The train journey took under half an hour but it was a mile's walk from Braeside to Sunderland Station and at the Newcastle end there was a rather longer trolley bus ride out to Jesmond. Allowing for waits at stations, the daily trek back and forth took the better part of three hours.

The result of this was that my social life was bifurcated. Bev and my other Sunderland friends went to the local grammar school, the Bede, as in due course did Alan. That was what Sunderland boys clever enough to have passed the eleven-plus exam did. And as when I had attended Barnes Primary School they met other boys on the way – girls too. The same applied to most RGS boys. Although drawn from a wider catchment area, a good proportion came from such solid middle-class enclaves as Jesmond itself and Gosforth just up the road, as did many of the girls attending the nearby Church High and Central High Schools.

Thus, in both Sunderland and Newcastle I found myself something of an outsider. Needless to say I did not journey back and forth alone. In the mornings I travelled up with a group of technical college students from Seaham Harbour. Some younger RGS boys got on at Seaburn and other stops along the way. When we managed to get a compartment to ourselves there was apt to be larking about. Sometimes this led to complaints from passengers in the compartments adjoining. Although such carryings-on helped alleviate the tedium of the journeys they were totally unrelated to anything that happened at either end.

ભ ભ

Yet, in spite of this, Bev remained my closest friend. Although we spent most of our time out of doors we were continually in and out of one another's houses. However, Bev spent more time in ours than I did in his for the simple reason that his father was a tyrant. Everyone agreed Mr Carss was a nasty piece of work. He was a small man, ferret-faced, who wore a flat cap and muffler. Once, around the time of Dunkirk, he had remarked to Father "Well, it looks like we're finished," a comment for which Father never forgave him. Mrs Carss, a small, kindly woman, always deferred to him. She did her best to be welcoming, but when he was at home it was prudent to stay away. The Carsses, seemingly having no friends or outside interests, believed in keeping themselves to themselves. As far as I can remember I was the only outsider ever to enter their house.

Bev suffered. Unlike my parents, who were happy to let me develop at my own rate and not unduly concerned if my school reports were poor – as for the most part they were – Bev's father drove him inexorably, demanding that he come top in everything and making his life a misery if he so much as dropped a place. As Bev was self-evidently the cleverest boy around it was hard to see what purpose this served. I was the slow one. Whatever I did, Bev could do better and in half the time. When I came up with a new idea, like making balsa wood gliders, roller skating, or writing a novel, in no time at all he would be so far ahead that there seemed little point in my continuing.

In time I came to suspect that there was more to his father's behaviour than sheer bloody-mindedness. Although, in terms of occupation and income, all the families in our immediate neighbourhood were middle class, our origins were mixed, some having come up in the world, others gone down. The Carsses had come up. How far they had come up I became vaguely aware of from the bicycle trips Bev and I made to his grandmother's.

She lived a couple of miles away in one of the rows of pit cottages in Silksworth. In spite of their rural-sounding names – Houghton le-Spring, Chester-le Street, Dalton le-dale, Hetton le-Hole – Durham's pit villages were essentially urban. In the case of Silksworth it was as if a section of Sunderland's docklands had been lifted up and magic-carpeted into the hills. Up there among the fields and hedgerows were the same rows of back-to-back houses, Methodist chapels, street corner pubs, fish and chip shops, mission halls and corner tobacconists as on the plain below except that, instead of ending at the dock gates, their cobbled alleys gave onto countryside where larks sang and ponies grazed. Along the river and around the estuary it was the giant derricks that dominated the scene; up in the hills it was the slag heaps and pit-head winding gear.

On the way up to his grandmother's Bev and I would pass coal-pickers, gaunt figures with blackened faces, straddling or wheeling bicycles draped with sacks of coal that they had scavenged from the slag heaps and were on their way to hawk around town. I presumed the heaps were safe although I never felt entirely confident of that as at night they glowed. On still days their sulphurous fumes could be smelled even in our living room. Once or twice, to test our nerve, Bev and I embarked on night climbs. As in a scene from Dante's Inferno we would stand on the summit, the ground glowing beneath our feet, and gaze down into the maw of the pit out of which all day long the steel buckets came jangling. Had the crust given way and we fallen into the burning core no one would ever have known what had become of us.

From Silksworth, on a clear day, one could watch the freighters passing up and down the coast. To the north lay South Shields and Newcastle, to the south Middlesbrough and Teesside. Along the roadside were benches where old miners with bad chests would sit and watch the passing scene. In the fields around were pit ponies put out to grass. Once we spotted one lying on its side gasping, its belly enormously distended. Thinking it needed helping to its feet or was about to give birth, we tried lifting it but it was too heavy. So we patted its head, offered it handfuls of grass, and murmured encouraging words, none of which did any good. We were about to give up when, suddenly, with a great spasm, it gave up the ghost. This left us nonplussed, feeling that an event so momentous ought to be reported to someone. But to whom? We told Bev's grandmother, who said not to worry as someone would turn up and it would all be properly taken care of. Probably it was old and had had a long and happy life down the mine.

Coal picker

Whenever we called she would be huddled over the fire with a kettle on the hob. The colliery gave her free coal to keep her little fire going the year round. She was always pleased to see us and to listen to our chatter. How, she would ask, was Bev getting on at school? She would give us glasses of lime cordial, after which we would freewheel back home down the hill. Years later, reading D H Lawrence's *Sons and Lovers*, I was reminded of the scene.

I recently came across figures showing that in the early Thirties there were around a thousand deaths a year in the coal mines and that in any given year approximately one in every five of those working underground was injured. So that was the life Mr Carss had escaped by doing well at school, going to university and becoming the elementary school teacher he was, no small achievement for someone of his generation and background. It also helps to explain his determination that Bev, his only child, should improve on what he had achieved by going one better. All the same, remembering the hearty miners tramping back from their shifts and thronging the local pubs there had been a price to pay in opting for the frozen, companionless middle-class respectability of Birchfield Road. Possibly that had contributed to his manic fury over Bev's loss of his tricycle. How many other such episodes there were I do not recall. Once he systematically smashed an entire chemistry laboratory that Bev had spent years assembling.

But it was over the issue of Mrs Blaikie's broken window that he out did himself. Who was responsible for the breakage would long remain a mystery. However there was never any doubt about the events leading up to it. As already noted, my father had a mould for making lead musket balls and Bev and I both had catapults. We also had moulds for making all sorts of other things – model field guns, lead soldiers, warships – melting lead being one of the things that children did in those days, the only equipment required, apart from the moulds, being a fire, an old kitchen ladle, and lead, which we could easily scavenge from bombed buildings. So there was nothing unusual about our spending an evening in front of our dining room fire melting lead in a ladle, pouring it into moulds and dividing the products of our labours at the end of the evening.

What was unusual was to have a policeman knocking at our door before breakfast the next morning. There had, it transpired, been a complaint about a broken window. I was duly summoned from bed and asked to identify the newly-minted lead ball in his hand. It looked, I agreed, remarkably like the ones we had just manufactured. Mine were duly produced and the match was identical. Was there anyone else who might be in possession of such an object? Having no alternative I went out onto the doorstep in my pyjamas and pointed out Bev's house. The policeman thanked us and departed.

Seized with curiosity I got dressed and went out, first to view the window, which turned out to be merely cracked, and then to knock on Bev's door. There I was confronted by a demented Mr Carss, still in his pyjamas, who screamed at me in such a way that I had difficulty making out what he was saying but eventually grasped amounted to a denunciation of me, my family, everything we stood for, but in particular for our conspiring to saddle Bev with a criminal record. Shaken, I returned home and reported what he had said to Mother. Father by that time having left for the Bank, she put on a coat and went around to Birchfield Road intent on putting things right. By the time she arrived Mr Carss had got as far as putting on his shirt although not yet his trousers. That did not deter him from giving a repeat performance of the one I had witnessed.

"There he was," Mother said, "with those little white legs of his, in his socks and suspenders, dancing up and down. I felt so sorry for Mrs Carss. She was in the hallway and did look embarrassed."

The upshot was that Bev was forbidden ever to have anything to do with me or my family again. It was an edict destined never to be lifted. Even at the age of eighteen Bev was reduced to crawling up our pathway on his hands and knees so as not to be seen from his parents' back bedroom window. Otherwise, however, it caused us little trouble as we soon devised ways of leaving messages and meeting by prior arrangement. As Mr Carss seldom left the house and had no friends there was little chance of our being surprised or of anyone giving us away. Who had caused us all this trouble remained a mystery throughout our childhoods and for long afterwards. I believed Bev's disclaimers and he mine. That being the case we ought to have been able to identify the culprit, who was, of course, my eight-year-old brother Alan, supposedly sick at the time but so eager to fire one of our bullets that he had crept out of bed while everyone was still asleep, taken my catapult, opened the front door, loosed one over the roof of the adjoining house, crept back to bed, and gone back to sleep, an act of folly he finally got around to confessing some 45 years later.

No one was surprised when Bev, having achieved distinctions in all his subjects, gained a place at King's College Medical School in Newcastle. What was a surprise was his defying his father by quitting medicine after a year and opting to read Chemistry, which had all along been his passion.

Meanwhile, local views on Mr Carss, now retired from teaching, had begun to change. Mrs Carss, for whom everyone had previously felt sorry, had taken to her bed and now everyone felt sorry for Mr Carss, trailing back and forth to the shops with his shopping bags and not looking too well himself.

"Perhaps," Mother said, "he'd been a good husband to her after all."

No sooner did he die, however, than Mrs Carss hopped out of bed, spruced herself up and had the house done over. "You wouldn't believe it," Mother said. "She's a new woman. I wonder what was the matter with her before? Perhaps she was just putting it on."

Through Bev I met other Bede boys, among them Robert Hartford. Although less intellectually gifted, he was in many ways like Bev, being an only son and the object of high parental expectations. Often the three of us went on bicycling expeditions: to Durham Cathedral; to a pond in Herrington to catch newts (common and crested); to the cliffs at Marsden to observe the nesting sea birds, and to Cherry Knowle, our local mental hospital, to observe the inmates, an unsettling experience in those pre-tranquiliser days. Locally it was still referred to as a lunatic asylum and its inmates as lunatics. "He's been to Cherry Knowle, you know," and "She looked as if she'd escaped from Cherry Knowle," were, and probably still are, common Sunderland expressions. I can't think that escaping would have been very difficult for no one seemed to mind our visiting the wards to observe the antics of the insane much as eighteenth-century sightseers had amused themselves by wandering around London's Bedlam. Another frequently-visited location was Penshaw Monument, a replica of the Temple of Theseus in Athens, built in honour of John George Lambton the first Earl of Durham, nowadays remembered for having once remarked: "£40,000 a year, a moderate income – such a one as a man might jog on with." Its modern equivalent, I suppose, would be somewhere in the region of ten million. Although not officially open to the public we also visited Lambton Castle, like Lowther Castle one of Robert Smirke's Victorian confections. It overlooked a wooded gorge through which the River Wear flowed pure and clear as it had done before the age of coal and steam. Apart from a bored janitor, it was at that time deserted, Lambton finding it more convenient to occupy the home farm up above. The janitor, having nothing better to do, took us on tours. Once, when I was there on my own, he scared me out of my wits by locking me, albeit only briefly, in the cellar. On another occasion we arrived as a partridge shoot was in progress. It was a windy day and the birds, driven by unseen beaters in the fields above, were travelling down wind at close to eighty miles an hour as they passed high over the wooded gorge, where Lambton picked them off one by one with all the assurance of a TV darts champion scoring his triple twenties.

Robert had an air pistol with which he once performed the magical feat of shooting a flying sparrow, but that was simply a fluke, as when another boy brought me to the ground with a bolas consisting of no more than his rugby boots tied together by their laces. There was also the occasion when we thought we had solved a crime. We had spotted a figure in a belted raincoat and trilby standing at the end of our street looking sufficiently gangster-like to persuade us that he was up to no good. So we took turns cycling around him, and then, with our heads bent over the dining room table, composed a description of everything from the colour of his hat to the size of his shoes. It so happened that that very night the house outside which he had been standing was broken into. As soon as we heard about it we bicycled in triumph down to Sunderland's main police station bearing our document. There we were shown into an office where a detective listened politely to our breathless tale, made some jottings on a notepad, thanked us for our efforts, said he did not think it necessary to keep our notes and seemed altogether less impressed by our efforts than we had expected. It later transpired that the house had been broken into by three young women who had hitch-hiked in from Durham and were presumably already in police custody at the time of our interview. It would not be my last encounter with such unlikely conjunctions.

The war over, our family holidays resumed. We were staying in a former gamekeeper's cottage in Hulne Park when we heard on the wireless that Hiroshima had been bombed. I remember thinking the moment I heard it that an entirely new era had dawned and that what had happened represented a development that might eventually be the undoing of us all. Now there actually *was* a weapon capable of doing what people at the beginning of the war had feared aerial bombing would do. Considering what countries had got up to with high explosives it was hard to believe they would suddenly begin behaving more responsibly now they had access to atomic weapons. Father and I argued about it, he seemingly unable to grasp that what had happened had much wider implications than the prospect of ending the current war. So far as he was concerned what had destroyed Hiroshima was just another big bomb. We had had other disagreements, as over my contention that battleships had been outmoded and that henceforward carrier fleets would determine who controlled the oceans. As happens to teenagers, it was beginning to dawn on me that Father's was not the authoritative word on everything.

The following year we stayed on a farm in the Pennines close to Cross Fell, the mountain that, back in that gloomy autumn of 1941, I'd seen magically turned white by an early snowfall. Once again I was in my element, taking the farm dog with me and scouring the fells. One day the whole family took a bus trip to Penrith and from there walked out to Hazel Bank. Except that the conservatory had been extensively smashed up and the kitchen garden fallen into ruin everything looked exactly as it had been when we had left it two years before. Seeing no one about I ran through the hall and up the familiar stairs only to find, in my bedroom, lying in my very bunk, a half-dressed land girl who, surprisingly, seemed not at all put out by my barging in on her. I took her down stairs to meet the family and together we took them on a guided tour. The gardener, I gathered, had gone to prison. Apparently he already had a long criminal record, a discovery that rather cast doubt on his tales about shooting lions in Africa. Otherwise it was all as if time had stood still.

The following year, 1947, we were back in Sea Houses where our arrival coincided with the visit of the Scots herring fleet. Every year the fishermen, and their wives who did the gutting and crating, would follow the herring on their migration around the British Isles. Father and I went out with them, sailing at dusk and coming back at dawn, night being when the herring shoals rose to the surface. Two boats would patrol together and when a shoal rose would encircle it with a net, lash the boats together, and winch in the lot, the final stage being to pull in the bottom of the net so as to prevent a single one escaping. A good shoal might weigh anything up to five tons. Once we had hauled them alongside we would use the winch to ladle them on board, each scoop sending a struggling mass of quicksilver fish cascading knee-high over the deck and down into the hold through two tiny apertures, leaving just the odd idler flapping.

Between times we would sit in the diesel-smelling cabin drinking mugs of strong tea sweetened with condensed milk. On occasion whales came by. Although we could not see them in the dark we could hear them blowing only a stone's throw away – a sound rather like a horse whinnying. Once a storm blew up and we had to put in at Amble 20 miles down the coast. I was never sick but Father often was. "We've been bloomin' mugs," he would say to me. The fishermen, overhearing, would laugh. For fear of losing his teeth over the side when he vomited he would take them out. I appreciated that these night trips were undertaken on my behalf. How many of my friends' fathers, I wondered, loved their sons enough to spend nights on the North Sea being seasick rather than in their beds? All the same, seeing him crouching there in an old overcoat, white faced and toothless, there were times I wished he was a bit more like the hearty fishermen.

Being deprived of the real thing, I became an avid reader of books about nature and the countryside. This was not an entirely new development. Before going to Penrith I had been a fan of "Romany," a radio personality of the time who appeared on Children's Hour and who allegedly travelled the country in a caravan with his spaniel Raq. It was his description of Gipsy habits that had given me the idea of trying to roast a hedgehog by wrapping it in clay. His real name was The Reverend G. Bramwell Evans and I actually got to hear him and have him sign one of his books when he came to Penrith the term I was at Beaumont.

But the writer closest to my heart was Denys Watkins Pitchford, who wrote under the pen name "BB," a keen wildfowler and author of such books as *Manka, the Sky Gypsy*, a story about an albino goose, and *Wild Lone*, which was about a fox. My favourite was *Brendon Chase*, an account of the adventures of three boys of about my age who ran off to live in a wood where they subsisted on rabbits, pigeons, pheasants and other small game that they shot using a .22 rifle. Eventually they managed to shoot a feral pig, which helped keep them fed through at least the early part of the winter. Unlike Paul Gallico and most other writers of animal fiction, BB was no sentimentalist. But what mainly attracted me to his work was that, as I could tell from my own experience, he really knew what he was writing about. I composed a fan letter that I was too bashful to mail. My father mailed it for me along with a short story I had written and received a reply to the effect that I was plainly "a young man of ideas and imagination."

What attracted me to BB's books quite as much as his stories were his white-on-black scraperboard pictures. Supposing them to be ink drawings, I spent upwards of two years trying to copy his style using a mapping pen, eventually becoming so adept at spacing black lines as to produce white ones. My subjects were, foxes, buzzards, rabbits, mountains, stone walls, fir trees and barns, all created out of my memories of Yanwath and the countryside around it. In the course of what, although I didn't fully realise it at the time, were acts of homage to that lost world, I accumulated scores of meticulously executed pen and ink sketches.

Drawing aged 13

I was already well embarked on this enterprise when I noticed that the Hancock Museum, just down the road from the RGS, was offering a prize for a nature diary covering the following year. The Hancock was the North East's leading natural history museum. In addition to its cases of stuffed animals and birds it had a gallery devoted entirely to prints, mostly rural scenes, by the eighteenth-century wood engraver Thomas Bewick. Here, then, was an opportunity to produce not merely a written diary but one illustrated with black-and-white drawings in the manner of BB and Bewick. So for the next 12 months I kept lists of all the birds and animals I'd seen, wrote up accounts of my various bird-watching expeditions and drew pictures to match.

When, the next January, I presented myself at the Hancock and was explaining to the woman at the desk that the envelope I was giving her contained my submission for the Hancock Competition a distinguished-looking old gentleman came up from behind and asked who I was. I explained that I was a pupil at the RGS.

"And what is your name?" he asked.

"Temperley," I said.

"No, no," he said. "I asked you *your* name."

"Temperley," I said. "Howard Temperley"

"Ah," he said. "You'd better come with me."

He led me into his Victorian-style office where, having settled me down in a chair, he introduced himself as George William Temperley and proceeded to ask me all sorts of questions about myself and my relatives. Concluding that we were related, he then went on to tell me about himself and his branch of the family. He was, he explained, the Honorary Secretary of both the Museum and the Natural History Society. He had started out as a corn merchant, that being the family business, but finding it sufficiently flourishing he had retired while still in his thirties and had since devoted himself entirely to ornithology. He had a son, a geologist in Kenya, who seemed unlikely to produce any male heirs, from which he concluded that there was a danger of our branch of the Temperley line dying out. "It is," he said fixing me with his earnest gaze, "all up to you and your brother."

This raised all sorts of issues that, at the age of 14, had never crossed my mind. I doubt they had crossed Father's either. Nevertheless I told him what had happened and in due course a letter arrived from George William suggesting a meeting. Temperley is not a common name and various attempts had been made over the years to trace the family's history. Armed with these, Father and I set off for Newcastle where we were graciously welcomed and our genealogies scrutinised with interest. Other meetings followed, how many I do not recall as I was not present at all of them, although I do recollect once visiting George William at his house in Stocksfield, a substantial sandstone residence not quite on the scale of Hazel Bank but sufficiently impressive to make us feel that inviting him to our little semi in Sunderland might not be a good idea.

How we were related soon became clear, although the connection was not close. Back in the early 1700s there had been a coal and lead miner who lived in Stublick House, near Haydon Bridge in the Tyne Valley, from whose three sons there descended three lines of Temperleys. George William's ancestors had moved, by way of farming, into corn trading, which was proving more profitable. Ernest Temperley, a descendant of one of the other brothers, had gone to the RGS and thence to Cambridge, eventually becoming the bursar of Queens College and founder of what George William referred to as "the Cambridge Temperleys." Of these there seemed to be a good number, the most famous being the diplomatic historian Harold Temperley, Master of Peterhouse. We came from the third and apparently least distinguished branch of the Temperley line. That we had such notable relatives was news to me and to Father. Indeed, if George William was to be believed, there was a distinct possibility that we might have even more distinguished antecedents in the form of the Timperleys, a Catholic family of ancient lineage who had fled East Anglia to avoid persecution at around the time the Temperleys turned up in Northumberland.

Although two years had passed since my leaving Penrith, the passage of time had failed to assuage my sense of loss. I yearned for the Lakes almost as much as, back in my Beaumont days, I had yearned for home. Still, around Sunderland, there was countryside of a sort. Amazingly, at the bottom of our street there was a farmhouse. Wordsworth never stayed there; had he done so I doubt it would have inspired any verses. Nevertheless, at milking time we could hear the cows mooing and a voice calling them in to be milked. The farmer, Mr Moorhead, did not look or act like a farmer. Presumably this was because the land he owned, surrounded as it was by middle-class housing, was enormously valuable simply as an investment. A portly bachelor, he seldom stirred out of doors, smelled of whisky and tobacco, wore a business suit complete with waistcoat and watch chain, and never did a hand's turn of work. He was, however, a genial sort.

Occasionally he lost his temper and chased us off his land, but mostly he did not mind our playing football in his field or making hideouts in his barn.

Drawing aged 15

The work about the place was virtually all done by a farmhand called Ikey who not only looked after the cows, pigs and chickens but came around the neighbourhood daily in a horse and cart delivering milk and eggs. Sometimes he would let one or other of us ride with him. Sitting in front when the horse defecated was an experience that took me by surprise. Once – it must have been around the beginning of the war – I spent the better part of an afternoon watching him with his arm stuck up a cow's rear helping to deliver a dead calf. It was a bloody business for which he apologised to my mother the next day, saying it must not have been a nice thing for me to watch. I'd not minded a bit having already discovered – I was possibly six at the time – that what happened on real farms was different from the way it was presented in children's books. It never occurred to me to ask how the calf came to be inside the cow; it being dead, the obvious explanation was that the cow had eaten it.

As Moorhead's farm was only some 30 acres it hardly qualified as countryside as I had come to know it around Penrith. Shallcross, was certainly no substitute for Cumberland's Eamont or Eden. Further out, battalions of new council estates were rapidly occupying the belt of green fields that lay between us and the pit villages. We regarded them as no-go areas on account of their being where the raggy boys lived. We called them "raggy boys" because they dressed, literally, in rags, trousers within trousers sewn together as a single garment and passed down from sibling to sibling. I doubted the stories that circulated about their mothers sewing them into clothes for the winter and their keeping coals in the bath were true. All the same, there was no question but that they smelled. It was the smell of poverty. One encountered it all the time, in trams, on buses, and at the cinema; it even impregnated the books I borrowed from Sunderland Public Library.

Years later, reading Arthur Koestler's *Arrow into the Blue*, I was struck by his description of the shock he had felt, looking down from his middle-class balcony, at the appearance of the industrial workers who in 1919 invaded the streets of Budapest. He concluded that they were what conditions had made them and that conditions would therefore have to be changed. I imagine they must have looked pretty much like the fathers of Sunderland's raggy boys. In post-war Sunderland, however, conditions *were* changing, and rapidly. The Attlee Government now ran the country and an active left-wing Labour Council controlled the town. The effects of these changes were everywhere apparent. Where Bev and I had once lain in that green meadow, and further out still where we had bicycled to catch crested and orange-bellied newts, the countryside was being bulldozed flat to make way for the onward march of the Council's estates.

Father, a reader of the *Daily Telegraph*, thought things were being carried too far. Nevertheless, he learned with ever increasing wonderment of his entitlement to glasses, false teeth and much else for which he had previously had to pay. Never having had any money to speak of he was not given to extravagance. The problem was that our doctor, Dr Punshion, a tall, impeccably-dressed figure, had chosen not to join the new National Health Service, the result being that not only would he continue to charge a fee for his services but that he was barred from prescribing the free drugs to which we would have otherwise have been entitled. For a while, mainly out of loyalty, we soldiered on paying for both. In time, however, such expenditures came to seem profligate, so we acquired a National Health doctor too, a Dr Williams, a younger and distinctly less well-tailored figure, who on his first visit produced an instrument that fell apart and necessitated his spending some time crawling under the bed retrieving the pieces. This confirmed my parents in their belief that Dr Punshion was a "real" Doctor and Dr Williams merely some sort of state factotum. How could a service that was free be any good? So up to the time of my leaving home we had two doctors, one to prescribe drugs, the other to deal with serious ailments.

Unlike Koestler, I felt no urge to join the Communist Party, although I did attend a number of Soviet-sponsored events aimed at persuading me to do so. The most impressive was a display of Cossack horsemanship at Ashbrooke sports ground, a sort of Wild West Show in which, among other things, riders demonstrated their ability, while at full gallop, to swing under their horses' bellies and come up the other side. I came away heavily laden with Moscow-printed pamphlets, among them *The Communist Manifesto* and Lenin's *What Shall Be Done?* Being not yet into my teens, I found them heavy going. So far as I was concerned the town's class, income and geographic divisions were as much a part of its social landscape as its collieries and shipyards were part of its physical. That was simply the way things were, as was the fact that I spoke and dressed differently from my contemporaries out on the estates and down around the docks.

Though lacking in opinions on social and political matters, I was fully prepared to do battle when, as happened from time to time, groups of raggy boys came straggling over the fields like marauding tribesmen to invade our territory. This was class warfare of a sort, but like our earlier battles on the way to and from Barnes Elementary School our encounters were mostly symbolic, the two sides hurling stones and abuse at one another from a sufficiently safe distance that no one got hurt.

Occasionally, though, things did get out of hand. Around bonfire night marauders would come down from the estates after dark and try to set light to our bonfire. This led to running battles and actual fisticuffs. In the course of one such encounter I pushed over a boy who hit his head on the kerb and went off bleeding. Being better nourished I was taller by a head than most of my working class contemporaries. This led to misunderstandings, as became apparent the next day when he and his parents came around banging on our door demanding money as a condition of their not going to the police to lodge a complaint on the grounds that I was an older boy who had harmed their little son. When, however, it transpired that I was actually younger than the boy I had injured, a claim that at first they refused to believe, they were distinctly put out of countenance. Eventually, Father, assuming his army-sergeant manner, ordered them off the premises, whereupon they departed grumbling and no more was heard of the matter.

For my thirteenth birthday I received an ancient but powerful air rifle with which I shot the rabbits that had been nibbling Father's lettuces and the wood pigeons that, when the weather turned hard, would descend in ravening flocks to consume the allotments' Brussels sprouts. With the meat ration down to four ounces a week these were welcome additions to the family diet. A year or so later, unbeknown to my parents, I acquired from the Irwins a long-barrelled 4.10 derringer pistol with an attachable wire butt that I kept concealed in the bathroom cupboard behind the birds' eggs. It might have proven a useful weapon for holding up banks or jewellers' shops but was no good whatever for shooting game. The Irwin boys had 12-bores and were good shots. I took it with me when I went out shooting with them on their farm at Ponteland and although they shot any number of partridges and pheasants I couldn't hit anything, so I traded it back for a young jackdaw.

I named the jackdaw Jacko and built a cage for him out of wire mesh and old tea chests. He was quite tame and would sit on my shoulder as I bicycled around. Mostly he ate creepy crawlies. He had sharp blue eyes and as I turned over stones would hop about, turning his head from side to side ready to pick up whatever was revealed. Wood lice were his favourites. I'd clipped one wing but as he was so tame I let the pinions grow back with the result that one windy day he took off over the housetops never to be seen again. I must have kept him for almost two years. I'd meanwhile started keeping pigeons but I was never as fond of them as I was of Jacko.

The winter of 1946-47 was exceptionally severe. Snow lay on the ground for the better part of three months as a result of which I earned enough half crowns clearing paths and driveways to buy a 12-bore of my own. It was advertised in The *Sunderland Echo* for £16.00 and I remember going out with Father to a tiny terrace house in Pallion, near the shipyards, paying over my earnings, and returning home in triumph.

At that time guns did not have the connotations they have acquired latterly, so for a fifteen-year-old to be seen carrying a shotgun on a bus or train, providing it was in a case, was not regarded as out of the ordinary. I imagine that most people would have regarded putting teenagers in charge of motor cars as being far more of a threat to public safety. In order to use a shotgun I had to buy a five-shilling licence. This involved filling out a form, but I do not recall that it required that I state my age. The ownership of rifles was, of course, more closely regulated and that of hand guns more restricted still. But shot guns were to be found in virtually every farm, the only requirement being that their barrels not be shortened, which would have indicated criminal intent. Otherwise the law was aimed at ensuring that the shooting of game – i.e. of pheasants, partridges and the like – remain the province of the well-to-do by requiring a hefty fee for the privilege rather than ensuring that guns did not fall into the wrong hands

കൊ കൊ

One neighbour who took a keen an interest in my sporting aspirations was Old Charlie Pickersgill. We always referred to him as Old Charlie to distinguish him from his son, Young Charlie, a handsome young man who had served as a captain with the 8th Army in the Western Desert. His mother once described him as "God's gift to Hollywood," a comment that made my mother snort. All the same, there was no denying that Young Charlie cut a dashing figure. Once or twice there were Desert Rat reunions across the road with loud music and the singing of bawdy songs that in other circumstances would have led to complaints. I suspect Father disapproved, but Mother, for whom such exhibitions of male camaraderie were a novelty, took an indulgent view. After all, these were the lads who had beaten Rommel and turned the tide of war; if anyone had earned the right to let off steam they had.

The Pickersgills also had a daughter, Ninkie. Like many teenage girls she was keen on horses and spent a good deal of time on Moorhead's farm helping groom Ikey's pony and milk the cows. Once, to my embarrassment, I surprised her with her blouse unbuttoned being cuddled by Mr Moorhead. She was a striking girl and by her late teens her voice could be heard throughout the neighbourhood as it went up and down the scales. According to her mother she had such exceptional talent that in the opinion of those best qualified to judge she was destined to become an opera star. This, too, was seized on by my mother as evidence of Mrs Pickersgill's presumption. What right had such a poor washed-out old thing to assume such airs? One simply did not boast about one's children until, with a bit of luck, they had actually done something worth boasting about, in which case one let it come out casually.

But awful though Mrs Pickersgill undoubtedly was, everyone loved Old Charlie. He never boasted or assumed airs above his station, but then he did not have to for he was plainly from a social stratum far above that of any of the other men in the neighbourhood. His manner, his speech, his dress all bespoke the country squire. Exactly what his origins were I do not know, although I understood he was related to the Pickersgills who owned Austin & Pickersgill's, one of the largest shipyards on the Wear and a major local employer. I do know that he had held the rank of Major in the Great War. According to Mother his marriage to Mrs Pickersgill, formerly a Miss Black and supposedly related to owners of the Binns department store chain, had been a major social event back in the Twenties.

In short, the Pickersgills had come down in the world. The reason was a matter of common knowledge: Old Charlie was a drunk. Most of the time he was confident, considerate, full of bonhomie, but every now and then he would go on a bender. A taxi would draw up and he would be carried up the path. On occasion he'd literally be thrown out onto the pavement. Once or twice we had seen him lying by the kerb or halfway up the pathway in a pool of his own urine. According to mother there had been times when he had lain like that all night. Whether this was because Mrs Pickersgill did not know he was there or did not see fit to go out and pick him up I do not know. Being barely into my teens I was in no position to form opinions about relationships between adults. People simply were as they were, which, in Mrs Pickersgill's case, meant being skinny and mean-looking. What did strike me, though, was that the house was filthy – the cooking pots covered with grease, the sofas with dog's hairs, un-plucked birds hanging from the ceiling, shooting sticks lying around – in short sunk in the sort of squalor you would associate with fallen gentry only instead of its being spread around a dilapidated manor house it was here confined within the walls of a single small suburban semi.

Mother once let drop that Old Charlie had been sent to Cherry Knowle, presumably to dry out. According to Father there had been a time when things had gotten so bad that he had been reduced to hawking women's underclothes door-to-door. Yet, for all that, he still managed, at least during the game season, to retain something of the lifestyle of the country squire. He even had a gamekeeper of sorts called Bill, really a retired dockworker but who knew the country around, would carry the game bags and help control Old Charlie's dogs. Whether Old Charlie paid the farmers for the shooting I was never told, although I do know he was always punctilious about giving them a half share of whatever we bagged, mostly partridges but with the odd hare or pheasant thrown in. The rest the Pickersgills either consumed themselves or gave to us and other neighbours. There would be a knock on the door and there would be Old Charlie holding up a rabbit or a brace of partridges.

I was initially recruited as a beater, but later, having acquired my own 12-bore, as a fellow sportsman. I could not have wished for a better instructor than Old Charlie. He had strict views on gun safety and knew all there was to know about rough shooting. In time I became quite a good shot although never half as good as he was. Occasionally I was brilliant but often I missed; he never took chancy shots and virtually never missed. He would bring along a hip flask and from time to time take a swig, but it never affected his aim.

As he lacked a car, and would doubtless have long since been disqualified had he possessed one, we always went by taxi, picking up Bill along the way. Most of the farms around Sunderland were small and in process of being further reduced in size on account of being built over. Altogether, I suppose, we must have had access to some five farms providing, in total, around 600 acres of rough shooting. One was next to Cherry Knowle where the inmates would cluster against the wire to watch so that any birds that came between us and them had to be let go. Another hazard was that some inmates had taken to lying in the kale so that just when we expected a covey of partridges to burst out one of them would pop up.

My partridge shooting days ended in 1951 when I left to do National Service. I met Old Charlie on visits home and gathered that he and Bill still went out as before. Meanwhile, another humiliation had befallen the family. Ninkie had not become an opera singer. Nevertheless, she had landed a named role in *White Horse Inn*, then on tour. This led to much boasting. Soon, however, she was home again and plainly in the family way.

"She's been a naughty girl and run away and got married," Mrs Pickersgill told Mother.

However, no husband was in evidence even after the baby was born, although, again according to Mother, "a matinee-idol-looking chap" had been spotted going up the path. Presently Ninkie departed to rejoin *White Horse Inn*, this time as a member of the chorus, leaving the baby in Sunderland. Next she and her partner were running a flourishing antique business; but then it transpired that her partner had mysteriously disappeared, the bailiffs had seized the antiques, and Ninkie was working in the fashion department of a Newcastle department store. Her mother's explanations for her goings on became more and more preposterous.

Old Charlie died while I was in the United States. I was touched to hear that he'd asked after me shortly before. When I returned for a brief visit in 1959 Young Charlie and his wife, an unassuming young woman of about my age, had taken over and completely redecorated the house. They struck me as a thoroughly modern young couple, eager for my approval and for information about what was available in the way of household appliances in America. The old furniture had all gone, along with the dogs, shooting sticks and the disgusting cage in which Old Charlie used to hang his game. I don't recall what they said had happened to Mrs Pickersgill, Ninkie and the baby other than that they had moved elsewhere.

When I next visited Braeside a new family was living in the house. Young Charlie and his wife, I was told, had started a travel business in Gosforth, one of Newcastle's swankier suburbs. So there the story of my dealings with the Pickersgills would have ended had I not been visiting Father some five or six years later, Mother having died in the meantime, and chanced to be in the street when a large and plainly expensive car drew up disgorging two fashionably dressed women. Even in the mid-sixties there were few cars in the neighbourhood and certainly no women dressed like these two standing with their noses in the air as though they weren't sure they approved of what they saw or knew where to go. Partly out of curiosity I went over and asked if I could help.

"Oh," the younger one said, "you must be Howard. I'm Ninkie. You will remember mother."

I gawped. It wasn't Ninkie who astonished me so much as her mother. That skinny old crone of fifteen years before had been transformed into a woman of quality. Put on weight, too. I had expected her to have been dead long since. We exchanged very few words. Yes, Ninkie was married; the baby was now at school, doing very well, quite a young lady now. That's all I remember apart from my sense that they saw themselves as slumming. What accounted for this transformation, whether it was Ninkie's marriage or Mrs Pickersgill's coming into her Binns inheritance I do not know. I left them walking up the familiar pathway and rapping on the door in front of which Old Charlie had been left lying in his pool of urine all those years before.

4: A SUPERIOR SORT OF MISFIT: 1947-49

ALTHOUGH BEV WAS plainly destined for high academic honours, my future remained much in doubt. School reports spoke of my appearing "preoccupied." Mostly it was sheer boredom but Penrith had not helped. In arithmetic, algebra and Latin, having never learned, or long since forgotten even the rudiments, I'd simply given up. I strove as best I could to conceal this by faking illness when exams came around and inveigling a classmate into helping me out with homework. Admirable though the RGS was in other respects it made no provision for tutoring drop-outs like me. Not until much later did I come to think of this as a defect. At the time I put it down to my own congenital stupidity. Selling matches outside the Odeon was what Slinker Owen, my Latin teacher, prophesied.

In sports, by way of contrast, I enjoyed considerable kudos. Being strong and physically an early developer I was on all the School teams appropriate to my age group. In rugby I was even a reserve for the County Under-14s but failed to gain promotion as it became increasingly clear that mere strength and determination no longer sufficed. Up to that time my technique had been simply to get hold of the ball and fight my way to the far end of the pitch, which meant breaking the rules about punching, hitherto not strictly enforced. However it got me into trouble with county referees and was in any case of little use against opponents who had learned how to tackle. My outstanding ability was throwing. At the age if 16 I came within inches of beating the School's 1911 record of 109 yards for the cricket ball and doubtless would have done better in subsequent years had I not wrenched my shoulder muscles showing off and was never able to throw as well again.

Father was inordinately proud of such achievements as I managed, and never took me to task even when, as in Latin and mathematics, I was routinely ranked 31st in a class of 31. All the same, he was plainly worried, the more so as his bank colleagues had taken to boasting about their children going on to colleges and universities, that apparently being the new fashion. In my case anything of that sort seemed an unlikely prospect, a view with which my teachers concurred. I was always surprised by how much nicer they were talking about me to my parents on Parents' Day than when they had me on their own. Normally they used such terms as bonehead, idler, and time-waster. Still, the message was the same: I was an out-of-doors sort of lad and perhaps ought to be looking for something in that line. But what? If only, like the Irwins, I had stood to inherit a farm the problem would have been solved. It was Larry Watson, my housemaster, who came up with the traditional solution for muscular academic underachievers, namely if there weren't jobs in Britain for lads like me, why not try the Empire?

Ah, the Empire! Out there, across the sea, there was a Greater Britain, a world of excitement and adventure. At the age of 14 nothing appealed to me more than the idea of pig-sticking and tiger-shooting. Having long since got over my terror of the frontispiece of Father's copy of *The Man Eaters of Tsavo*, I had gone on to read Jim Corbett's *The Man Eaters of Kumayon*, Frank Buck's *Bring 'Em Back Alive* and other works of that genre. My first ever earnings, gained by picking potatoes in the war, I had blown on a book called *"Mauled by a Tiger."* In Penrith's Alhambra I had sat through two entire showings of Kipling's *The Jungle Book*, and had even dreamed of one day turning up at School with a scar or limp and casually observing "He was a big chap that tiger. Came at me out of the bamboo. Had to finish him off with my knife." Catching rabbits in the Lake District was all very well, but for large animals and real bushwhacking adventures one had to go abroad and where better than the Empire? What else, after all, was the Empire for?

So it was with such ideas in mind that Father and I made a trip to the Sunderland Labour Exchange, an unlikely place from which to launch a career of derring-do. Nevertheless, the man behind the desk managed to fish out a Department of Labour pamphlet entitled *Careers for Young Men Overseas*. Back home we pored over its pages.

There were, it transpired, any number of careers for colonial administrators, foresters, veterinary officers and agricultural scientists, all of which appealed to me, the only problem being that in every case save one they required degrees or diplomas of some kind or other. The single exception was rubber planting in Malaya, the only requirement for which was being "a young man of character and determination." That sounded like me. It also turned out to be a career about which, surprisingly, Mother was well informed, having once been courted by a rubber planter home on leave and anxious to acquire a wife to take back with him to Malaya. Why she had declined his offer I was not told, but it was just as well for news had lately reached us that he had died in a Japanese prison camp. Nevertheless, she produced photographs showing a handsome white-suited figure lounging on the veranda of a smart-looking bungalow or standing in front of rows of grinning native servants, all of which led me to wonder why on earth she had married Father.

Rubber planters returning home on leave still called in at the Bank. It was no surprise, therefore, when, shortly after our trip to the Labour Exchange, Father announced that he had invited one over for a chat. What was more surprising was his bringing home a bottle of whisky in preparation for the visit, suggesting that he was rather worldlier in his approach to such matters than I'd supposed. Either he had heard a thing or two about rubber planters or had made a shrewd assessment of this particular one, a heavy-breathing, elephantine figure who arrived by taxi and duly lumbered into our living room.

Judging by the loose way his clothes hung about him he had at one time been even fatter than he now was. Seated precariously on one of our dining room chairs he gratefully accepted the offer of a whisky, and did not demur when a top-up was proposed. There followed a lengthy discussion as to the virtues of different brands of whisky, the prices at which they could be purchased in Malaya (astonishingly low), and the iniquity of the taxes which Labour was loading onto the British public (extortionately high), which made him wonder whether he would come back to England on his next leave. And who would be the loser? The Attlee Government. It was cutting its own throat.

Having got this off his chest and again assured Father that he was a man of unusual discrimination so far as whisky was concerned, meanwhile gratefully accepting a third top-up, he turned his attention to me. What was it that interested me in a career as a rubber planter?

"Are there," I asked, "any tigers on your plantation?"

This took him aback. Tigers, it emerged, did not feature in the day-to-day affairs of his particular plantation, although some of his "boys" had once claimed to have seen one down by the creek. This was disappointing. I could see that he was not the sort who would relish spending a night up a tree with a goat tethered underneath and a flashlight attached to his rifle But what about other rubber planters? In response to further questions, he said that although there were wild pigs he personally had never gone in for pig-sticking, nor, so far as he was aware, had anyone else in Malaya. He didn't go in for duck or pheasant shooting either. In fact, wildlife didn't appear to feature at all in his scheme of things or in that of rubber planters generally. Finally, leaning forward and fixing me with his slightly bloodshot eyes, he said, "The important thing for young lads like you is - keep off the native women."

I was astonished. Here was a side to life in the tropics never mentioned by Colonel J H Patterson, Jim Corbett or the authors of any of the other big-game-hunting books I'd read. Nor could I recall Biggles having encountered temptations of that sort, or any of John Buchan's characters either. In fact it struck me as being totally at odds with the legends of exploration and endurance, bugles and cavalry charges that I had come to associate with the Empire. All the same, it added a whole new dimension to my concept of life in the tropics.

So how rubber trees were tapped, who did the tapping, what happened to the sap after it was brought back from the forest and how and where it was turned into useable rubber remained aspects of planting about which I had failed to ask and was destined never to learn. I often thought about those "native women," though.

❦ ❦

What with my being beaten up by my cousin Elizabeth and wounding Dora Smith, my relations with the opposite sex had not up to that time been happy. In fact, they had been pretty well non existent as neither I nor any of my close friends had sisters and there being no girls of my age living in our immediate neighbourhood. From the age of eight onwards I had had brief crushes on girls, demure little creatures I'd glimpsed in the distance but never had the courage to approach. Unlike Father, who took no interest in such matters, Mother quickly wheedled the details out of me.

However, when I was around the age of 13, Robert and I – Bev having his mind on higher things – began taking Sunday afternoon strolls in Barnes Park where we encountered groups of girls similarly engaged. I took a shine to Pat Short and after a while we paired off. What she talked about I do not recall, but I was into Alexandre Dumas and duly set about telling her the plots not only of *The Three Musketeers* but also of *Twenty Years After* and *The Viscomte De Bragelonne*. As she did not appear to be much of a reader, pop songs being more her line, I doubt she was much impressed. The main problem, then and later, was of finding something to do other than walking around duck ponds and sitting on park benches. I recall visiting her house, but not whether she ever visited mine.

What did one do with girls? I had a shrewd idea about what I wanted to do, but as I later found, taking them home was no solution. With Bev and Robert there was no problem: one melted lead, mended bicycles, built buggies, fired air guns, put carbide crystals in pop bottles so they exploded, or climbed on the shed roof to feed the pigeons. These were not, or so it seemed, things one did with girls dressed up to the nines that one encountered strolling in the park on a Sunday afternoon. Dare one even invite them home? It was not that my parents would have been unwelcoming, but not being much used to entertaining the chances were that they would be as unsure of what to do as I was. Did one show visitors into our ice-cold drawing room with its velvet settee and unplayed piano or into the tiny living room where we huddled around the fire for warmth and where as likely as not they would be confronted by a cloud of pipe smoke and Father in his slippers reading the paper? An additional embarrassment was our toilet, an old-fashioned affair with a chain that in order to flush required a special knack known only to the family. Father was always promising to get it attended to, but in the meantime such visitors as attempted to use it could be heard tugging away to no good effect, occasionally dislodging the plunger from its socket in the process. After listening for a while Father would intervene. "No need to pull so hard," he would say reprovingly. "Look, it just needs a gentle touch," as with a deft double tug he would set the water cascading.

So far as girls were concerned it was the church that eventually came to my rescue. Ours was the Parish of St. Nicholas and every Saturday night there were dances in the Church Hall run by the Vicar, the Reverend Peter Talbot. Bev, Robert and I shambled along. None of us knew how to dance, but the Vicar was a hearty sort and managed to get us to join in so that after a while we more or less learned the Quick Step, the Gay Gordons, the

Polka, and the Waltz. As the evening wore on the windows would mist over and the atmosphere would grow heavy with the smell of dust, perspiration and fumes from the paraffin heaters.

In general the girls were better dancers than the boys, most of them having attended dancing classes. If I'd had any sense I'd have done the same. In fact, I did a couple of times but found them embarrassing and, claiming that it was all rather sissy, gave up

The best dancer of all was Shuna Spencer, with whom I fell passionately, insanely, in love. One day I walked exultantly all the way to Durham thinking of nothing but Shuna. I wrote a poem about her, which wasn't any good and that I doubt I would have had the courage to send her even if it had been. I tried to be philosophical. Was I being irrational? The Reverend Peter Talbot, I noted, had warned us about the dangers of mere physical attraction. In the diary I was keeping at the time, along with other mawkish teenage ramblings, I wrote an account of earlier encounters with Shuna leading up to the moment when – it must have been Christmas Eve 1946 – I had seen her with a group of carol singers and realised she was not like other girls. I wondered if I was being irrational. After all, I wrote, "I know almost nothing about her. She is almost too beautiful."

On moonlit nights I stood looking at her house. Shuna knew nothing of this. So, far as she was concerned I was a clumsy oaf who had twice asked her to dance, trod on her toes, and with whom she had no intention of ever dancing again. Besides which she had her own circle of friends whose social life centred on Ashbrooke Sports Club where she played tennis. I did not play tennis; I wandered around the countryside with firearms killing small creatures.

What was I to do?

My first plan was to strike up a friendship with her brother. I scarcely knew Peter Spencer, who was a year younger than me and went to the Bede School, but I'd met him on occasion and heard mention of him from Mother, who often ran into Mrs Spencer while out shopping. (I also gleaned from her the information that Shuna was named after the Scots island of that name where the Spencers had spent their honeymoon and where, more likely than not, she had been conceived). Peter, I gathered, was keen on model trains. I neither knew nor cared about model trains. Nevertheless, screwing up my courage, I knocked on the Spencer's door. It was opened by a somewhat distracted Mrs Spencer. While Peter was being summoned Shuna came stamping down the stairs, her face set in anger, and without looking at me disappeared somewhere into the back regions.

Evidently there had been a family row going on. Presently, Peter appeared, looking puzzled. I duly said my piece about being interested in model trains and was taken down to the basement where, arranged on interconnecting tables, he had assembled an elaborate array of lines, signals, stations, locomotives and goods yards. Even before he began demonstrating its many wonders it was plain to me that my ruse was a ghastly mistake. To make matters worse, he began asking me about my trains. I said mine was a very modest set-up compared to his, but I'd been thinking of expanding it, and without waiting for him to advise me as to how that might best be done, thanked him profusely, and fled.

When I informed Mother that I had chanced to bump into Peter and that he had invited me to see his famous model railway she let drop another interesting piece of news: Shuna was beginning confirmation classes. Had I, she wondered rather doubtfully, ever thought of being confirmed? I hastened to ensure her that I was very keen on the idea, in fact couldn't wait to be confirmed.

Nothing could have been further from the truth. I'd begun having doubts about religion around the age of nine and was now a hardened unbeliever. Life at Hazel Bank and pictures of wartime atrocities had effectively disabused me of any belief in the providence of a benign ruler. The main thing, though, was that I could not see where religious instruction fitted in with the physics and chemistry, both thoroughly materialist, that I was taught at school. So why, I'd taken to asking, shouldn't everything be materialist?

"Ah, but what about the spirit?"
"What spirit? When someone died could you catch it in a bottle?"
"Well, there was the mind."
"Wasn't the brain made of matter?"
"What about thoughts, feelings…?"
"Well, mightn't they just be something that well-organised matter did?"

Having simply put two and two together I could hardly lay claim to having performed any great feat of imagination. All the same, I was very proud of it, believing I'd thought it up all on my own and even imagined myself eventually going on to make myself famous by revealing it to the world. It was a matter of sweeping away all the flimflam and getting down to the bedrock.

Although nominally Anglican, mine was not a particularly religious school. Being one of the few true believers on the staff, the task of teaching RI mostly fell to Tucker Anderson. As he had doubtless heard it all before, I imagine he was amused rather than shocked by the line I was taking. It did, however, shock a number of my contemporaries, several of whom, coming from families of a religious persuasion, felt conscience bound to remonstrate with me. I remember, in particular, one Parents' Day looking across the hall and seeing the most persistent of them, Leon LeDune, an owlish boy with two owlish parents, he with arm outstretched and finger pointing in my direction, and I could tell from their expressions what they were thinking: I was a bad apple and what's more destined for damnation.

I cannot believe that at my first confirmation class I was so stupid as to seek to impress Shuna by trying out my materialist notions on the Vicar of St. Nicholas's. On the other hand I would not rule out the possibility, for, as I've lately heard, there's a theory that the human intellect is like the peacock's tail in that it was initially developed for purposes of sexual display rather than for its practical utility. Whatever the case, I can't see myself letting such notions as are laid down in the 39 Articles pass unquestioned.

"Does resurrection of the body mean that the same atoms...?"

"How could Christ have died for sins I haven't yet committed?"

I can't recall Shuna saying anything. In fact I can't remember anyone other than the Vicar and me saying anything at all and I'm not sure which of us said the most.

At the end of the class, feeling pretty pleased with myself, I was standing modestly aside while the rest filed out, my intention being to catch up with Shuna and walk her home, when I felt the Vicar's hand on my shoulder.

"You are," he told me, "obviously a very intelligent and thoughtful young man. I was very impressed by the questions you asked."

I swelled with pride.

"However," he went on, "it just so happens that I'm starting an adult class next week and I really think it would be more appropriate if you were to attend that."

So that was how I came to be inducted into the mysteries of the Anglican faith along with about the strangest group of people that you ever saw. I persevered thinking that when it came to the actual confirmation ceremony there might be some sort of party, either before or after, that would provide an opportunity for a casual word with Shuna, but again I had miscalculated. It wasn't just our two groups who were being welcomed into full membership of the Church; there were hundreds of us from all over the town and far beyond. Moreover, we were segregated by sex, the girls in their pretty white dresses over on one side and me with my miserable lot of freaks on the other.

Thus ended my first great passion. Years later I heard Shuna had married a gym instructor and gone to live in Australia, where no doubt she cut a dashing figure.

୨୦ ୨୦

It was about that time that I was buoyed up to receive a letter informing me that I had won the Hancock Prize. It came in a parcel along with a magnifying glass to which was attached a note in George William's hand suggesting I might care to turn my attention to botany. However I had by now acquired my 12-bore and set my mind on undertakings of a quite different sort, botany, to my way of thinking, being an occupation more suited to young ladies. Besides, I had already begun work on a second and altogether more ambitious nature diary containing poems, evocations of nature, and, now I had discovered how they were done, scraper-board drawings of snow scenes, hunters crouched in ditches and skeins of geese flying over moonlit marshes.

I had also, on the recommendation of BB, lately begun reading Richard Jefferies, Henry David Thoreau, James Fenimore Cooper, and Wordsworth. The Americans were too philosophical for my taste. Woodsmen would not have talked like that. Also, from his description of Natty Bumppo's marksmanship, it was plain that Cooper knew nothing whatever about firearms. Even at close range to have shot a bird with a musket ball would have been something of an achievement. To hit a nail at a hundred paces stretched the imagination. But to select *two* birds *flying in opposite directions* and kill *both* with a *single* musket ball *at the moment their flight paths intersected* so far exceeded Robert's and Lord Lambton's achievements that I doubted anything like it had happened in the entire history of the United States, or of the world for that matter. Jefferies and Wordsworth were an altogether different proposition as was reflected in my new journal's more high-flown passages. Inspired by the sight of a flight of geese on 28 February 1947, I wrote in my journal

Pen and ink sketches drawn age 16

On Tuesday I was at the snipe marsh, the grass was white with hoar frost; there was thin, cats' ice around the pools. Snipe were constantly getting up – little warm birds against the cold background. Then, high overhead a long strung out skein of geese passed over, bugling to each other. I thought of the clamouring skeins on a winter's gloaming and of the whistling wind. How wild and free must be the lives of these wildest of all birds, always moving, now Spitzbergen, now the Solway, now the Zuider Zee, beating on, on, on, the wind whistling in their pinions…

My 12-bore having been acquired as a result of winter snow-shovelling meant I had to wait until the opening of the partridge season the following September to use it. Even then I could only use it when Charlie Pickersgill invited me, it being far too powerful a weapon to be used on Father's allotment or even on Moorhead's farm. It was one thing to use my air rifle to pick off the rats that swarmed around Moorhead's manure dump, but to go blasting away with a shotgun was something else again.

What principally kept me on tenterhooks throughout the spring and summer of 1947, however, was the prospect of wildfowling. BB had written vivid descriptions of his exploits up around Holy Island on the Northumbrian coast. So, too, had Abel Chapman, a turn-of-the century hunter-naturalist whose handsome volumes, illustrated by W H Riddell, show the area as teeming with wildfowl. That summer I hiked up from Sea Houses where we were holidaying and got as far as the Beacons on Guile Point, the finger of land that stretches out towards the southern end of Holy Island and from there was able to survey the immense area of sand and mud that extended northward all the way to Berwick. Apart from a few shelduck and waders there were no wildfowl to be seen at that time of year, but in my imagination I conjured up images of the vast skeins that would be filling the winter skies a few months hence. So there it was, all laid out before me on that bright August day, the place I'd read and dreamed about – castle, harbour, sands, mudflats. A new adventure was beginning.

There remained the problem of finding somewhere to stay. The Irwins had a punt house on the mainland, but that was of no use to me unless they were there and had offered to put me up. There were no hotels nearby and even if there had been I would not have been able to afford them. Consulting a Youth Hostel map, however, I discovered there was Youth

Hostel at Fenwick on the Great North Road right opposite the mud flats. Youth Hostels, the brochure said, were intended "to help all, especially young people of limited means, to a greater knowledge, love, and care of the countryside." Well, mostly it fitted.

It was plain from the expressions on the faces of the young couple in charge that I was not their usual sort of guest. For a start I was not wearing cycling gear. Being roughly halfway between Newcastle and Edinburgh I imagined that that was what most of the hostel's visitors wore. Nor, for that matter, did I look like one of those bare-kneed mountain hikers whose pictures decorated the walls, although being on a coastal plain I don't imagine too many of them came that way. Least of all did I look like one of those carefree lithesome figures whose image the Youth Hostel Association sought to project as being off on a sunny day to enjoy the delights of the British countryside. For there I was just off the bus, a scowling sixteen-year-old clad in a dirty army greatcoat and layers of sweaters looking more like one of Tito's partisans than like a regular youth-hosteller. Worse still, I was carrying a canvass bag containing what was plainly a gun.

By way of contrast, the couple confronting me might well have stepped out of one of those very posters. I could imagine their first encounter as having occurred on just such a happy jaunt, golden haired youngsters leaning over styles to consult their maps or straddling their crossbars to admire the view.

First one then the other examined my membership card. I could see they were nonplussed. I had read the membership rules and nowhere was there any mention of firearms. Intoxicants were forbidden, there were restrictions on smoking and portable wirelesses and members were enjoined to uphold the Association's "reputation for sensible behaviour in the countryside." Well, I did not drink, smoke, own a wireless, and as for behaving sensibly in the countryside – that was precisely what I intended. I was there to enjoy the great out of doors – in fact, I was about to do so, or so it seemed to me, in a far more meaningful way than those idiotic groups I'd seen from the bus, heads down, arses up, peddling like crazy among the cars and lorries. What kind of enjoyment of the countryside was that, risking your life breathing petrol and diesel fumes? How many of them, I wondered, wrote poems about their experiences or kept nature diaries filled with meticulously executed pen and ink drawings? They were town people with no more experience of, or interest in, real outdoor life than the London advertising agency that dreamed up the posters on the walls. While they were sitting around of an evening cooking their tinned meat and vegetables I'd be out on the marshes. As I wrote in my journal that evening, "Those long-haired vulgar cyclists, what do they know of the full hunter's moon reflected on the glittering mud?"

This was pure conjecture. Being a weekday in December no one else was staying. As I had not booked in advance I was told that there would be no meals available. OK, so they were not going to make me welcome, but they were not going to throw me out either. With nothing to live on but two sandwiches, a packet of biscuits and a tin of pilchards it was going to be a hungry week. I paid my nine pence, tramped up to the empty dormitory, changed into Wellington boots, slung my game bag over my shoulder, tucked my gun, still in its canvas bag, under my arm and headed downstairs. Instead of wishing me luck they looked ostentatiously in the opposite direction.

In spite of this frosty reception it was a moment I'd dreamed of all year. Back in February I'd written in my journal,

> As I watched those gulls flying through the filtering snow, silhouetted against the leaden sky, I longed to be away from these houses, away on some lonely mudflats with only the sea birds and wildfowl for company.

Well, hungry and unwelcome though I felt, that was what I was now doing. The sight did not altogether disappoint. As I wrote in my journal that evening,

> As I topped a rise, the whole Island and the Slakes lay below me under the palm of my hand. It was here that Abel Chapman stalked the Brent [geese]; it was here that so many of my favourite authors had adventures that made me thrill with excitement as I read of them. I imagined great skeins of wildfowl etched against a winter's sky

No such great skeins were visible on this occasion – or on subsequent ones either – at least not in the teeming numbers described by Chapman or as drawn by Riddell.

Nevertheless, like Chapman and the other Victorian hunters whose books I read at the Newcastle Literary and Philosophical Society, I believed in the limitless bounty of nature. Chapman had been a punt gunner, which is to say he had shot his ducks and geese with a three-inch canon mounted on a flat boat, routinely killing thirty or forty at a time. Rex Irwin, the twins' father, towards whose punt house I was now walking, held the record, having bagged some 130 widgeon with one shot. Theirs was wildfowling on the grand scale. That it reduced the total number of wildfowl to any significant degree had not occurred to them – or, indeed, to me – any more than the notion that catching fish would deplete the number of fish in the seas.

Nor do I recall such issues being discussed in *The Field, Shooting Times, Country Life* or any of the other sporting magazines laid out on the long table in the reading room of Newcastle's Lit and Phil that I would stop by to consult on the way home from school. These tended to be more concerned with pheasant rearing, fox hunting, and deer stalking than wildfowling. I had nothing against shooting deer or pheasants; nor, having read my Siegfried Sassoon, against riding to hounds, although the tips on estate management and the organising of shooting parties hardly seemed relevant to one in my position. Still, the advertisements for Scottish shooting estates, lavish oil paintings, and Louis XV furniture offered a tantalising glimpse of what life was like for those at the top.

Intriguing, too, were the soft focus portraits of young women, occasionally in riding gear, gracing the frontispieces of such magazines. These I took to be country house versions of tabloid pin-ups. Mostly, they were the daughters of titled folk or senior military officers. Some had double-barrelled names; one, Jane Vane-Tempest-Stewart, had a triple-barrelled one. Hers was a name to conjure with, one that that impressed me all the more as I was studying the English Civil War at the time and so knew something about the parts that Vanes, Tempests and Stewarts had played in that conflict. Even more intriguing than her name's historical resonances, however, was an accompanying statement to the effect that her family home was in Seaham. I had been to Seaham; the students I commuted with to Newcastle came from Seaham; everything I knew or had heard about Seaham pointed to one inescapable fact, namely that Seaham was a dump. So what would such a striking-looking young woman, who from her appearance it was hard to imagine living anywhere north of the Wash, find to do in Seaham? Go fox hunting among the slag heaps? Distribute alms to the poor? Sunderland was bad enough, but no one in their right mind would live in Seaham other than out of dire necessity, which hardly seemed likely to apply in her case. It was a puzzle.

That wildfowling seldom featured in these magazines I attributed to the editors' regarding it as rather a plebeian branch of shooting, otherwise a distinctly up-market sport. Because everything below the tide line was open to all and sundry, anyone with a gun licence could go wildfowling. It was thus a very different proposition from standing in one's tweeds in a stubble field and potting driven pheasants, an expensive occupation requiring the hiring of beaters and usually a generous payment to the landowner. Wildfowling was also, particularly for those who ventured out onto mudflats, a dangerous and dirty occupation. Pheasants, like the barnyard fowl they resemble, are extremely stupid. Duck and geese, on the other hand, are wild and very clever, which makes hunting them that much more of a challenge. If pheasant shooters look down on wildfowlers, the same is true the other way around.

But what at that age persuaded me wildfowling was superior to bicycling and hiking – and to organised pheasant shooting for that matter – was that I saw it as a way of satisfying a primal human urge to hunt. In fact it was about as close it seemed to me as one could get in modern Britain – deer stalking aside – of satisfying that primitive instinct. Its principal disadvantage, at least for shore-shooters like me, was that for most of the day, unless the weather is unusually stormy, nothing happens. It is at dawn and dusk, and at night when the moon is up, that wildfowl fly. On a clear night the birds can see you a mile away. Best of all for wildfowling is a windy moonlit night when the birds fly low and are visible silhouetted against a layer of cloud. But, as always with hunting, conditions are seldom right, and even when they are, the moments of high excitement are interspersed with long periods when nothing at all happens. These I would fill in by tramping along the coast and over the dunes to Budle Bay on the look out for whatever else might be worth shooting – rabbits, hares, partridges and the occasional wandering pheasant. As all of these, apart from rabbits, were technically game, I could have been prosecuted, but the war and social change had rendered the old Game Laws redundant. No one ever enquired if I had a game licence. The butchers in Newcastle's Granger Street Market to whom I would take my bag on the way to school on Monday mornings certainly never did. With domestic meat strictly rationed they were pleased to have something to sell and what they paid me for what I had shot helped cover the cost of the bus fare and cartridges.

𝄞 𝄞

But here I am anticipating. That first trip I was lonely tramping up and down the coast on my own. However, I had brought a notebook in which I scribbled reflections on the immensity of the universe, the insignificance of man, the ugliness of his works, the glories of nature, and the stupidity of Youth Hostel wardens, all to be incorporated into my second Hancock submission. Sometimes I drew sketches, for I was determined that the new version should be even more handsomely illustrated than its predecessor. Occasionally I broke into verse:

Far, far away,
In the faint light of day
The grey gees are gathered
In gabbling array.

Meanwhile, back at the Youth Hostel, the wardens were growing increasingly tight-lipped, never missing an opportunity to tell me that they were fully booked for the weekend. I suppose they had been up in the dormitory, which was taking on the appearance of a butcher's shop or gamekeeper's gibbet on account of all the furry and feathery corpses strung up around my bed. Although I had taken care to see they didn't drip blood on the floorboards by arranging newspapers underneath, I could see that from the warden's viewpoint it did not look like the sort of thing youth hostelling was supposed to be about. In the event I stayed there only three nights, by which time, having consumed the sandwiches and pilchards, I was prepared to give up. As a last resort I knocked on the door of the crossing keeper's cottage to ask if anyone there knew where I could get a meal and bed. That was how I made the acquaintance of Ma Schooler.

"Aye," she said, "I'll gie ye a bed if nae one else comes."

So I went back to the Hostel and collected the game and the rest of my clobber.

"I hope you are not thinking of coming back," the hostel woman shouted after me. "We're fully booked for the holidays."

So I never did go back, not to the Youth Hostel anyway. I offered two rabbits to Ma Schooler. "They'll allus make a meal," she said. "I suppose ye'll be going out tonight?"

I said I would.

She gave me dinner before I went out and was impressed by how much I ate. "They must have been starving ye at that hostel." I told her they hadn't been feeding me at all, and the reason why.

"Aye," she said, "there's some folks funny like that."

The next morning I stopped at the farm to make sure I knew which was the Irwins' punt house and was invited in. On the wall I recognised a photograph of an old fisherman and commercial wildfowler with a long white beard, a picture I had seen in wildfowling books. It was Selby, Abel Chapman's Old Man of the Marshes. There were lots of other sporting memorabilia including a huge mounted head of a bison. Chapman had been all around the world slaughtering lions, elephants, pretty much anything that came his way – museums were stuffed with his trophies – so presumably this bison was one he had shot in America.

On my last day I met Dr Basham and his partner, joint owners of the punt house next to the Irwin's. The pair were soaked to the skin having been out near the Island when their punt was swamped. Left stranded by the tide they had spent hours dragging it across the mud. I helped them pull it in the last few hundred yards and tip out the remaining water. They were staying on the Island and but for their misadventure would not have come over to the mainland. They brewed up some tea, but there was no milk and the only implement for stirring in the sugar was a rusty nail. So it was I spent the afternoon sitting on the foreshore drinking black tea and talking over wildfowling matters while the tide crept in over the mud. It was almost dark and beginning to rain by the time the water was high enough for them to raise their sail and head off into the night. Out on the island the lights were coming on. Ah, this was the life! As I noted in my journal that evening, "They are men after my own heart, quiet, educated and strong [with] a touch of the stuff that makes men go off into the Antarctic to discover the South Pole."

Ma Schooler was always welcoming and fed me well. Once when she had other people staying I had to sleep on the floor of her garden shed, a structure situated within feet of the main Edinburgh-London line and so flimsy that when the expresses passed, as they regularly did at around 80 miles an hour, it felt as if the whole structure would be carried away.

Meanwhile I had lost touch with the Irwins, the twins having left school. Early in the 1948 season, however, tramping back along the shore I saw their punt house window lit up. Pat, the oldest brother, was there on his own and invited me in to stay. He'd left school several years before and was now farming. So too, I gathered, were the twins. However, we arranged that in future we would keep in touch and that I'd co-ordinate my visits with theirs. This saved me having to carry my sea boots and oilskins back and forth every time. Later I acquired a key of my own and so could stay there even when they were not around.

Night on the mudflats. Drawing aged 16

Back home I fashioned a pair of wooden patens allowing me to go out on the mud. There were many different kinds of mud. Far out, if one dared venture that far, it gradually gave way to sand. That closer to shore had an oily, glutinous, jelly-like quality and so soft that if one fell over it was almost impossible to get up without the help of a pole or shovel. Should the worst come to the worst the solution was to roll or crawl to one of the creeks as they had pebbled bottoms. The principal dangers were getting cut off by the tide or getting mud into the barrel of one's gun, in which case it might explode. As all of our shooting out on the mud was necessarily at night, finding what we had brought down was difficult. In the morning herring gulls would patrol the mudflats looking for dead or wounded birds. It was a common sight, especially after the punt gunners had been at work, to see solitary wounded birds sitting on the tide, each with a herring gull in attendance.

The Irwin's punt house was no more than an elongated tar-paper shack set on the foreshore. Three-quarters of its length was taken up with housing the punt itself, never used in my time. However, the other quarter, which was partitioned off, had a wooden floor, a collapsible table, a double bunk, an acetylene lamp on a hook and an iron stove that properly stoked with coke gave off a good heat. Nevertheless, living conditions were primitive. The only fresh water came from a nearby stream that flowed through a farmyard, and as there were no toilet facilities, the convention being that we used the sheltered end of Basham's punt house. Ours and the Basham's were the only two punt houses on our side of the mudflats, but the Bashams also had one out on the Island and there must have been others too for from time to time we would hear the boom of their guns.

Wildfowlers proved a companionable lot. Tramping up and down the coast I struck up a friendship with Jim, a retired miner from Ashington armed with an old-fashioned hammer gun. We were to spend many hours together sitting in ditches waiting for the evening flight. He told me he was a communist, and although he didn't admit to having personally written SECOND FRONT NOW or YANKS GO HOME about the place, he plainly sympathised with the lads who had. His version of history bore little relation to the one I was being taught at school. By his account we lived in a world shaped by vast and sinister forces. Nothing happened by accident, or at all events nothing that could not be readily explained in terms of some conspiracy theory. What were the Tories but a sort of Mafia gang? Had I seen the famous picture of Churchill, complete with cigar and Thompson submachine gun, looking like Al Capone? Did I not know that he had once ended a dockworkers' strike by threatening to have the Royal Navy shell Liverpool? But, although the Tories were the worst, Labour was scarcely better. Look what they had paid the mine owners when they nationalised the pits. Bloody fortunes! If there had been a just settlement that money would have gone to the miners. Basic to all his thinking was the notion of property being theft. "Dinna believe what they tell yer," he would say. "The country won't be free until the likes of us can have a go at the Duke of Northumberland's pheasants." Come the Revolution, it seemed to me, there would not be many pheasants left. Nevertheless, one of his comments took me aback.

"They'll be Lambton pits down where you come from," he said.

"Lambton Castle is there," I said, "but I don't know about the pits."

"Aye, but I imagine he owns most of them. Like up here it's the Percys."

"You mean the Percys own all those collieries, the ones I saw from the bus?"

"Whey aye man, where do you suppose they get all their money from? It's from us miners."

This was news to me. The impression that I had got from Father's tales of his youth had led me to think of the Percys as stalwart defenders of rural England, a view strengthened by my own experiences of holidaying in and around Alnwick. It was what, as I understood it, British history was all about – town versus country, industry versus agriculture, the Commons versus the Lords. I had supposed the Percys, Lumleys, Lambtons, and, over the Pennines, the Lowthers, all of whose handsome estates I had visited and admired, to be countrymen at heart and thus defenders of the old rural order. Latterly, judging by what I'd seen and been told, things had not been going too well for them on account of income tax and death duties. All around

Teenage drawing of Jim from Ashington

England their stately homes were being abandoned, sold off, torn down, turned into hotels, their estates transformed into golf courses, theme parks, and housing projects. It was part of an ongoing process, the march of Blake's dark satanic mills over England's green and pleasant land. And who was responsible? First it had been the capitalists, now it was the Socialists.

Who the Socialists were was clear enough. They were the Attlee Government, much despised by Father, who were now running the country, and the Sunderland Council and its counterparts elsewhere who were busily engaged paving over the countryside with housing estates. But who exactly were the capitalists? I imagined figures of the kind portrayed by cartoonists, men with immense waistlines holding bags of money – in fact, figures like Sir Arthur Sutherland and the other RGS Governors in their frock coats, striped pants and mayoral chains who, looking uncommonly like George Grosz's Weimar plutocrats, trooped onto the School platform every speech day to tell us to work hard and play hard in the expectation of one day becoming like them. It was hardly a prospect to thrill. Still, there was no denying that they had been remarkably generous to the School, giving us swimming pools, rifle ranges and other amenities. Latterly, however, there had been a series of civic scandals, extravagant even by Newcastle standards, beginning with the discovery that they had stolen a fire engine, not by leaping into its cab in their civic regalia and driving away Keystone Cops-fashion, although the result was much the same as if they had in the sense that they had acquired the vehicle illegally, sold it on to Liverpool and trousered the proceeds. Their main offence, however, had been failure to pay income tax and trading on the black market, both on such a scale as to warrant a number of them spending time behind bars.

Now here was Jim telling me that the big fish weren't this self-made lot but those whose hereditary estates and titles had led me to think of them as defenders of rural England. He laughed at my incredulity. "It's capitalism, man, that's how it works."

"I knew they owned the land."

"Whey aye, man. They owned the land and so they owned the coal. Yer divvn't get to live the way they do just growing turnips."

It made sense. *Somebody* must have made money out of the mines and not much of it seemed to have come to Sunderland. I was reminded of Bev's and my visits to Penshaw Monument built in honour of the Earl of Durham (he who jogged along on his £40,000 a year), with its plaque noting the generous contribution made by his "loyal tenants," a term I had associated with thatched cottages, swallows nesting under the eves and chickens running around the yard. Now I realised that it applied to the miners in the pit villages spread out on the plain below. I had always thought of them as workers, but now I came to think of it I realised they must have been tenants too. It made me wonder how voluntary their contributions had been.

I asked Father if the Percys were colliery owners. He supposed they would have had many interests and that coal might have been one of them, although it must have been run separately from the Estates Office in the Castle or his father would have mentioned it.

I consulted the School's copies of *The Dictionary of National Biography* and the Lit and Phil's copy of J. U. Nef's *The Rise of the British Coal Industry*. There I found that the first Duke, Hugh Percy (he of the Brizlee tower), owed his great fortune largely to coal, which was what was meant by his having "developed the resources of the Percy estates." I also discovered that he was not, properly speaking, a Percy at all having been born Hugh Smithson and adopted the name Percy on marrying the Percy heiress. (He had also fathered an illegitimate son, James Smithson, who hated him and left such fortune as he inherited from his mother to the United States, which used it to establish the Smithsonian Institution.) I further learned that the Lumleys and Lambtons, by developing the Durham coalfield and shipping its produce to London, had pretty much created Sunderland.

Flipping through Nef's index I came across other names I recognised. The Lowthers, I discovered, had been dominant figures in the development of Cumbria's Whitehaven coalfield. Another name that caught my eye was Vane-Tempest-Stewart, which turned out to be the family name of the Marquises of Londonderry, who were, or at all events had been, the largest coal owners in whole of England. Suddenly the young lady's connection with Seaham was explained. She did not *live* in Seaham, her family *owned* it – the town, the harbour, the shipping, in fact the whole caboodle. At one time they had had 4,000 miners labouring for them and bringing in a cool £60,000 a year. They owned lots of other places too, many of them in Ireland but some in other parts of England. Nor did it appear to be the case, as mostly it had been with the Percys, of their being landowners who let out their coal seams in the same way they let out arable land. The Vanes and the Tempests had started out as coal men and risen through the trade. They were coal owners through and through.

This turned my notions of the world upside down. Jim was right. It was coal money that had paid for Lowther and Lambton's fairy-tale castles and enabled them to live in the style they did. I pointed this out to Father, but he was unimpressed, regarding the aristocracy as part of the natural order. He also had firm views on the perils of wealth, thinking no doubt of cases he had come across during his time in the Bank of sons squandering their fathers' hard-earned fortunes – clogs to clogs in three generations. Occasionally he would lecture me on the subject. In return I would say that the Lambtons and Lowthers did not seem to have done too badly for themselves – or the Percys for that matter. "Ah," he would say, "that was different; they knew how to handle money, they'd been born to it." I was not so sure. For sheer profligacy the families I'd been looking up took some beating, the Lowthers in particular. What the 5ᵗʰ Earl got up to had filled the tabloids of his day!

I told Jim about what I had found. "Well, bugger me!" he said, "yer not as stupid as yer look."

❧ ❧

Needless to say I did not win the Hancock Prize the second time around. No personal greeting or explanation accompanied the manuscript. It simply arrived through the mail with a printed compliments slip on which someone had typed in tiny letters: "With thanks."

For a couple of years I neither saw nor heard from George William. However, one day while the Irwins and I were up at the punt house we heard voices outside and on going out found him standing in the middle of our latrine area. He was with a group of elderly bird watchers peering out over the mudflats through their binoculars. I introduced myself, but scarcely had he had time to take in who I was than a voice called out: "Someone has been here!" whereupon they fell to examining their shoes. I had been in the middle of asking George William if had seen any interesting birds when he turned his back on me and started shepherding his elderly flock back onto the sand and along the foreshore. The Irwins, who had watched all this from a distance, thought it was hilarious. "Someone has been here!" one of them would shout, and they would dissolve in laughter.

I had begun to wonder about the Irwins. I was also beginning to wonder about Abel Chapman, whose home address, I noted, had been Silksworth Hall and whose exploits had presumably been made possible thanks to the labour of the likes of Jim. In fact, having lately been given Peter Scott's *Wild Chorus* as a birthday present, I was beginning to wonder about the whole wildfowling enterprise. We seldom saw any Brent geese, which in Chapman's time had come in vast numbers. Thirty years before, he had regularly counted as many as 10,000 wintering around Holy Island. Elsewhere he had encountered wildfowl in even greater numbers. On his first winter in southern Spain he and his companions had shot over 5,000 head of wildfowl using shoulder guns alone. It was all very well his opposing wildlife conservation on the grounds that, as he put it, "The Laws of Nature will always take precedence over the laws of man," but one could not go on slaughtering wild creatures on that scale without its leading to a diminution in numbers. I was becoming petty sceptical about BB's "balance of nature" theories too. As Peter Scott pointed out, many species were simply being exterminated.

I called on George William at the Hancock on later occasions, mainly in the hope of proving that I'd not turned out quite as badly as he must have supposed. By way of redeeming myself, I also agreed to carry out periodic censuses of the bird population along the Durham coast between Seaham Harbour and Blackhall Colliery, no small penance as each census required a day-long tramp along what must surely be Britain's most desecrated shoreline. This was Vane-Tempest country (the Seaham colliery was actually called "Vane Tempest"). Here they had made a practice of getting rid of their slag by simply tipping it in the sea. Up to that time my bird watching expeditions had taken me to places of scenic beauty. The birds themselves, I now discovered, were less discriminating, not minding the sight of blackened beaches, derelict factories, rusting machinery, rotting wooden piles, or rubbish dumps – in fact they positively *loved* rubbish dumps.

George William was always courteous when we met, but never as warm as at our first meeting. He died in 1964. I later borrowed his family tree from the nephew to whom he had left it and passed on a photocopy to one of the Cambridge Temperleys whom I had lately met and who had embarked on yet another attempt to compile a family genealogy, only this time in a thoroughly professional manner using the computerised records of the Mormon Church. His findings effectively scotch George William's notion of the Catholic grandees of Hintlesham Hall, Suffolk, transforming themselves into the Protestant coal- and lead-mining Temperleys of Haydon Bridge. Until evidence is found to the contrary is found it may be assumed that local church records are correct in showing the East Anglia Timperleys as having taken themselves off to France to join the Old Pretender and that the Northumbrian Temperleys were pretty much a cross section of the Tyne Valley's population. Whatever the mists out of which my mother's family emerged, it is plain that my father's was solidly North Country English.

Not surprisingly, my wildfowling excursions impinged on my School activities. Being away so many weekends meant missing Saturday sports fixtures. Accounting for these absences meant concocting ever more implausible excuses leading to a showdown with the games master who vowed that so long as he was in charge I would never again play for a School team. This was fine by me. I'd much sooner be out on the marshes with a gun than travelling to and from windswept rugby pitches. There was a similar bust up with the master in charge of the School's Officer Cadet Force, which I had ill-advisedly joined without realising that it would be like the boy scouts only worse. I wanted to be out of doors doing things rather than sitting around in an uncomfortable uniform being instructed on how to do them.

Thus released, I began branching out in other directions. My winning of the Hancock prize had caught the attention of M G Robinson, the Senior English Master, who was a keen bird watcher, and to my striking up a friendship with his protégé, David Boll. David was in many respects a Newcastle counterpart of Bev, having a record of academic brilliance, an overbearing schoolmaster for a father (our gloomy Head of Mathematics), and an unhappy home life. That he had a gift for writing was evident from his articles in the School magazine, *The Novo,* of which he duly became Editor. He was also a leading figure in the School's debating society, in fact, one of the principal intellectual luminaries of an unusually brilliant year. It was no surprise when, in his second sixth-form year, he won an open scholarship to Balliol.

That he took any interest in me, a B-stream pupil two years his junior was flattering. True, I knew as much as he did about birds. I had also read widely in my own idiosyncratic way, although by no means as widely in English literature as he had. Early on in our acquaintance he asked me what poets I admired. Remembering father's recitations, I told him Sir Walter Scott. "Ah," he said with what seemed like approval, "so you're a Scott Man." This and other Oxford-sounding pomposities he had obviously got from MGR. All the same, I thought it sounded rather grand.

While it is easy to appreciate why I was impressed by David, it is less easy to understand what he saw in me. In part it may be explained by the fact that he and I were just about the School's only knowledgeable birdwatchers. Although I do not precisely recall the circumstances, it was probably on one or another of MGR's bird watching expeditions that we first met up. Once acquainted, we began organising trips of our own, initially as day outings, later as camping expeditions. In the years that followed, we must have camped dozens of times, mostly on our own but sometimes with other boys. One favourite location was Kielder Forest, up on the Cumbria border where there were reputed to be Golden Eagles, although we seldom saw them. Twice we went to Inchnadamph in Sutherland where there genuinely were eagles as well as ptarmigan, herds of red deer and much else not found in the vicinity of Newcastle. We climbed Suilven and most of the other mountains thereabouts; we also had an old man row us over the Kyle of Durness to visit the aptly named Cape Wrath. At the bar of the Inchnadamph Hotel we made the acquaintance of the local gillies from whom we prized out stories about the Whitbreads, Grosvenors and other local landowners. Lady Mary Grosvenor, according to her gillie, spent half the year in the wilds of Kenya and the other half in the wilds of Scotland, travelling between the two by aeroplane and chauffeur-driven car.

"Aye," he'd say, "all she ever thinks about is shooting. And she'll go up a hillside like a man. Nothing she likes better than going off in the snow with a rifle and a mule. She'll stalk a stag all day, shoot it, cut its throat and bring it back all on her own."

It struck me as an enviable lifestyle. By his account she would travel to and from the airport with the blinds pulled down so as not to witness the horrors of modern Britain.

On these expeditions we mostly slept in my parents' beach tent, a flimsy affair that let in the rain and was no defence against midges. We also lacked proper sleeping bags, making do with groundsheets and blankets pinned together. Camping had not yet become popular so there were no organised campsites, at least not in the places we wanted to go, but farmers would generally let us camp in the corner of a field in return for our buying their milk and eggs. If the weather turned nasty, they'd also usually let us take refuge in a barn or outhouse.

With David as my mentor a whole new world opened up. In some ways it was like Hazel Bank all over again, not simply our roaming the countryside but my mixing with boys far senior to me, the difference was that those with whom I was now mixing were the School's high achievers. One would later become the nation's Lord Chief Justice, another its Banking Ombudsman, and yet others High Court judges, television producers and media personalities.

In spite of the discrepancy in age and achievement, my relationship with David was not entirely one sided. There were things I knew that he did not. So far as literature was concerned I deferred to his judgment, much as, I presumed, he deferred to MGR's. Many speak of the way their lives have been transformed by a charismatic school teacher. That was arguably my experience, only at one remove and allowing for the fact that we were perfectly capable of branching out in ways of our own, as into the work of various Continental writers. In fact it was Father who, having once read *Crime and Punishment*, put me onto reading Dostoevsky, from which it was a natural step to go on to Tolstoy. Still, it was the case that what David got from MGR he passed on to me with the result that by the time I was in the fifth form I was roughly acquainted with the current literary canon, solemnly ploughing my way through Joyce's *Ulysses* (still officially banned) and even dipping into *Finnegan's Wake*. Some of this was a waste of time. On the other hand, it was immediately evident to me from *Portrait of the Artist* and *Dubliners* that Joyce's writing was of quite a different order to anything I had come across before. The same could be said of Graham Greene and Evelyn Waugh. I also liked Auden insofar as I could understand him. Pound and Eliot were another matter. The former I found totally incomprehensible and the latter puzzling. What was this Waste Land he went on about? My impression was that people down south led rather privileged lives. Judging by his photograph, Eliot looked like a bit of a toff himself. Had he deigned to come up our way I could have shown him what a real waste land looked like. Had he, I wondered, ever visited a pit village or a dockyard? This, however, was David and MGR's territory, so I kept my scepticism to myself.

Nevertheless, I was quite capable of taking issue with David over other matters, as over Freud's Ego, Super Ego and Id, which impressed him but struck me as airy-fairy notions. Having become an avid reader of books on popular science I'd been entirely won over to Behaviourism. You could measure conditioned reflexes in a way you couldn't measure Egos and Ids. More fascinating still was the smattering of information I'd picked up regarding relativity and quantum theory. Unlike the basic physics and chemistry I was studying for School Certificate, I found advanced science every bit as intellectually stimulating as anything in literature. So far as I was concerned George Gamow's *Mr Tompkins in Wonderland*, with its trains travelling at the speed of light and stop-watch observers positioned on platforms, besides being scientifically accurate, stretched the imagination quite as much as anything in fiction – or verse for that matter.

It was also the case that David's thick-lensed glasses and receding chin made him look like an intellectual nerd of the kind portrayed by cartoonists, which may explain why, given the choice, the prettier girls seemed to prefer me. Picking up local girls was more his line than mine. Nothing much ever came of it. Still, I remember his once being chagrined when we camped in a barn outside Alnwick and two girls he'd chatted up took to standing outside chanting "Howard, Howard, Howard" rather than "David, David, David." I was unhappy for another reason. The barn belonged to an old friend of my father's, who had agreed to let us use it on the understanding that we were interested in birds of the feathered kind. I was not best pleased, and neither was Father, when a letter arrived describing what had transpired in rather exaggerated terms and saying that we would not be welcome thereabouts again.

At the end of my fifth-form year, by which time David had won his Oxford open scholarship and was waiting to go into the Army, he, I and another boy spent three weeks bird watching in France, first in the Auvergne and later in the Camargue. Again, it was all done on the advice of MGR, who was familiar with those areas. Originally there were to have been more of us but the others pulled out leaving only David, me and a slender, rather girlish-looking fifteen-year-old named Robin, who also wrote for *The Novo* and was plainly destined to be one of the School's future intellectual luminaries. Whether the School or our parents were suspicious of these relationships I've no idea. My brother remembers on the eve of my departure my mother saying "Now, Howard, I've never talked to you about sex," and my replying, "Oh mother, for heaven's sake," at which point she gave up.

It was only many years later, when David confessed (he had earlier put it into a novel), that I became aware that he had a crush on Robin and that they had been up to more than I realised at the time. As has generally proven the case with such entanglements, I'm astonished in retrospect at my naïveté. We had been sharing the same hotel rooms, haylofts and youth hostels for three weeks and all I noticed was a certain amount of private giggling. We are told to trust our instincts in such situations. Well, I knew what my instincts were telling me and the message came over loud and clear. Quite simply they were both much cleverer than I was – better at card games, more fluent in French, quicker witted and so living on a different plane from slow-thinking types like myself. As with Bev, it was not something I resented, simply a fact of life. All that holiday I lived in dread of what I would find when I got home and saw my School Certificate results.

DAVID AND ROBIN IN FRANCE

My lack of perceptiveness as to what was actually going on may be attributed to the fact that nothing of that sort had arisen in the course of my relationship with David. Yet there is no denying that ours was an intense relationship. I remember being extraordinarily nasty, out of what I now realise was pure jealousy, to a boy who tagged along with us up in Inchnadamph.

Apart from David's infatuation with Robin I know of no other such carryings-on between older and younger boys at the RGS. Doubtless some of our contemporaries were gay, but if that was the case I was unaware of it and so, quite conceivably, were they. As ours was a day school the lack of girls was not as acutely felt as at boarding schools. All the same it was a problem, and during the brief interval between the time boys reached puberty and the time when they came to think that they were too old for wrestling on the School field there was a certain amount of groping that went on, but – and here again I may simply be displaying my naïveté – my impression is that it quickly died out.

My first orgasm occurred in the back tier of benches in a lecture theatre as a result of just such a groping encounter. It was an experience for which I was totally unprepared. This was quite some time before my meeting up with David and the other events I have been describing. I do not recall the name of the other boy, but he was evidently more versed in such matters than I was. The experience filled me with excitement and terror. Suppose the Physics master had looked up from his experiment and seen the expression of total astonishment on my face. I presumed I would have been expelled from the School. My whole life would have been blighted.

The more I thought about it the more shameful and foolish it seemed. Yet, wracked with guilt though I was, there was no denying that it had been an exciting experience. The boy concerned showed no interest in repeating it, besides which I found it was an experience that could perfectly well be achieved single-handedly.

As to what the School would have done had I been discovered I can only speculate. These were uncharted waters. A possibility that never occurred to me was that I would have been judged the innocent party, as in a sense I was. More likely, as would prove the case some years later when I took to arresting soldiers for similar acts, the authorities would simply not have wanted to know about it. Being a relatively humane school, I'd like to think the most probable outcome would have been a quiet talking to by Tucker Anderson. Although I rarely saw him now he was back in charge of the Junior School it was plain when I did that he still took a paternal interest in my goings on.

But, whatever the likely outcome, there was no doubt in my own mind that I had committed an act of unspeakable wickedness. Being an atheist I was not troubled by thoughts of Hell. What troubled me was what the act revealed about me in the here and now. In the course of our Sunday morning walks it emerged that Father thought Oscar Wilde a very wicked man, although what exactly he had done, except that it had involved a Lord Alfred Douglas, was never exactly spelled out. So where did that leave me? If Wilde deserved punishment, then I must deserve punishment too. Homosexual acts were still deemed criminal offences and those found guilty of committing them continued to be sent to prison. The Sunday papers were full of such stories.

It never occurred to me that my confusion was anyone's fault but my own. Sex was an unspeakable subject, both in the sense that the acts concerned were physically disgusting and in the literal sense that it was something that should not be spoken of in public, or in private for that matter, and hence a mystery one was left to uncover as best one could from, novels, newspapers, lavatory walls, and the confidences of one's schoolfellows. Yet it was obviously important. George William Temperley had implicitly spoken of it when he talked about continuing the family line, which could only be achieved by – well, you know what. Those medieval couples whose likenesses, carved in stone or etched in brass, lined the aisles of Durham Cathedral must have got up to it. The same applied to Mr and Mrs Carss, Mr and Mrs Pickersgill. Even my own parents must have got up to it. Did any of them encounter problems of the kind I'd been warned about by the owner of the two dogs back in Eamont Bridge? As I knew hardly any girls I'd no idea what their thoughts were on the subject, although from what I knew about the thoughts of boys I assumed theirs must be rather purer.

That it was a subject about which the whole of society was in collective denial never occurred to me.

In retrospect I wonder if my seniors weren't as confused as I was. What, for example, did my parents make of Darcy? Darcy was Mrs Whitfield's sister and thus the aunt of the Whitfield boys over the road. Darcy had a man's haircut, wore a collar and tie, spoke with a man's voice and walked with a man's swagger. She also did manly things. She owned an open convertible almost as large the ones from which Hitler had reviewed parades, and would arrive wearing gauntlets and goggles looking like Amelia Earhart. Most remarkable of all was her habit of bringing with her a succession of fluffy female companions to whom, when we boys gathered around to admire her remarkable automobile, she would solemnly introduce us.

Yet, flamboyant lesbian though she obviously was, my parents invariably spoke of her with reverence. That was because they revered education and Darcy was one of His Majesty's Inspectors of Schools. In their opinion it was scarcely possible to achieve higher distinction, educationally speaking, than that. Lacking much in the way of formal education themselves they thought of teachers as brainy. Darcy was a super teacher, a queen bee of the teaching profession, a teacher of teachers, and her fluffy young companions were apprentice teachers, doubtless benefiting from her instruction. All of this was of course, lost on me. I suspect it wasn't until after I'd left school that Mr Tooby, an irreverent neighbour from down the road, alerted me to the possibility that she might have been instructing them in more than I had supposed.

In my final Middle School report Larry Watson noted, evidently without much conviction, that "He is the type of boy who <u>might</u> blossom in the VI." Admittedly I'd never taken seriously the notion of my winding up selling matches outside the Odeon, but it was easy to imagine other outcomes only marginally less disagreeable. As compared with the prospects of proven high-flyers like David and Bev mine looked distinctly looked unpromising.

Allocating positions on the basis of talent rather than birth or wealth made sense. But what if one lacked talent? To while away one's life in a mundane job performing tasks one disliked and probably wasn't very good at! It didn't bear thinking about.

5: ALMOST AN INTELLECTUAL: 1949-51

MY WILDFOWLING DAYS ended abruptly in December 1949. As usual, I had caught the bus after school on the Friday, got off on the Great North Road, walked down past Ma Schooler's cottage, crossed the rail line and cut across the fields to the Irwins' punt house. It had all become so familiar that I didn't need a torch even though it was pitch dark. Eric had got there a couple of hours earlier and had the stove already lit.

On the Saturday an easterly gale blew up making the birds fly low. That night we were awakened around 2.00 am by the sound of greylags in the nearby creek, but they must have heard us moving about because they took off before we got the door open. Hoping that they would return the next night we decided to stay on an extra day.

Again the same thing happened, only this time we took more care. By the sound of it there were even more geese than the night before. As we crawled out of the door and along the beach more and more kept coming in. Eric had the big 8-bore. Between us we got six and the next day another one that we had wounded came in on the tide. What with the duck, waders and rabbits we had shot during the day it was the largest bag we had ever made.

So it was that, heavily laden, tired, hungry we set off for the bus stop shortly after dark on the Monday. As in some old black and white film I can remember every freeze-framed detail – wet tarmac, telegraph poles, our leaning against the gale, Eric holding the crossing gate as I went through, and the train that came from nowhere, a sudden roaring, glittering apparition that in a second was gone – and then the silence, the empty road stretching ahead, the empty track down which the train had disappeared, and Eric vanished.

I walked a hundred yards down the track and there was nothing. A man came by on a bicycle to whom I told my story, who pushed his bicycle through the gates and rode away. At the cottage Ma Schooler came shuffling to the door. The storm had brought down the telephone lines and I'd need to go to the signal box.

Down the track, further than I could have imagined, there lay a goose and then other scattered objects that I couldn't properly see it being so dark. Finally, a good quarter of a mile from the crossing, there was a pale shapeless object that I took to be Eric, or what remained of him, tied up in his fisherman's-knit pullover. In all that dreary wilderness there was not a light to be seen until, beyond a wood, there appeared a tiny golden cube that seemed magically suspended in air. Having climbed the wooden stairs and pushed open the door I was met by a thick fug of pipe smoke, rows of levers, a glowing stove, and a signalman with his feet up reading the paper.

Then things began to happen. The Edinburgh express was stopped. A bunch of jolly railwaymen appeared. (Where could they have been?) And off we set, they in oilskins, flashing torches, me in an old army greatcoat leading the way, not looking where they played their beams.

Leaving them to their task, I made my way back to the cottage to find the police already there. What was my occupation? Why wasn't I at school? Did our parents know where we were? Could I describe the man on the bicycle? Then in barged the jolly railwaymen wanting cups of tea. There was a hand they had not been able to find but it would turn up in the morning. Having satisfied themselves that it was all straightforward, the police let me go. So I found myself standing alone at the side Great North Road, waiting for the bus Eric and I had been hurrying to catch three hours earlier. After a while the police car come by, paused as if some discussion were going on, and then sped away.

In Newcastle Central Station a man bought one of the geese I was carrying saying it would do for his Christmas dinner. It was midnight and my parents had long been in bed by the time I got home. Father came down in his pyjamas and instantly realised that something awful had happened. All the way home my one thought had been that I would have to inform the Irwins. So, simply telling him that Eric had been killed, I grabbed some coins and headed for the telephone box at the end of the street. It turned out the police had already rung, so the Irwins knew that Eric was dead but not that I had been with him or the details of how it had happened. While I was explaining all this, reassuring Eric's mother that his death had been absolutely instantaneous, Father in his dressing gown was dancing around outside like a moth around a lamp. Having dealt with the Irwins, I set about reassuring him that it was not, as he'd naturally assumed, a shooting accident. Eventually, having I got him calmed down and off to bed, I sat for a while with Mother, ate a bowl of cereal, had a bath and went off to bed myself.

My own calm still strikes me a little eerie. Plainly I was in a state of shock, but perhaps, too, it had something to do with my Hazel Bank training. "Nothing worse than this will ever happen to you," the headmaster said when I went back to school on the Wednesday, which would have been reassuring if I had believed him. A classmate's contribution "And the poor bugger never had a woman," struck me as more apposite.

It was all gone over at the inquest – the stormy night, trouble with the signal lamps (oil lamps on the front of a London express!), the train's late departure from Berwick, and the question of whether the pedestrian crossings should be manned (obviously impractical given that there were dozens, perhaps a hundred, between Berwick and Newcastle). Before the proceedings started a man came up to me in great agitation. At first I could not make out who he was but it eventually transpired that he was the train driver. Why he was so profusely apologetic I couldn't understand given that what had happened was no more his responsibility than that of the passengers in the carriages behind. I was continually surprised at the way others regarded it all as more extraordinary than I did. Having been brought up under the shadow of one war and lived through another it came as no surprise to be reminded that death could be sudden and arbitrary. But what haunted me, then and for some time after, was my failure to denounce British Rail for not putting proper lights on the front of its trains. I'd meant to; in fact I'd steeled my self to stand up and say my piece the moment the opportunity arose, but it never did. The oil lamps having blown out, there were no lights at all on the front of that train, nor, in that gale, was there any sound as it bore down on us at something close to a hundred miles an hour.

And so I was left with a sense of guilt at not having done what the occasion required of me. That Eric died and I survived, that he held the gate for me rather than I for him, was pure chance. Shuffle a pack of cards and deal them out and the chance of their coming out in a particular way is less than one in a billion. Still, they have to come out some way and that was how they came out in this instance. It could equally well have been both or neither of us. Thinking back to that winter's night of 60 years ago, it is not just that hurtling mass of steam and metal that comes to mind but what went before and came after: the geese coming in, our staying on an extra day, the fumbled lock, the pause at the stile to catch breath, all the circumstances leading up to that fatal conjunction of metal and flesh; and then the ripples spreading outward, the woman Eric didn't marry, the children he didn't have, the house where someone else is living.

By the time of the inquest the wildfowl season was at an end. I never saw or heard from the Irwins again. I doubted they would want to be reminded of me. In any case, by the time the next shooting season came around I was too involved in other things to spend time hanging around mudflats.

Years later I was reminded of my wildfowling forays when I saw John Huston's film of Arthur Miller's *The Misfits*, a tale of loners in Reno, Nevada, who head off into the wilderness to round up wild horses. They believe they are living the carefree, footloose life of the Old West, but this is 1960s America and the wild horses they team up to hunt are to be sold for dog food. Whatever the Old West had formerly been, this is plainly a debased version of it. Few wild horses are left and what the cowboys are doing is wanton and cruel.

Huston would have been hard-pressed to find a role for Marilyn Monroe on Northumberland's mudflats. Still, the film's message applied to us as much as to his cowboys. Years later I read that Old Selby, Abel Chapman's hero, had in one season, single-handedly, eliminated six percent of the world's pink footed geese. He, of course, was no romantic, just a commercial wildfowler. Thanks to changes in the law the geese not only survive but multiply. As in Abel Chapman's day vast skeins of them now fill the winter skies, while ducks swagger about in public in a way they would never have dared to do wartime. Long gone, however, are those shoals of herring that migrated annually around the British Isles. Gone, too, are the hardy fishermen I so admired and who fished them to extinction.

My School Certificate results had been waiting for me when I got back from France. By RGS standards they were mediocre. I had gained no distinctions, failed French and mathematics and not even bothered to take Latin. The only good news was that I'd achieved credits in everything else, including Physics and Chemistry, which was a surprise. Still, for someone entering the Arts Sixth, it hardly amounted to a ringing endorsement.

Yet, in spite of that, things began to look up. Independent thought was now encouraged and rewarded with ticks and comments in a way that had not been previously. MGR was a charismatic teacher, in perpetual motion, striding about the classroom in search of the right adjective or adverb. "You say Prince Hal was 'playing at being serious.' Yes, very good. But how would you describe Falstaff? A rogue? Well, he was that, but wasn't he something more? Wasn't he playing a role too? 'Lord of Misrule.' Yes, very good. Excellent." Sammy Middlebrook, the Senior History Master, a more august figure, was not a classroom performer. His expertise lay rather in the meticulous annotating and marking of our essays. I can picture him now with his glasses pushed up on his forehead, weary-eyed from the reading and annotating of so many essays. But come up with something good and you could be sure that Sammy would spot it and reward you with one of his ticks. MGR might inspire, but Sammy had been there for ever and represented the gold standard so far as essay marking was concerned. A remarkable number of Britain's leading historians – Sir Richard Southern,

Marcus Cunliffe, Jack Lively – had been his protégés. Get an A- from Sammy and you were up there with the greats.

I was not at that level, but I was getting B++ and even, on occasion, BA, which was as good as anyone in my year was getting. Although David was now in the army he came back occasionally on leave. Once, around breakfast time, he astonished Mother by appearing from our garden shed looking distinctly bedraggled having taken up with some local girl and lingered too late to catch a train home. Finding me just completing an essay for Sammy, he offered to rewrite it for me. He wrote in a strange cramped hand and his spelling was worse than mine, but there was no doubting that his prose style was much better, as proved the case when I submitted a fair copy and was rewarded with an A- together with a pat on the back from Sammy. It was the most useful lesson I was ever taught.

A week or two later, impressed by the work I'd been turning in, Sammy took me aside to ask how I would feel about trying for an Oxbridge scholarship in my second Sixthform year. It would be a risk because it would mean I'd be working mostly on my own; it would also mean that I'd not be following the Higher School Certificate syllabus like everyone else. I needn't come to school if I didn't feel like it; the important thing was that I should keep the essays rolling. In short, he and MGR would treat me as if I was a university undergraduate.

Thus began what I look back on as the most intellectually stimulating year of my life. Because Oxbridge scholarship exams were broadly based it meant that, with Sammy and MGR's approval, I could study and write about practically anything I liked. Suddenly all the reading I'd done became relevant, not just Evelyn Waugh's and Graham Greene's novels, but George Gamow's *Mr Tompkins in Wonderland*, C E M Joad's *Guide to Modern Thought* and George Bernard Shaw's *Prefaces*. A new discovery was L Susan Stebbing's *Thinking to Some Purpose*, a work which delighted me by deconstructing speeches by politicians. Effective oratory, I discovered, was no guarantee of honesty, Churchill being as adept at eliding awkward questions as all the rest. It was a principle that applied to politicians of all persuasions, autocrats and democrats alike.

For a while I was haunted by what I took to be the insurmountable problem of acquiring the Latin and French demanded by Oxford and Cambridge. After five humiliating years I was no closer to mastering them than I had been at the beginning. Yet, after a mere three months, with the help of a little private tuition, I succeeded in getting the School Certificate qualifications I needed.

As I imagine was the case with many grammar school boys in the 1940s, my counter-culture was, in fact, culture. As my horizons expanded I took to listening to the BBC's Third Programme. This was something of an imposition on the rest of the family. Wasn't I getting above myself? Promenade Concerts they could put up with; Aristophanes with his wailing choruses they found harder to take. Did I really like that stuff? The truth was that I didn't, although I aspired to. The Third Programme also broadcast lectures. The nearest I came to drugs as a schoolboy was listening to one by a canon of Christ Church, Oxford, who by way of experiment had taken something (LSD? mescaline? magic mushrooms?) at teatime one Sunday. However it was not until evensong a couple of hours later he had felt its full hallucinatory effects (hearing colours, seeing sounds), all of which he described in thrilling detail. A time was coming, he prophesied, when drugs would replace alcohol. The notion of drugs becoming readily available and of our all being able to go on psychedelic trips like the good canon struck me as an exciting prospect, but neither then nor later were they destined to come my way.

After working at home all day I would go out, often after dark, and climb Tunstall Hill or wander the town's alleys and back roads. There was, I discovered, an inconspicuous door into Backhouse Park that was never locked. The Backhouses had been rich Quakers whose mansion, along with its landscaped gardens, banks of rhododendrons and cedar trees, was the nearest thing Sunderland had to a stately home. Nearby were bombed houses where I could squeeze through the wire and climb the shattered staircases to rooms where people had once slept and where ivy now grew through the window frames. To test my nerve I sought out the spookiest places, opening cupboards never quite sure what they would reveal or what might fly out. Up a muddy lane to the north of Tunstall Hill there was a ruined farmhouse where bats flitted about and a pair of owls nested. Next to it was a barn where on a still night small creatures could be heard rustling in the hay. In the course of these late-night wanderings I was never surprised by a hand descending on my collar or a policeman with a torch looming up to ask me what I thought I was doing. In fact, I never met a soul.

တတ

But if my academic work had taken a turn for the better the same did not apply to my relations with girls. Having given up on Shuna, I heard it whispered that Margaret Carter had developed a similar crush on me. The Carters, makers of Carter's Bread, owned the town's largest bakery and lived in a large Edwardian house off Alexandra Road. Margaret, too, was large in a big-boned way, good at sports and with Christian leanings. She was a year older than me, preparing for her Higher School Certificate at Sunderland Girl's High School and planning to go on to study Art at one of the local art colleges.

If what I had been told was true, as it appeared to be, I had less cause to feel self-conscious talking to Margaret than to other girls. On the other hand, it didn't seem as though we had a great deal in common. She listened tolerantly enough to my disquisitions on the wonders of relativity as described in *Mr Tompkins*. I explained how a man with an acceleration equivalent to twice the force of gravity could travel immense distances and return at some date in the far distant future. With the help of diagrams I would eagerly demonstrate how, by measuring a ray of light entering his spacecraft, he could prove that light was bent by gravity. When I asked her questions about what I'd been explaining she would say she wasn't sure but liked hearing me talk. What she talked about I do not recall.

She was more than willing, however, to be led to some of the dark places I had explored in the course of my late night wanderings, including the hayloft up on the hill. There things did not work out as planned. I will spare you the details. Let me simply say that what I found mortifying at the time appears more comic in retrospect, not least the losing of my trousers. In a pile of loose hay a pair of trousers easily goes missing; and on a freezing cold night without the assistance of a torch they are not easily found. The more we searched the more hopeless it seemed until, just as Margaret was about to depart to filch a pair of her father's, they turned up.

Sin, I've heard it said, is its own reward; it is virtue that needs the green stamps. I had set out to sin – desperately wanted to sin – but it was premature ejaculation, not virtue that had prevented me from doing so. There had been no reward; no green stamps either. It was the worst of all outcomes, and it was entirely my fault. Big hunter, big intellectual, big flop!

It was a fiasco from which my relationship with Margaret never recovered. I had completely lost my nerve, at least so far as Margaret was concerned. We tried again, but in similar circumstances and to no better effect. Suppose it went on happening? In the whole of my reading the only character I'd encountered with a problem at all like mine was Joyce's Leopold Bloom. What made it all the worse was there was no one I could talk to about it: certainly not my parents; plainly not the Reverend Talbot after all his talk about the right place for sex being in marriage; not my friends, who would think I was pathetic; and least of all Margaret herself who – and I could hardly blame her – was becoming distinctly annoyed over my ineffectual goings on.

So there I was, barely seventeen, an angry woman on my hands and nothing in prospect but a lifetime of humiliation. Then, just when it seemed things could get no worse, they did.

The idea of having a fancy dress party came from some of the girls, and as Margaret was the one with the largest garden it was decided that it should be held there. I had never been to a fancy dress party and did not relish the prospect of having to dress up for one, but as Margaret had been cast in the role of hostess and as I was supposedly her boyfriend I could hardly refuse. I consulted Mother who said she would look around. Out of cupboards she produced miscellaneous items including a disintegrating fur coat and various other objects that ought to have gone to jumble sales. So it was in these that I set off for the party. It was a perfunctory effort, but I reckoned it would do.

As soon as I got there I realised I'd made a mistake. Not that, in most cases, the outfits amounted to much, but everyone else had gone as something – cowboy, pirate, detective, or whatever. Margaret confronted me.

"What are you supposed to be?"

"I don't know," I said. "You said it was a fancy dress party and I just thought these clothes were fancy."

"Why have you come dressed in women's clothes? Why, I wonder, would you want to dress up as a woman?"

I suddenly realised, thinking back to some of her earlier remarks about my friendship with David, the lines along which her mind had been working. Was this something she had dreamed up all on her own or had her friends put her up to it? Either way, I was appalled. Had I been more confident I would have told her to go to hell and walked out. But what basis had I for saying she *had* got me wrong? It had not been my intention to dress up as a drag queen but, seeing myself through her eyes, that was what I had contrived to do. People went on about the mysterious power of the unconscious. Maybe Freud was right. How much did I really know about myself?

How little I knew about her was revealed not long after when I called unexpectedly and glimpsed a woman in a nurse's uniform hurrying a strange looking figure into another room and abruptly shutting the door. It turned out that Margaret had a Down's syndrome sister about whom she had never told me.

But what finally put paid to the whole miserable business was Polly.

Polly was extraordinary, six feet tall in her stilettos, with a huge head of blonde hair, long painted finger nails and enormous ear rings, her style was straight out of Vogue. She went to the same school as Margaret but was two years her junior. What they made of her there I can't imagine. She had a friend called June who was good looking enough, but it was Polly people turned to look at, women as much as men. When she went to get a Poly-photo for her passport they blew it up to giant size and put it in their front window. Sunderland had never seen the likes.

I got to know Polly very well over the next two years. She was a year younger than me, which means that she and June must have been scarcely sixteen when they turned up at St. Nicholas's. I was mesmerised from the moment they walked in the door. Dressed like that they were plainly on the hunt and Robert and I were only too happy to be hunted. Perhaps my dancing had improved, anyway Polly seemed not to mind, and afterwards I walked her home. We were standing uncertainly on the doorstep as I dithered over whether to kiss her, shake hands or simply back away when the door suddenly opened to reveal an angry looking Mr Carr who grabbed Polly by the elbow, asked her what the hell she meant by coming home at this hour, glowered at me as the presumed culprit, and without a further word slammed the door in my face.

That more or less set the pattern as far as my relations with Mr Carr were concerned. He owned or managed a string of pubs and looked the part. With an ample belly, tight waistcoat, watch and chain and glowering expression he was not a man to be trifled with. The house, on the other hand, was full of tiny ornaments and fragile glass objects presumably collected by Polly's mother, a gossipy woman who reminded me of Jane Austen's Mrs Bennett. She would flutter her eyelids as she talked and was not above flirting with her daughter's admirers. There was also a younger daughter, Bunty, a normal, sensible, hardworking girl with a pigtail and university aspirations. I often wondered what she made of the other three.

I can see why a father with a daughter who looked like Polly might be worried, though in fact she had her head well screwed on. Abandoned scenes in cobwebby barns up muddy lanes were not her style. Looking the way she did required discipline, attention to detail and quite a bit of money. As regards the latter I can only assume her mother took her side for I didn't see her father volunteering. All the same, a lot of beer would have had to be drunk in Mr Carr's establishments to pay for Polly. Thursday nights were "hair nights" and nothing would induce her to change her schedule. She was also very good at keeping me up to scratch, seeing I walked on the outside of the pavement and allowed her the window seats on trams and buses. In this, as in everything else, her standards were exacting. Once she told me she would rather be killed than lose a finger.

Yet in spite of this she was not averse to late-night walks in Backhouse Park, the unlocked door I'd discovered being providentially set into the park wall only a stone's throw from her house. This became a regular routine, a fact not easily concealed from Mother when the weekly wash contained shirts and handkerchiefs extravagantly smeared with lipstick.

Sometimes we went to the cinema, sometimes to dances, on occasion to the Illuminations at Seaburn, Sunderland's version of the Blackpool Illuminations and quite possibly borrowed from there. In time she got a driving licence and took me on trips up into Northumberland and along the Roman Wall. Once I took her to a Sixthform dance where she caused a sensation with her three-inch heels and elbow-length gloves. No sporting triumph ever won me a fraction of the kudos I gained by appearing with Polly. My parents were no less dazzled.

"Oh, lad," Mother said afterwards. "You'll have trouble with that one."

And so it proved. Yet rocky relationship though it was, I suspect it suited us both very well thanks to the limits she put on it and the fact that, unlike what had happened with Margaret, it was all pretty much out in the open. Mother was fascinated. Father, being a restless sleeper, had taken to sleeping in Gladys' old bedroom and Mother liked reading late, so when I got home I'd regularly go up and fill her in, more or less, on the evening's events.

The first hitch occurred one day when, as arranged, I went to collect her and I was told by a flustered Mrs Carr that she had phoned to say she would be late. Where was she? She wasn't sure but she had phoned from somewhere up near Hexham. When eventually Polly turned up it was in a car driven by a young man in a business suit. This was unfair competition. What had a sixth former with a weekly pocket money allowance of five shillings to offer as compared with what was, as it turned out, a quantity surveyor?

I wrote a piece for *The Novo* about it but heavily disguised – supposedly it concerned a woman fraternising with the officers of an occupying army – so that no would know what it was *really* about. As it turned out, no one knew what it was *supposedly* about either, but as I was now Editor of *The Novo* what got published was up to me. It was a position I had attained partly on account of having written an earlier piece, also inspired by Polly, called "The Advertising Woman," a collage of descriptions of elegant women doing the sort of things models do to sell products, like draping themselves over the bonnets of cars and holding up packets of detergent.

The quantity surveyor, as I duly learned through June and Robert, did not last long. However, hardly had normal relations been resumed than an even more formidable rival appeared on the scene in the form of a handsome Sikh with a Rolls Royce and a turban. He was, as I duly learned, taking a degree in mechanical engineering at Sunderland Polytechnic and, like Polly, had become one of Sunderland's more striking figures. Also like Polly, he had gone to get a passport photograph with the result that a blow-up of his handsome turbaned head duly appeared alongside hers in the photographer's window.

This was about the time I went into the army. Polly had meanwhile left school and was training as a secretary. We never corresponded, or rather she never responded to my letters, but when I was home on leave I would call her and we would go out together. Once Young Charlie Pickersgill mentioned her to me, from which I gathered she had moved on into the local sports club and cocktail party circuit. The only time I felt really betrayed was on the eve of my embarkation for Egypt when, on returning home, I discovered that Robert had been taking her out. The scheming bastard, I thought, he's getting above himself. June was his girl. She was Polly's side kick just as he was mine, but evidently he didn't see it that way. What right had I, he wanted to know, to think I had a prior claim? Reasonable question though this was it made me so angry that I grabbed him by his lapels, held him over some railings and threatened to throw him into the stairwell below. Why I should have been so angry, and who exactly I was angry with puzzled me. For her to take up with the Sikh was one thing (it was, she assured me, a very *old* Rolls Royce) but for her then to parade around with Robert of all people seemed unworthy.

After I moved to America I lost contact with her. When I returned in 1959 I knocked on the familiar door and was asked in for tea. According to her mother, she had got a job as departmental secretary in the University of Newcastle's Department of Chemistry. There she had met a research scientist who had asked her to marry him and go out to the States. At first she had refused but, after thinking about it for a while, she had changed her mind and that was where she now was. Once, in Charlottesville, Virginia, I thought I saw her going into a rather handsome house in one of the streets just off campus. I was with my wife, who said I should stop the car and enquire but I'd probably made a mistake. No one at the university knew of a tall English girl who fitted her description. I wish now I'd gone back and rung the door bell. She certainly gladdened my life. Wherever you are Polly, I wish you well.

I did once reencounter Margaret. It was in the early 1960s; we were both back in Sunderland visiting our parents. She was on the lawn with a pram, I was walking by and we recognised each other at the same instant. It seemed churlish simply to walk on so I crossed over and lifted the latch on the garden gate. I was not well received. However, she introduced me to her husband, an art teacher she'd met at college. As I left she asked in a sneering sort of way "How's your funny friend," meaning, presumably, David. I said he was, like me, married and a father. Margaret is one of a group of women I try not to think about.

I took the Oxford Modern Subjects exam in the Headmaster's Office. The first paper, a three hour essay, had the names of all the colleges at the top and underneath various instructions and at the very bottom, in tiny print, a single word: "Circuses." For three hours I struggled – Roman circuses, bread and circuses, animals in circuses, circuses I had seen. Somehow I just couldn't get a handle on it. The other papers were better. I thought I had done well in one with an essay on Graham Greene and in another in which I had to compare a photograph with a reflection in a mirror. I did less well in one requiring that I paraphrase Ulysses' "alms for oblivion" speech from Shakespeare's *Troilus and Cressida*. Nevertheless, I'd done well enough to merit an interview and was duly summoned.

Up to that point I had thought of Oxford as a goal to be attained rather than as a place in which to live and study. In my mind's eye it was an institution of monkish ritual and awesome learning, an enlarged version of Durham with even more Gothic arches, ecclesiastical spires and terrifyingly intelligent people.

My initial encounter with it failed to dispel this impression. The School had put me down for Magdalen, my headmaster's old college. The rooms I was allocated were bare and cold as a mausoleum. I switched on the tiny electric fire and allowed it to remain on throughout my stay, but such warmth as its single bar produced failed to penetrate into the bedroom and even in the sitting room proved no match for the chill that seeped in from the walls.

My first interview was with C S Lewis. I'd read his *Screwtape Letters* and had imagined him as looking like Voltaire or some old Jesuit – thin faced, stooped, quizzical. In reality he wore tweeds and looked like a red faced farmer, albeit one who had just received a rather stern letter from the Inland Revenue. In front of him was a large brown envelope the contents of which he leafed through until, with a grunt, he extracted what he was looking for. This turned out to be my paraphrase of the Ulysses speech which, stupidly, I had failed to look up in the meantime. What exactly had Shakespeare meant when he said "And give to dust, that is a little gilt, more laud than gild o'er-dusted"? What, in general, was Ulysses getting at? It was an inquisition from which I did not emerge with credit.

My second interview was at Balliol. On the way I peeked into the envelope. On the bottom of the Shakespeare passage Lewis had written "He has not understood it." My Balliol interview could hardly have been more different. Instead of the peremptory Lewis I was questioned by a group of dons who seemed scarcely older than I was and who appeared to be thoroughly enjoying themselves. When they asked me about Shakespeare I piously trotted out T S Eliot's comment about the want of an "objective correlative" sufficient to account for Hamlet's behaviour, at which they laughed their heads off. This gave me the impression that Eliot was taken less seriously at Balliol than at the RGS. A college full of young dons prepared to take an irreverent view of such pontifical figures as Eliot impressed me as being a college after my own heart. In retrospect I suspect it may have been me they were not taking very seriously. Whatever the reason for their jollity, I warmed to them in a way I hadn't to Lewis.

Thinking I'd given a pretty good account of myself at Balliol put me in a suitable mood for taking the Magdalen History Scholarship exam, timed to coincide with the Modern Subjects interviews. The questions suited me. One allowed me to write at length about *War and Peace*, concerning which I had formed the view that, in spite of Tolstoy's masterly command of detail, his historical theories were nonsense. This was January 1951, two years before the publication of Isaiah Berlin's *The Hedgehog and the Fox*, so I had not got it from there. Somehow, all on my own, in however bumbling a fashion, I had come to much the same conclusions as Berlin.

The day after I got home a handwritten letter arrived from Bruce McFarlane, the senior Magdalen history tutor, mentioning in particular my Tolstoy piece and saying that the college had awarded me a Demyship, namely an open scholarship. In his autobiography William McGonagall notes, "The most amazing incident in my life was the time I discovered myself to be a poet, which was in the year 1877," which pretty much sums up how I felt in 1951 on discovering myself to be a Magdalen demy, the difference being that whereas McGonagall was mistaken with regard to his gifts as a poet I cherished no illusions about mine as a scholar. If my contemporaries were astonished – as many were – they were no more astonished than I. Plainly a mistake had been made.

My parents, who knew nothing of such matters, took it all at face value. Their numbskull had turned out to be an egghead. They were all the more impressed when a formal announcement arrived with my name printed alongside those of the year's other two History Demies: Prince Rupert of Lowenstein and Simon Wyndham Lewis. They did not take kindly, however, to a telegram that arrived from David saying CONGRATULATIONS. ALMOST A BOLL. Who did he think he was? I tried to explain that whereas he had been awarded a Domus scholarship by Balliol I had only got a Demyship from Magdalen. They said they couldn't see the difference. On reflection I wasn't sure I could either.

With an open award to Oxford I automatically qualified for a State Scholarship and so did not have to take Higher School Certificate. That was fortunate as I had done virtually nothing by way of preparation. However, with National Service looming, I did re-take School Certificate Mathematics, which I had failed at 16, thinking it would help me get a commission in the Artillery, and duly failed again. For the next forty years I would wake up haunted by dreams of exams not properly prepared for. Somewhere, deep down inside, I knew that things weren't as they should be. One day I would be found out.

6: EMPIRE TROOPER: 1951-53

CONSCRIPTION HAD BEEN going on for so long that service in the military had come to be seen as a natural rite of passage. Virtually all my male relatives had been in the armed forces at one time or other, Father and Uncle Walter for four years, Uncle Gordon for five. And now here we were at war once again, this time in Korea, in consequence of which National Service had been increased from eighteen months to two years. Still, compared to them, I was getting off lightly.

Most national servicemen were called up shortly after their eighteenth birthdays, exceptions being made in the case of medical and dental students like Bev and Robert on the assumption that they would be more useful to the military after they had qualified. Though I had hated the regimentation of the RGS Officer Cadet Corps, and indeed regimentation of any kind, I was resolved to make a go of the real army. Perhaps they would send me to Korea and I would have a chance to test my courage in action.

I found that by volunteering to be called up early I could choose the branch of the military in which I served. Having time on my hands I set about reading up on the subject. From Basil Liddell Hart and Heinz Guderian I learned that armour was the key to modern warfare. Britain's great mistake at the beginning of the war had been to deploy tanks in support of infantry rather than in the form of armoured divisions. Forward-thinking British strategists had been among the first to recognise the potential of massed armour, but, typically, we had left it to others to put their ideas into practice. If armour was what counted, that was where I wanted to be.

ᦉ ᦉ

My medical was in Newcastle Drill Hall. From its looks it had not had a lick of paint since Northumberland's brave lads had marched off to the Great War, or possibly the Boer War before that. Its cavernous interior was equally dingy. Most times, I imagined, it would have echoed to the shouting of orders and the stamping of boots. Now it was eerily silent. In the centre a man had set up a mini laboratory on a couple of trestle tables and was busily at work with test tubes and pipettes. Around the hall were offices, their doors painted the same frog green as everything else. In front of each there stood little queues of pale naked men

"In there; clothes off; shoes and socks too. Put them in the locker. Report to the first office on the left. Quick about it"

I stripped off and lined up with the other newcomers, peed into a flask and padded barefoot over the boards to add my contribution to the chemist's collection. And so for the next two hours I made my way by stages around the hall. I imagine that queuing with other naked figures was less of a novelty for me than for most, the RGS having had advanced views on such matters as nude swimming. All the same, I found myself discreetly glancing around, as I noticed others were also doing. I was, I discovered, one of the tall, skinny, hairless variety.

And so for the next two hours, as I made my way gradually around the hall, I was reminded of the scenes of purgatory I'd seen on the walls of French churches with angels soaring up above and devils with tridents prodding the damned into fiery holes down below except that, unlike either, our examiners seemed merely bored. One tested my eyesight, another my hearing, this last by going to the other end of the room, turning his back and whispering, a form of testing which, seeing how hard of hearing I latterly became, strikes me as having been a bit lackadaisical. There was one test, however, that I did query at the time. It was the one in which the examiner held my testicles and had me cough. This, I have since been reliably informed, is a standard test for hernia. In the next office other tests were carried out after which the examiner held my testicles and had me cough.

"Funny thing," I said, "the man in the next office just had me do that."

My examiner chuckled. "Did he by George! That wasn't authorised. Next door on the right."

And so, in August 1951, almost ten years to the day since I had crossed the Pennines to join the RGS in Penrith, I took the same route, only this time to start my basic training at Carlisle's cavalry Barracks. There, along with some 200 other raw recruits, I was taught how to march in step, mark time, about turn, present arms, climb ropes, perform chin-ups, whitewash the coke in the coke bucket, square-off my spare socks by inserting little bits of cardboard and perform other tasks of a kind it was thought might contribute to the defence of the nation. Had anyone, I wondered, pointed out that armies were onto Behaviourism long before Pavlov?

We were a mixed lot, mostly from the Borders, the largest contingents being from the Clyde and Tyneside. The Glaswegians lived up to their reputation for lawlessness. Two days into training a police van arrived and carted off a number of them for something that had happened on the eve of their joining up.

We lived in so-called spiders, groups of Nissan huts linked together by corridors leading to common ablutions and toilets. The dominant figure in mine was Jock, thick-set, broad shouldered and loud mouthed. It was he and a group of his fellow Glaswegians who organised our hiring a wireless that belted out the Radio Luxemburg's top ten – *Mona Lisa, They Tried to Tell Us We Were Too Young, One of the Rolling Kind* – from reveille to lights out. Each Nissan had a two-bunk section set apart for an NCO, but as one lance corporal sufficed for our eight huts, Jock and one of his buddies seized that section in mine.

Initially most of our time was taken up with square bashing. Our drill sergeant had a tragedian's voice and an inexhaustible fund of obscenities. Day after day he chased us up and down the parade ground. "Don't worry your balls will fall off," he would shout. "They're all sewn up in a little bag." He seemed to make a point of picking on John Raisman, the son of the

Vice-Chairman of Lloyds Bank. John had arrived in a chauffeur-driven Bentley, leading the corporal at the gate, supposing he was some sort of dignitary, to call out the guard. Being only lately down from Oxford, John was older than the rest of us, and having already acquired something of the weightiness and solemnity of the oil company chairman he was destined to become, gave the impression of being even older than he was. This so impressed the lad in the bunk next to mine that he enquired whether perhaps we oughtn't to address him as "Mr Raisman." The drill sergeant was less deferential. "What's the matter, trooper," he would shout. "Can't get your arms and legs to work together?" John, it must be said, was not well coordinated, but the same applied to the rest of us. We were, the sergeant told us, the worst intake ever to have come his way. We marched like ruptured ducks, our boots weren't properly polished, our flesh was dirty, our beds shambolic. We were a shower.

Officers were remote figures. Practically the only one we saw was a melancholy-looking lieutenant who, like some Renaissance prince, strolled around the perimeter of the parade ground trailed by a Russian wolf hound. From time to time there were breaks for gymnastics, small arms training and films showing – in gruesome detail – the effects of VD. This last was also a subject touched on in religious instruction, for although all seven deadly sins were mentioned, lust was dwelt on at such length as to pretty much crowd out the others. Some men, we were told, were attracted to women because they looked sexy. Others – Oxford professors were specifically mentioned in this context – were attracted by qualities of mind. But these were the wrong reasons. What mattered were unions of "the soul." And what was the soul? Long silence. Most were fast asleep. Slowly it dawned on those of us who weren't that an answer was required. As the silence dragged on even the sleepers began to stir. Suddenly the lad next to me, a former deckhand on a Tyne tug boat, blurted out.

"Why, Sir, it's your real self."

The Padre's face lit up. He had talked to many intakes and at last someone had given him the correct answer. The lad glowed with pride. One of us had finally got something right.

I had assumed that our drill sergeant's fulminations over our inadequacies were routine hyperbole. This turned out not to be the case, as was brought home to us when the intake that had arrived a fortnight later was allowed out of barracks before we were. Once we were allowed out, however, we made up for it. With some two month's accumulated pay in their pockets, our lot headed for the pubs down town only to come staggering back hours later, some clinging to railings for support, others getting down on all fours to vomit.

Used to living on pocket money, I found myself, even on a private's pay, better off than previously. Most, however, were used to earning considerably more. The majority were also smokers. I had first tried smoking as a nine-year-old at Woodland House when I was evacuated there from Hazel Bank during the scarlet fever scare. The Miss Kidds would leave their cigarettes on the mantelpiece, and being accustomed to digging into one another's packets never noticed when I dug into them too. Sitting under the bushes I would savour that delicious dizziness that comes the first time you inhale. Now, while others took themselves off to town, I would go to the camp library and relax in the same way. At first it was a rare luxury, but in time the dizziness and relaxation became harder to attain while the need to smoke increased until I found I could not concentrate on any task without a cigarette in the corner of my mouth. Returning from all-night exercises I would find my fingers stained yellow right up to the knuckles.

In spite of our collective inadequacy, three of us, John Raisman, Archie Wigglesworth-Hamilton and I were chosen to go before the War Office Selection Board (WOSB) as potential candidates for officer training. The prospect of our elevation did not make us popular. We were, it must be said, an odd trio: Archie with his preposterous name; John, in spite of all our gymnastics and square bashing, still looking like a recruit to Dad's Army, and me, forever eager to prove myself by doing daring things. Apparently Archie's family, who lived in Chester, had at one time been every bit as grand as their name suggested, but having latterly fallen on hard times were now poor as church mice. Nevertheless, they had scraped together enough money to pay for a public school education in the course of which he had somehow contrived to acquaint himself with some of Soho's shadier establishments, a list of which he kept in his wallet.

As candidates for officer training we were naturally anxious to impress our superiors by proving ourselves model soldiers. So while the rest were off boozing, we potential officers – "fuckin' POs" as we were known – stayed behind.

It was on one such evening, as the three of us were polishing our brasses and blancoing our belts, Radio Luxemburg belting out pop songs as usual, that I had the bright idea of switching to the Third Programme, where, as it turned out, there was a Promenade Concert on. As the pub goers came straggling back from town they could hardly believe their ears.

"Fuckin' Hell, what's this? Who the fuck put that on?"

"It's a Promenade Concert."

"Well, turn the bloody thing off."

It wasn't just the music they objected to – although there was that – but the fact that it looked uncommonly like a PO coup. We were getting above ourselves, acting as if we were already bloody officers. Still, nobody did anything until Jock arrived. Weighing up the situation in an instant, he strode to where we were sitting and switched to Radio Luxemburg. I got up, shouldered him aside, and switched back. After some more shouldering back and forth we stood glowering at one another.

"So," he said, "ye want a fight then?

"If that's what you want."

"Well we can't fight now. See ye after lights out, 'round the rifle range."

Word soon went around that Jock was going to fight one of the fuckin' POs. Come lights out, I went down to the end cubicle where I found him so deep in drunken slumber I had trouble shaking him awake. At first he didn't seem to know who I was or what I was talking about.

"We were going to have a fight."

"Oh. Aye, aye."

It had been a hot day. I was in plimsolls and dungarees. I'd boxed at school and imagined a similar sort of bout, Marquis of Queensberry fashion, albeit with bare knuckles. Jock had other ideas. Putting on two sets of dungarees, he stamped his feet into his boots, buckled a belt around his middle and wrapped his buddy's belt around his fist with the buckles on the outside.

By this time quite a crowd had gathered and others came flocking to join it as we set off along the side of the parade ground towards the small-arms range. It was a bright moonlit night.

We had gone more than half way when Jock said "I'm no a fighting man, but if you want a fight I'll gie ye a fight."

"I'm not a fighting man, but if you want to fight..."

And so instead of turning off at the range we walked on. This drew protests from the crowd behind.

"Hey, you've gone too far." "The range is this way." "Where are you going?" "I thought you were going to have a fight"

Meanwhile we were agreeing that as neither of us was a fighting man we would not have a fight now, but should either of us ever turn into one, or even feel the slightest bit that way inclined, the other would be morally obligated to do battle.

Next morning, needless to say, we were back to Radio Luxemburg.

I later crossed paths with Jock in Egypt. We were walking in opposite directions along the road between Fayed and Fanara. By that time he was a lance corporal in the Royal Dragoon Guards and I was a second lieutenant in the Mauritian Guard. We joked about what had happened. Looking back it is plain that not only was he a natural leader in the way I was beginning to suspect I was not, but that he had shown better judgment in avoiding a situation that would have got both of us into big trouble and me, more likely than not, badly injured. Hazel Bank had taught me to stand up to bullies; it had not taught me discretion. Shortly afterwards a similar misjudgement would very nearly get me killed.

In spite of my shortcomings, which came to light only later, I passed WOSB with flying colours. Unlike most WOSB candidates, who, when it came to giving their required lectures, talked about their hobbies, beekeeping or whatever, the subject of mine was "The Use of Armour in Modern Warfare." I gave them my considered views on the theories of Liddell Hart, Heinz Guderian and such other authorities as I had consulted, described how Guderian's Panzers, coming down through the Ardennes in 1940 had sliced through the British and French infantry, and concluded with a graphic account of how, in the summer of 1943, Rokossovsky's T34s had come over the Urals and destroyed Manstein's armour at Kursk. These were, I argued, the crucial turning points in the war and standing proof that massed armour was what counted. I was later told that I had passed WOSB with about the highest marks possible.

From Carlisle I went to Mons Barracks in Aldershot for officer training. The big man there was Regimental Sergeant Major Brittain, credited with having the loudest voice in the British Army. Coming from so portly a figure it was surprisingly high-pitched. He had lately had a cameo part in *They Were Not Divided* a film about Brits and Yanks in World War II currently showing in town. If he caught anyone on parade peeking out of the corner of his eye he would shout: "Don't look at me! If you want to look at me, go to the moving pictures."

His other favourite line with officer cadets was, "I will call you 'Sir' and you will call me 'Sir.' The difference is that when you call me 'Sir' you will mean it."

The first couple of months were mostly spit and polish. I had trouble with my spit. At least that was the conclusion of those in my hut, who pointed out that, as the boots and polish were the same as everyone else's, it could only be the spit. The sergeant threatened extra drill. "In the British Army it is forbidden to burn your boots. I am not telling you to burn your boots. But if your boots aren't bright and shiny tomorrow you're up in front of the Adjutant for jankers," which was to say extra drill.

So I bought a candle, two tins of Kiwi polish, a new duster from the NAAFI, hung my boots up by their laces, buttered them liberally with polish and sat up well into the night slow-frying them. It wasn't until the next morning that I realised the full enormity of what I had done. True, they gleamed like patent leather, but they were rock hard and shrivelled in a way that reminded me of the shrunken heads I'd seen in museums. Nevertheless, they passed inspection next morning and saw me through the weeks that followed, requiring no more than a little dusting now and then to bring the toecaps up bright as glass. And so it might have continued had

R S M BRITTAIN

we not been sent on a cross-country exercise the day before the formal parade that marked the end of our officer basic training.

Until then I had been making do with my second-best boots, but with them thoroughly sodden and muddy I had no option but to take down my best. These, I now discovered, were not only hard as clogs but shrunken to the point that there simply was no way that I could get my stocking feet into them. Nevertheless, without socks and the help of some borrowed Brylcream, I eventually managed to wriggle my bare feet inside. So along with the rest, holding our rifles between pieces of toilet paper so as not to put fingerprints on the polished wood, I hobbled down to the parade ground and lined up. Going through the necessary motions for the inspecting officer proved no problem. It was after he had departed that the trouble began. Being a cold, wet morning, RSM Brittain decided we needed warming up with half-an-hour's brisk drilling. As we strode through puddles, stamped, wheeled, and about-turned I became aware that my boots were loosening up. The explanation, I discovered glancing down, was that narrow slits had begun to appear in their uppers. By the time we were dismissed these had grown into two gaping grins through which my pale wet toes were clearly visible.

My crime was never discovered. As we went on leave the following day I took the boots back home with me. There I found a replacement pair left over from my brief spell in the school cadets. They were RAF boots, which is to say that they differed from regular army boots in having uppers moulded out of a single welt. Still, I reckoned they would serve and polished them up accordingly. For the rest of my non-commissioned career they were the subject of repeated questioning. Inspecting officers appeared mesmerised by them. There, among the serried rows of toe-capped boots, were mine.

"You were issued with these boots?"

"Yes sir."

"Where did you do your basic training?"

"In Carlisle, sir. 67th Training Regiment"

And off they would go shaking their heads. No one noticed my brasses, blanco, or the rest of my kit. With those boots I could get away with anything.

ক্ত ক্ত

It was only after I returned from leave that I began to have second thoughts about having chosen the Armoured Corps. The first day back we were given mechanical tasks to perform. They were graduated according to difficulty, the simplest involving reassembling a bicycle pump. It was the only one I completed, albeit wrongly, having inserted the washer back to front so that it sucked instead of blew. Worse still, I discovered I loathed everything to do with tanks and armoured cars – their cramped interiors, their noisiness, the poor visibility they afforded, the tendency, especially around nightfall, of their radios to drift off station, and my inability, even at the best of times, to hear what was coming over them. Pig iron warfare I have heard it called. Worst of all was my discovery that I was simply no good at it.

A typical situation would be this. I'd be out on Salisbury Plain supposedly in charge of four tanks, in reality armoured cars, with my head out of the turret and clinging on for dear life. The instructor in his Land Rover would be up on a hill watching. Around my neck would be two identical microphones and sets of earphones, one for communicating with my driver, the other for talking to the other vehicles. Also around my neck would be a Perspex holder containing an Ordinance Survey map of the Plain on which I had crayoned the coded letter equivalents of the map's reference numbers. The enemy, we were told to assume, were devilishly clever, listening to every transmission and with the same map in front of them that we had, so any slip would instantly give our position away. (It was even hinted that our *real* enemy, namely the Russians, might be listening in and cataloguing our individual voices and styles. If so, goodness knows what they made of mine.)

So there we would be, bouncing over the plain, four vehicles abreast with me supposedly in command, when suddenly, on a hilltop directly in front of us, the enemy would appear. "Driver right," I'd scream. My driver would continue driving ahead. Realising what had happened I would tear off one headset, put on another, and repeat the order. Instantly we would lurch to the right.

Reverting to the previous headset and microphone I'd shout "Enemy on hilltop twelve-o-clock. Head for wood at…"

That was when my real difficulties began. Pulling up my map case I'd first try figuring out where the wood was on the map. That accomplished, I'd write down its numerical coordinates. Finally, using my code grid, I'd get down to substituting letters for numbers, all the while clinging on for dear life. By the time I'd done that my driver would have completed at least four full circles in full view of the astonished enemy, the instructor, and my fellow potential officers, delighting in the knowledge that their own chances of qualifying for one of His Majesty's commissions were improving by the minute.

I managed better at gunnery, firing off shells at £200 a time, an exercise in profligacy that allowed me to spend roughly the equivalent of my three-year Oxford scholarship in less than ten minutes. Aiming the heavy gun, or the machine gun for that matter, required little skill and absolutely no muscle control; one simply lined up the instruments and pressed the button. While others were firing I would sit on the front of the tank so as to feel the reverse force of the muzzle blast and catch a glimpse of the outgoing round. If, as I now suspect, I was already growing hard of hearing, this folly presumably hastened the process.

Throughout officer training the ever-looming fear was of being "RTU'd" (returned to unit), a fate Archie and I narrowly avoided. So while John, still looking as though he ought to be in a suit and bowler rather than in a beret and battledress, departed to join whatever fancy regiment he had already got lined up, we embarked on our second round of tank training. What the army ought to have done was put me in the infantry, but infantry training was at Eton Hall. Mons being essentially armour and artillery, and with my having failed my School Certificate mathematics (twice), there was no question of the artillery taking me. My Oxford scholarship was obviously an aberration. It had taken the army to find me out. Doubtless Oxford would shortly do likewise.

Sergeant Major Brittain had latterly begun taking a paternal interest in me. He had picked me out to be one of the two standard bearers at our final passing out parade. This was on account of my build rather than my aptitude for drill, as became apparent when, instead of getting better I seemed to be getting worse. Finding that bullying did no good, he tried being fatherly. That helped, and on the day it went off well enough.

That evening we hired a bus and went out to the Boar's Head to celebrate. Archie, for whom passing out had been even more of a close-run thing, was unaccountably absent. Back in barracks, slamming doors, we heard his weak voice. He had fallen asleep and lain in the bath for five hours. We watched him, Lazarus-like, rise from the cold water and begin peeling off grey layers of epidermis.

Passing through London on my way home next day I bought an officer's cap, shoulder pips, and a swagger cane. With time to spare before catching the night train from Kings Cross I went sight seeing, fell asleep in St. Paul's and was shaken awake hours later by a church warden to be told that the Cathedral was closing and it was already dark.

೪೦ ೪೦

I travelled out to Egypt in His Majesty's Troopship *Empire Trooper*. It was an old ship, captured from the Germans early in the last war, its bathroom fittings still labelled *Warm* and *Kalt* instead of Hot and Cold. There were some 70 of us officers in First Class, waited on by Lascars, and around 1,000 other ranks dispersed less commodiously elsewhere. Ours must have been one of the last troopships ever to sail from Southampton.

My Lascar, who was called Ali, woke me at 6.00 am every morning.

"Tea, Master."

"Huh?"

"Master, Master, it's morning tea, Master."

"Oh, yes, er, thank you."

He would come around again at intervals to make sure I didn't miss breakfast, which consisted of four courses served by men in white uniforms.

"Sugar, Sir? Milk, Sir?"

After breakfast we would stroll on deck or sit in deck chairs and read.

Lunch was much like breakfast, except that we were expected by that time to have changed into blazers and flannels. After lunch was siesta time; the Lascars disappeared and we dozed in our arm chairs. For dinner we dressed smartly, either in blues or service dress, after which we played cards or chatted until late. On the decks below the men could be heard singing. Once, when it was thought they were going on too long, our senior officer, a colonel, went down and conducted them for a while before telling them to go to bed, which they all meekly did.

There can be few more abrupt social transitions than that from private soldier to commissioned officer. At the end of my embarkation leave I travelled to London by first class sleeper. Only a month before a female redcap had given me a dressing down for strolling across Trafalgar Square with one hand in my trouser pocket. Now, strolling down Whitehall, I received an equestrian salute from the mounted guardsman outside Horse Guards' Parade. In due course batmen would black my boots, iron my tropical uniforms and bring me early morning tea; drivers would sit in their vehicles while I pottered around in libraries; men twice my age would respectfully await my orders. On the *Empire Trooper* I learned to summon waiters by snapping my fingers (a practice that I later discovered did not go down well with the Irish waiters on the *Queen Elizabeth*).

Ours might be a threadbare army but the officer class knew how to look after its own.

Thus, at the age of eighteen – the age at which freshmen nowadays go to college – I found myself being treated with a deference I would seldom encounter in later life. Over drinks in the ship's saloon I confided my unease over this sudden and bewildering change in status to another subaltern. "Look," he said, "when it comes to actually fighting a war it's the likes of us, not those cautious old-timers, who will lead the charge. Look at them – they may look impressive with all those pips and crowns on their shoulders but they're a lot of family men worried about their wives and kids." Leading charges, I reflected, was something I might be quite good at.

৩৯ ৩৯

So, like generations of subalterns before me, after a pleasant ten-day cruise I found myself arriving in Port Said and gazing down over the rails at the bum boats selling cigarettes, tobacco, whisky, jewellery, watches, dirty books and saucy postcards. I, too, marvelled at the Egyptians' skill at placing people by their accents. "From Glasga are ye?" Or, to another, "Whey aye, an' I can tell you're a Geordie." A Gully-Gully man came on board and produced enough new-born chickens from his mouth and ears to stock a battery farm.

No cavalry regiment having agreed to take me I had volunteered for the Mauritian Guard, rather romantically imagining that, like Beau Geste, I'd be out in the Sahara defending mud forts. It turned out to be nothing of the sort, our principal duties being to provide labour and guard petrol dumps, wood yards and installations along the Canal. Lowly occupations though these were they did at least keep us usefully occupied, in which respect we were better off than most of Britain's Middle East Land Forces.

At that time – it was the early summer of 1952 – the fear in government circles was presumably that the Soviets would invade the Middle East through Turkey and deprive the West of its oil. Our 80,000 troops strung out along the Canal were supposedly there to prevent that happening. Our right to occupy the Zone, so we claimed, derived from a 1936 treaty negotiated with the Egyptians at a time when it was feared that Mussolini, having already invaded Ethiopia, might try invading Egypt too. It gave us a 20-year lease, which we were eager to retain but which the Nationalist (Wafd) government claimed had been terminated in 1951. Eager to get us out, it had shut down railways and roads, withdrawn labour, and sent in army volunteers disguised as civilians to foment riots, blow up installations, plant roadside bombs and snipe at vehicles. Shortly before my arrival there had been a pitched battle with the Ismailia police in the course of which five of our troops and 42 Egyptians had been killed.

I knew none of this. All I knew was that the situation was tense; that all major towns apart from Ismailia were out of bounds; that even the most innocent-looking Egyptians might be terrorists; and that unspeakably awful things had been done to such British and Mauritian troops as had fallen into their hands.

Driving south from Port Said I passed camp after camp strung out along the main Port Said-Suez road. Most were little more than collections of tents surrounded by coils of barbed wire. But what principally struck me that first morning was the quality of the light and the oddity of the scene. Just two weeks before I had been in rainy England. Now here I was in what looked like a brilliantly-illuminated stage set, arranged as if for the enactment of a nativity play, onto which our military had somehow inadvertently blundered. Here were men on tiny donkeys, robed figures leading camels, women in burkhas selling fruit, groups of little white-washed mud houses set among palm trees, in short, a scene looking for all the world like one of those painted oilcloths that had decorated the walls of St. Nicholas' Church Hall at Christmas. But here, too, was the British Army in all its might – tank transporters, armoured cars, columns of men marching – familiar enough sights at home except that here they were all decked out in light sandy colours. Ancient and modern, European and Arab, a strange commingling, each group going about its business as if the other did not exist

But what gave it all a truly surrealistic touch was a third element. For there I'd be, observing the view, camels in the foreground, sand-coloured 15cwt trucks driving by, palm trees lining the road, the white sands of the Sinai Desert stretching into the distance, when there would be the blast of a ship's siren and between me and the nearest a row of palm trees, towering over the scene, would come the vast hull of a ship bound for Singapore or Bremen, alert, uniformed figures on its bridge gazing ahead through binoculars, idle sailors leaning over the rails, just as if they were somewhere far out in mid ocean.

🍠 🍠

Fanara lies half way between Port Said and Suez, a mile or so west of the Great Bitter Lake. To get to 2055 Mauritian Guard Company our three-tonner turned off the main Canal road, followed a dirt track leading in the direction of the Lake, bumped over a level crossing, passed an encampment of the Kings African Rifles, a lumber yard, some railway sidings, skirted an Arab graveyard and drew up at the camp gate, a hundred yards or so short of the row of palm trees marking the course of the Sweetwater Canal.

After saluting and shaking hands with the Company Commander, Major Cook, I was handed over to his second in command, Captain Sammy Achanah, a tiny Hindu officer, to be shown around.

"You like chocolate?"

I said I was very fond of chocolate.

"Oh then, you come with me."

He took me to the only timber-built building in the camp.

"You like Christmas pudding and boiled sweets?" he asked as he unlocked the door.

I said I liked all of them.

"Very good, well you will not go short of them while you are here." Climbing up some step ladders he began pulling out various jars and boxes. "If ever you find you are running short, you just come to me."

ço ço

The camp, home to eight officers and around 800 men, occupied some three acres of what had previously been waste land. At its centre was a parade ground roughly the size of a football pitch around which clustered the larger marquees that served as mess halls and cook houses. Radiating out from these were lines of sleeping tents, all neatly divided into sections marked by rows of whitewashed stones. At its rear of the camp abutted onto the Sweetwater Canal, so called because it brought the fresh water from the Nile that was used to irrigate the fields of maize and cotton stretching down to the shores of the Bitter Lake a half mile or so below.

Strung out along its far bank and thus only some twenty yards from our perimeter was an Arab village, or more precisely a straggling row of mud-walled hovels whose occupants led lives entirely independently of ours, but who presumably were as aware of our marching around as we were of their bicycling and driving their herds of goats back and forth along the canal bank. Besides irrigation, they depended on the canal for virtually everything – their washing and cooking, the mud bricks out of which they constructed their huts, and for disposing of their rubbish and dead animals. It must have been one of the most bacteria-laden stretches of water anywhere. From time to time a pervading stink would alert us to the passing of a decomposing camel or mule. Once, a dredger came by, throwing up sludge in such quantities that the villagers had to burrow through it to get to their doorways.

View across Sweetwater Canal

My arrival coincided with the beginning of Ramadan. Every morning I would wake to the wailing of a muezzin, and as the weeks passed we marvelled at his ability to keep it up day after day. At one point he developed a cough and for two days we basked in the unaccustomed silence, but then his loudspeaker crackled into life once again and he was back in better voice than ever.

Living in such close proximity to an Arab village, even with the Sweetwater between us, made us vulnerable to attack. Had anyone been disposed to lob hand grenades into the camp, or let rip with a machine gun they could have wreaked havoc.

Poor though they were (and to judge from the number of tiny graves in the graveyard there was a horrendous level of infant mortality), our neighbours' lives seemed jollier than ours. On festive occasions we would see torchlight processions passing along the far bank. From time to time platforms would be constructed where, from sundown until well into the night, musicians, sitting crossed-legged like snake charmers on an upper dais, would play endlessly repetitive tunes while belly dancers took

145

turns performing on the stage below. Our troops would line up along the perimeter wire to watch. Sometimes, after dinner in the Mess, we officers, still in our tight-necked blues uniforms, would draw binoculars from the Quartermaster's store and join them. The villagers would beckon us over, but we never went, there having been altogether too many stories of soldiers going to villages and winding up dead in the canal.

Commanding troops whose language we could not speak and did not properly understand led to difficulties. My French was poor; that of my fellow British officers virtually non-existent. Fortunately our Mauritian officers were bi-lingual, and our NCOs spoke English after a fashion. All the same, it was embarrassing hauling someone up before the Major on a charge without being able to report accurately what had been said. Like the population of Mauritius itself, our troops were a mixture of Africans descended from the slaves introduced by the French prior to the Napoleonic wars, and Indians and Chinese descended from the indentured labourers later brought in by the British. So far as I was aware these ethnic differences did not give rise to any antagonism, although living as we did in the Officers' Mess we were not well placed to judge what went on in the lines.

Our Group Headquarters was up on the highway half a mile or so away. Major Cook took me there for dinner on the night of my arrival. The Colonel asked me what I would like to drink. Mine not being much of a drinking family, I was momentarily nonplussed, but remembering how we had always enjoyed a bottle of port for Christmas I asked for port. It was evident from the Colonel's expression that it was not a choice of which he approved. Eager to save me embarrassment, Major Cook observed that taking port before meals was an old French custom.

While the port was being brought the Colonel asked me where I came from. I told him Sunderland, at which he snorted. Nevertheless, having once started down that track I stuck to it every time I dined there, although I could see from his expression, as he watched me out of the corner of his eye that he disapproved of such eccentricities.

Some weeks later, on hearing that I had applied to go on a Christian Leadership course, he raised the issue again. I had applied for the course, not out of any eagerness to save souls, but simply because a letter had come around explaining that it would be a week spent, largely in meditation, on the shores of Lake Timsah. As most of my time was spent, meditating to no good purpose, in a tiny tent containing precisely one collapsible chair and one trestle table, I reckoned I might as well do so in more agreeable surroundings. I had been assigned the job of looking after the Company's pay, but as my corporal, who had been doing the job for years, found my intervention a hindrance I simply let him get on with it. So I would repair to my tent over the newly-swept sand at precisely 7.00am every morning and fill in my time as best I could by writing letters and brushing up my Latin. What does a scholar need, I asked myself, but writing materials and time to develop his thoughts? The trouble was that I had no thoughts. Even writing letters was difficult and translating Virgil tedious beyond measure. Often, as the morning dragged on, my incoming footprints would be the only ones visible on the sand. Towards noon, in the sticky closeness of my little tent, I would find sweat getting into my eyes and dripping onto the papers in front of me, its blotches still visible on letters I wrote home.

My application, I discovered, had lowered me even further in the Colonel's estimation. Even worse than having someone from Sunderland lay claim to old French customs was having one who made a parade of his godliness. Cornering me in the Mess, he expressed his views trenchantly: "God-bothering eh! I hope they'll teach you that no bloody English gentleman drinks bloody port before dinner." I stuck to my old French custom a little longer but eventually switched to sherry, which I found I actually preferred.

My course took me to Ismaelia, the only town of any significance in the Zone that British troops were allowed to visit. In earlier times it had been the practice for passengers whose ships were passing through the Canal to stop off there for duty-free goods. With its expensive shops and public squares it still retained something of its former elegance. The people seemed welcoming too. So it was a surprise when I and a number of others were in the town one afternoon when people came pouring out of their houses, shouting and waving and pushing us about. What had brought them out onto the streets and made them so aggressive we had no idea, but sticking together we managed to shoulder our way through and make it back to camp where news had just come through of King Farouk's overthrow.

Back in Fanara my mail was waiting. Among the letters was one from Mother, miffed to hear that a girl called Joanna had received more letters than she had. Joanna was another of the St Nicholas girls. It was a relationship of which my parents disapproved. Her parents were divorced, her father having been a former bank colleague afflicted with "sticky fingers" and who had latterly been reduced to playing the cello in a band that toured the local pubs and dancehalls. Apparently she had called at Braeside not long after my departure to check on my address, but I never heard from her. Mother further reported that she had bumped into Polly, who also claimed to have written. "I do not think these young ladies speak the truth," was her comment. She had, she said, had a dream on the subject.

> I couldn't go to sleep, but at last I did drop off only to dream that you came home and brought your wife. She was the daftest little girl it would be possible to find if you combed the world. The funny part was I was not at all worried but only thought – well it won't last six months. When I woke up I laughed and thought, I will amuse Dad & Alan with this in the morning, but you know how it is – you go to sleep again and when you wake up you can't remember the details.

On my return from Lake Timsah I found myself in charge of Company transport. This had the advantage of getting me out of my tiny tent. We had a dozen or so Bedford 3-tonners and around half as many Morris 15cwt trucks. My principal occupation was dealing with work tickets. Theoretically, before starting out on a trip, every vehicle was supposed to have a work ticket, signed by an officer, showing the amount of petrol in its tank.

On its return, a second entry was required to show the miles covered and the amount of petrol remaining in the tank. As finding out how much petrol there was in a tank required using a dip stick, and as vehicles were running in and out of camp all the time, this was impractical. I, therefore, signed and filled in forms on the principle that, on average, a three-ton vehicle did 9.5 miles to the gallon. Trouble arose when vehicles consumed more fuel than anticipated with the result that, on being filled up, their tanks were shown as having more petrol than they could physically have contained. This required going back and amending the consumption figures. Fortunately work tickets were printed on recycled paper which meant that it was possible, using a razor blade, to go back over previous journeys and adjust the figures so as to make them appear plausible, a relatively undemanding task that kept me busily occupied for many happy hours.

The main benefit of being transport officer, however, was having a motor cycle. After my incarceration in the tiny pay tent this gave me a sense of freedom. There were always excuses for going off to Moascar or Tel el Kabir for morning coffee. Getting on those long, straight desert roads and opening the throttle wide was in itself a liberating experience. At seventy miles an hour an oncoming vehicle would first appear mirage-like in the shimmering heat, an image that wobbled and bulged, seemingly hanging above surface of the road before suddenly resolving itself into a perfectly ordinary Bedford truck or Daimler armoured car and whizzing past.

I never fell off, at least never at speed. My only mishap occurred at a level crossing waiting for the barrier to lift. In acknowledging a salute from a passing soldier I inadvertently took my hand off the clutch and careered into the ditch. I recall looking up at his astonished face, his hand still in the saluting position, and his asking "Are you all right sir?" Two Egyptians, plainly under the impression I was drunk, helped us drag the machine back onto the road.

My superiors in the Mauritian Guard had all held grander ranks in the war and were not disposed to let me forget it. They had re-enlisted not because of patriotism or love of the military life but out of financial necessity. Major Cook, an Irishman given to exclamations of "Holy Mary mother of God" and the like, was typical. He had once been an acting lieutenant colonel in the Artillery and would happily spin yarns about the Normandy landings and his days in and around Hamburg. After the war he had started farming in Ulster but found it hard going; now his wife was running the farm with the help of subsidies from his pay packet. He did not take kindly to serving with Mauritians. Some had mutinied in the war and the memory lingered. This was brought up one day when we discussed what we would do if the Egyptian Army attacked. I said that obviously we would arm all the troops, but he thought it might be best just to arm the NCOs and didn't appear too happy even about that. Plainly he did not have much faith in the men he commanded.

Still, it was a surprise on returning from the cinema one evening to find him at the camp gate with a revolver in his hand. Even more astonishing was the garbled story he told about Sergeant Moutou having threatened to knife him. Where was Moutou? He said he didn't know but he had heard he had barricaded himself in the Sergeant's Mess. I couldn't believe my ears. Here was the camp's senior officer about to flee on foot across the desert to the protection of Group Headquarters on hearing a rumour that an angry sergeant intended knifing him. Someone would have to take charge.

I walked over to the Sergeant's Mess. There I met Sergeant Major Thimah who gave me a more coherent account than I had had from the Major. Apparently Sergeant Moutou had got drunk, said he intended to do away with the Major, gone to the kitchen to get a knife and been locked in by the other sergeants. Peering through the serving hatch I could see him slumped on the floor and looking distinctly the worse for wear.

Having failed to learn my lesson from the Jock episode, I climbed through the serving hatch talking to him all the time much in the way one would talk to a nervous horse. Squatting down I patted him on the shoulder and asked him to give me the knife. He shook his head. So then I did a very stupid thing: I grabbed him by the wrist with both hands. Suddenly he came to life and I realised that he was stronger than I was. I shouted for help as we rolled over and over. Quite what happened next I don't know except a band of people led by Sergeant Major Thimah came pouring through the serving hatch and he was disarmed. More by luck than good management I sustained no injury apart from a cut on my forearm.

The story quickly got about and I was hailed as a hero. Even the Colonel went out of his way to congratulate me. I'd joined the army intent on performing acts of valour and now I had actually performed one – except, as CSM Thimah and all who witnessed it must have known, I had behaved very stupidly indeed.

Life in 2055 Mauritian Guard Company was in many ways much as life must have been on an old-style Mauritian plantation. There was Major Cook, uncertain of the loyalty of the black and Asian troops he commanded and whom he sent off every day to labour in the nearby timber yards and railway sidings much as in former times old-style plantation owners back in Mauritius had despatched their ancestors to work in the cane fields. And there were we, mostly white officers, the counterparts of those emigrant Scots lads recruited back in the old days to keep the books and help maintain discipline on the plantations.

For this latter purpose the threat of extra drills sufficed, the only whips in evidence being those used by Egyptians marshalling local labourers to work in the timber yards. Compared to the fine old plantation houses of Mauritius, our Officers' Mess, being simply two rows of tents and a marquee to which our Company carpenters had added a wooden veranda, was a poor affair. Nevertheless, it offered scope enough for Major Cook to play the role of petty tyrant. Liking his creature comforts he was quick to note any shortcomings on the part of the mess staff. As a result there was a rapid turnover of mess stewards. My arrival happened to coincide with the sacking of one, for what reason I do not recall. His replacement, Corporal Montezuma, was a young, eager and plainly very intelligent Anglo-Indian, and for a while the Major basked in contemplation of the shrewd choice he had made. Meals were served on time, guests treated with appropriate deference, officers' mess accounts added up correctly. Then, as the weeks passed, small deficiencies were noted. A table cloth was stained. The milk for the coffee had not been warmed. Reprimands turned into tirades. Gradually Montezuma began to lose his nerve; jugs began falling from trays; he trembled as he poured coffee. I tried reassuring him and putting in the odd word on his behalf, but the Major was implacable. I was summoned to witness the final dénouement. It was as if he had already been condemned, for instead of the smiling, white-coated figure with whom I was familiar he was marched in looking as I had never seen him before in full army gear and made to stand to attention. Although there was no evidence against him to speak of, he was accused of stealing from the Mess. It was hardly a charge he could refute standing there before us in his shiny boots. The intention had been to elicit a confession; instead he collapsed. The Major claimed the collapse was faked; I thought it genuine. Whatever the case he was reallocated to a labour platoon and replaced by another likely lad whom the Major had spotted.

Primitive though life was in certain respects, it was positively sybaritic in others. Each officer had a batman responsible for everything from bringing him tea in the morning to making his bed and seeing that his boots (in my case still my RAF boots) were properly polished. There were also waiters, cooks, and men to sweep the sand. Had I, as originally planned, become a rubber planter I could not have wished for more.

The first few months I shared a tent with a Lieutenant Dabby Singh. We were like a cuckoo clock in that I liked sitting in the sun to get brown whereas he was eager to appear as pale as possible. Thus, when the sun was shining he would lurk inside the tent, and when it clouded over I would retire and he would take my place. He went to great lengths in devising ways to lighten his complexion by squeezing face cream through a cloth which he used a face mask at night. So far as I was concerned this was just another of his foibles, like standing on his head, something he did for ten minutes every morning under the impression that it was good for his circulation and increased the activity of his brain. It was only years later, when news reached me of his having died of a heart attack in London, that

I paused to reflect on what had made such an ebullient character, a Sikh, ashamed of the colour of his skin.

Apart from signing and doctoring work tickets there was not a lot for me to do as Transport Officer that Corporal Moocarme could not perfectly well do on his own. I therefore took to going around on my motor cycle inspecting guards and working parties. Much as I would have welcomed hard physical labour the men would not let me. "Oh no, sir," they would say, pushing me away if I so much as offered to lend a hand. To engage in physical labour was to lose caste. The reason Corporal Moocarme and the other clerks with whom I worked grew long nails on their little fingers was to show they were of a status that absolved them from having to perform such work. Whether this was a practice that had originated back in the days of slavery or one imported by subsequent waves of indentured workers brought in from India is one of the many things I now wish I had enquired into.

How little I understood about what went on was brought home to me when a private in one of the platoons of which I was nominally in charge shot his platoon corporal. There was no dispute as to the basic facts. Coming back from guard duty, Private Rajabally, instead of turning in his rifle, had gone to the tent where Corporal Lochun was sleeping and there shot him dead. As Rajabally's platoon officer I was told to put together a case for his defence. As my French was no better than School Certificate and as he spoke no English whatever, I took interpreters along, although had I spoken fluent Creole I doubt I would have managed any better. He simply refused to cooperate.

On being arrested he had been taken to No 50 Military Correction Establishment at Moascar. Military prisons are places of furious activity. Unlike civilian prisons, where prisoners spend long periods in their cells, the routines employed in a military prison resemble those used in basic training except that, as in a speeded-up film, everything is done at the double. When not jerking about like marionettes, prisoners could be seen busily digging holes in the sand and filling them in again. As Private Rajabally was still awaiting trial he was not subject to this regimen. Instead, I found him crouched in a tiny cell, depressed and withdrawn. Had the corporal treated him badly? Had there been family feuds back in Mauritius? Had he been sexually molested? Was there *anything* in the way of mitigating circumstances that might account for what he had done? Apparently not, at least nothing that he was prepared to share to me.

The idea that I, a nineteen-year-old subaltern, was to represent a man on a charge of murder was, of course, ridiculous. In the event, a barrister was flown out from England, a jolly man with a fund of funny stories, who kept us up late. I attended the trial, but was no wiser at the end than I had been at the beginning. Others far senior to me had interviewed Rajabally and got no further than I had. Words had been spoken the day prior to the shooting; he had spent the night brooding on them; so he had simply come back and shot the corporal. Murder being a weighty matter, I had assumed its causes must be correspondingly weighty, but this appeared not to be the case. He was, accordingly, found guilty and sentenced to death – presumably one of the last times that a judge in a British court put a black cloth on his head and pronounced such a sentence.

That, however, was all a charade. We had been forewarned that should that be the verdict his sentence would automatically be commuted to life imprisonment. As it happened I ran into him some six months later on a troopship bound for Mauritius, where he was to serve the remainder of his sentence. He was one of a group of prisoners engaged in making balls for games of deck cricket and looking a lot more cheerful than when I had last seen him. In spite of his now having nothing to lose he could give me no better account than at our first meeting as to why he had shot the corporal.

Homosexuality, at least in the eyes of the army, was also a weighty matter. When I arrived in the Zone there was much talk of a case still pending that concerned a colonel's carryings on with his Mauritian batman. The batman had already been tried and found guilty, which did not bode well for the colonel. Nevertheless, in defiance of the rules of logic, he was duly acquitted.

With 80,000 troops and perhaps 1,000 (mostly respectable) service women in the Zone, sex was bound to be a problem. However, as it was a problem that was supposed not to exist, there appeared to be no agreed codes of practice for dealing with it. I first encountered it shortly after my arrival when, in the course of one of my nightly rounds as guard officer, I surprised two sentries away from their post and with their trousers down. It was not the sort of thing I could ignore, so I put them under arrest and had them sent back to camp. The Major, not best pleased at being woken up, suggested I call the duty doctor. He turned out to be a newly arrived national serviceman. I told him what I'd found.

"What do you want me to do?" he asked.

"Hadn't you better look at them?"

"And what will that show?"

"Didn't they teach you anything about this at medical school?"

"No," he said.

Nevertheless, he peered at their nether parts which looked perfectly normal to both of us. The next day they were both up before the Major for having been temporarily absent from their posts and given some minor punishment. This was the formula adopted on subsequent occasions.

The most dramatic of these was the time I arrested an entire guard of some dozen men for what appeared to be the same thing. Arriving at the Lido on the Bitter Lake around mid-morning I could see men, hastily fastening their trousers, running from the bath house towards the guard room. Hearing my motor cycle the corporal rushed out of the guard room calling "This way, sir, you come this way." Instead I made for the bath house where there was an old Arab and other young men buttoning up their trousers. Exactly what they were up to I never did discover. However, I told them they were all under arrest, got another guard to take their place, and called the Military Police to take away the Arab for examination. There was talk of a court martial and the Special Investigations Branch of the Military Police took statements, but apart from the corporal being demoted nothing came of it.

༒ ༒

Female prostitutes were also a problem, partly for health reasons. Three had set up shop after dark in the Arab graveyard that lay between us and the railway sidings. My first encounter with them occurred one night when I was again orderly officer and heard a rifle shot from that direction. On hurrying over I was told by one of my sentries that he had fired at an African soldier who had refused to halt when challenged. At least that was his story, but quite a lot of other things seemed to have been happening, for why were the three prostitutes also there? They were a pathetic trio, each with her little mat, the oldest being perhaps 17 and the other two possibly 13 and 11. It looked as though they had set up shop and been entertaining a contingent of men from the King's African Rifles in the area that my sentry was supposedly guarding and that he had fired in the air to scare them. I was puzzling over what to do when Chick Butters turned up. Chick had lately replaced Sammy as our Company's Second in Command. He had been a regular soldier since before the war, and had once been the heavyweight boxing champion of the Guards. Not only had he met a lot of prostitutes in his time but, from the way they greeted him, he seemed to have already made the acquaintance of these particular ones. Suddenly a tense situation was transformed into an occasion for joking and bottom pinching. Plainly Chick was much more accustomed than I was to handling such matters, so I left him to it.

Chick also taught me another lesson, which is the difference between having dabbled in a sport and coming up against someone properly trained in it. Chick was not a professional boxer, but he had fought professionals and been trained by them. Although I was physically at my prime and he well past his there was simply no contest. "Come on," he would say, "hit me," and I would genuinely try, but I might as well have been an 8-year-old flailing at him with my fists as he laughingly parried my blows. Fortunately, he never tried to hit me. I later had a similar experience playing against an Olympic table tennis player from whom it might be thought I would, if only by some fluke, have gain a point, but I don't believe I ever did

It so happened that I was again orderly officer when an Egyptian was caught leaving camp with something he had stolen and dragged in front of me. Handing him over to the Egyptian police was not an option as we had previously expelled them from the area, killing a number in the process. If there was a procedure for dealing with petty thieves, word of it had not reached 2055 Mauritian Guard Company. I enquired of the Major and was told to take him down to the Vehicle Park and teach him a lesson. But how? The Egyptian was a sorry looking creature, undernourished, unshaven and shaking with fright. I do not know which of us dreamed up the notion but as some sort of punishment was called for I thought I'd try having him stand in the sun holding a five-gallon jerry can of petrol over his head. I showed him how to do it and then had him copy what I had done. Both CSM Thimah and I had canes and we stood over him shouting and looking threatening so as to give the impression that if he didn't do as we ordered we would beat him. This made him tremble so much that he kept dropping the can. As I would not allow anyone to hit him it was all rather a fiasco. Finally we took him to the gate and told him to bugger off, which he lost no time in doing.

Mostly, though, life followed a regular pattern. In the morning I would busy myself with my work tickets or ride around on my motor bike. After lunch I would sleep or go swimming at the Officers' Club, and in the evening I'd read, write letters, or go to one of the open-air cinemas. Excited though I had been by my first glimpse of Egypt, the novelty soon wore off. As day followed day, each an exact replica of the one before, I found the prospect of ever more like them extending indefinitely into the future wearisome beyond measure and longed for the changeable skies of England.

To relieve my boredom, I took to climbing Mount Shubra, commonly known as The Flea, a rocky protuberance near Fayed. As a climb it was no challenge at all, being no more than some three hundred feet high. However, it was the only place of any elevation on the whole of that sun-baked plain. From its summit one could see the entire Zone, including the ships strung out along the Canal, with the white sands of the Sinai Desert stretching out beyond. The Flea also happened to be a place favoured by senior officers for walking their dogs. One was a Colonel Dickson. What exactly his job was I never discovered although it seemed to have something to do with intelligence. He and his wife lived in a smart house with a green lawn and sprinklers, quite unlike any other residence I'd seen in the Zone. In time we became friendly and they took to lending me books. I told him I felt at a loose end, so much so that I and had lately volunteered to go to Korea. He doubted anything would come of that as they were looking for infantry officers. I also said I would be due for leave around Christmas and had wondered about getting to Jerusalem. The normal thing would have been to go to Cyprus, but that struck me as unadventurous. He said there were flights to Jordan and that he could get me onto one.

The plane was a twin-engine Avro Anson. We flew over the Sinai Desert, miles and miles of nothing but rock and sand. The only other passenger was a brigadier on his way to liaise with the Arab Legion. He pointed out Petra as we flew over it. At one time, he reckoned, the land must have been much more fertile than it was now for why else would anyone have bothered to build a city in the middle of nowhere? He was the first person to alert me to the possibility that the deserts I had been seeing must at one time have looked quite different and that the change might, in part at least, have been caused by over-grazing.

The view from the plane window as we flew into Mafraq could well have been copied from an advent calendar. There were the rolling hills, the shepherds and their flocks, the little white houses surrounded by palm trees looking just as they had done in the picture books of my childhood. All that was needed to complete the picture was a star low on the horizon and three stately figures on camels. A more innocent scene would have been hard to imagine.

I knew, of course, that there had lately been trouble in these parts, although what it had all been about I was not at all sure. Still, there was something to be said for starting out with an open mind. As a young Englishman up to no mischief I assumed I would be treated with a measure of deference wherever I chose to go. Egypt, of course, was different. In Egypt there was a low-level insurgency going on. The Egyptians wanted us out. But Jordan was our ally. Why, we practically owned the place! Its monarch was currently at Sandhurst and so by way of being a fellow officer. A British general, Sir John Glubb – commonly referred to as Glubb Pasha – commanded Jordan's army, the Arab Legion. And here was I being flown in courtesy of the RAF who had a base there. I hadn't even bothered bringing a passport. Being British – and a British officer to boot – was surely enough to satisfy any Arab authorities I might encounter!

The bus journey was straightforward. Descending from the bus at Jerusalem, however, I became aware that my presence was causing a stir. People pointed at me; one ran indoors and brought out others to look. When I stopped to ask directions people behaved oddly. It wasn't until I got to Christ Church Hostel that I discovered the reason for this commotion. Had nobody told me to change out of uniform? Nobody had told me anything. It turned out that no one dressed like me had been seen on the streets of Jerusalem since the ending of Britain's UN Mandate five years before. I was an apparition, a ghost out of a vanished past, a reminder of the time before the City was divided and before there was a state of Israel.

Over the next three weeks I was at the receiving end of a succession of reminders that my assumptions, whatever basis they may have had in former times, were now decidedly out of date. To be English, I discovered, was no longer a guarantee that one would be regarded as a representative of the world's officer class.

This was brought home to me the next morning when, sallying forth resplendent in my Magdalen blazer (a prudent investment made with the thought that it would come in useful later), I got into even worse trouble. Immediately upon stepping into the street I found myself besieged by guides intent on showing me the Stations of the Cross. That was not why I had come to Jerusalem. I had come to see the Jerusalem of today. I was not a pilgrim; I was not even a Christian; I was not particularly interested in Jerusalem's history, at least not in the sort of history the street guides were likely to tell me. I had come to Jerusalem to see *real* history, namely what was happening now. Yet there seemed no way of shaking them off. I tried explaining; I raised my fist; I shouted. None of it did any good. Finally, by way of impressing them with my determination, I strode out of Jaffa Gate and headed downhill towards what I took to be a residential area. Suddenly I was all on my own. Looking about I saw that some of the houses lacked roofs and windows. However, there appeared to be no builders about, or residents for that matter. Looking back, I could see that a little crowd had gathered and were staring at me. Some waved; one or two shouted. Reluctantly I retraced my steps to be once again surrounded by guides. Didn't I know that that was Israel over there, that there were machine guns all along the other side of the valley? I looked but could not see any. It appeared a perfectly ordinary little valley, albeit somewhat overgrown and oddly deserted. All the same, looking more closely I could see that the reason the houses lacked roofs and windows was not because they were under construction but because they had been shelled. However, there were no notices, no fences, in fact there was nothing at all – presumably for political reasons – to indicate where the frontier ran or even that there was a frontier.

A year or so later I came across a brief newspaper item about a young American being shot doing pretty much what I had done.

Having learned my lesson, at least for the time being, I meekly agreed to be shown the Stations of the Cross. After that, none of the guides bothered me, although I sometimes ran into the guide who had shown me around and we chatted. It was as if newcomers had to pay a toll by submitting themselves to being shown the Stages of the Cross, after which those who so wanted would be left alone.

Such opinions as I had formed prior to my arrival favoured Israel, mainly on account of my having read Arthur Koestler's novel *Arrival and Departure* in which Palestinians are represented as untrustworthy and lethargic and Jews as idealistic and hardworking. Instead of following the Jews' example and making the desert bloom, the Arab nations had banded together with the intention of wiping Israel off the map. It was a case of David versus Goliath, the Jews, as usual, being the underdogs, only now standing up and gallantly defending their rights. Newsreels and newspaper articles reinforced the familiar stereotypes, showing Israelis labouring on their kibbutzim or seated around their communal tables with happy smiling faces enjoying the fruits of their labours. Pictures of Arabs, on the other hand, showed them as either angry or pathetic. Basically the message was that Israelis were people like us, Western, civilised, people one could rely on, in contrast to Arabs, who were something else altogether. It was all so obvious that I was surprised to find that virtually everyone I talked to in Jerusalem, including the good natured couple who ran Christ Church Hostel, took a different view. Didn't I remember the blowing up of the King David Hotel, the murdering of the British sergeants? There was, it emerged, another side to the story.

Jerusalem at that time was full of refugees, not only Palestinians but also many Eastern Europeans, stateless persons washed up there by the war, every one with a tragic tale to tell. Being kindly, the hostel couple had taken a number of them under their wings. I was invited to tea by a Romanian who had attempted to corner the market in dog skins. He had bought them by the truck load, but the market had fallen and now, hanging in racks from his ceiling, they took up fully a third of the tiny single room in which he lived. Another was a Pole, who because I was destined for Oxford, pressed on me a manuscript which he hoped I might use my influence to get published. It was, I discovered, an exposition of current Arab Nationalist thinking, the notion being that under the leadership of Egypt's General Neguib Islam would become a power to be reckoned with in the world, a third force capable of standing up to the United States and the Soviet Union. Given the inability of the combined Arab nations to defeat Israel, this struck me as an unlikely proposition.

Nor did meetings with Palestinians much incline me to favour their cause. Mostly these came about as a result of my having been taken up by the Brauns, fellow guests at Christ Church Hostel. Professor Braun was on sabbatical leave from the Free University of Berlin where he specialised in medieval Persian literature. They invited me to join them on their trips in the course of which we visited most of the towns on the West Bank, from Nablus in the north to Hebron in the south. Generally we went by taxi, old American jalopies and mini-vans in which we travelled crammed in with other passengers carrying baskets of poultry and sides of meat. Professor Braun spoke fluent Arabic, so along the way would strike up conversations which he would translate for me. Other passengers, hearing us talking, would ask if he was English.

"No, no," he would say, "I am from Germany."

"Ah, Hitler, there was a man! He killed six million Jews. Pity he did not kill all of them."

"You are lucky you did not have to live under him."

"Here, you see this house? Here we kill twenty Jews."

"You killed twenty Jews there?"

"Yes, and you see down there, down in the valley, thirty more." He mimicked a man firing a sub-machine gun. "Brrrrrr. One day we go to Haifa, finish the rest. Brrrrr"

Together we visited one of the refugee camps, that being one of the accepted things visitors to Jordan did in those days. We had been advised to arm ourselves with packets of boiled sweets. Evidently that was expected, for immediately on our taxi stopping we were besieged by swarms of clamorous children holding out their hands, so many and so demanding that it was impossible to do anything other than throw the sweets in the air much as though we were feeding ducks or pigeons and watch the children scrabble for them. The few adults around seemed to regard it all as perfectly normal. The camp we visited was largely made up of old 8th Army tents. Evidently army rules had been laxer in those days for many were imaginatively decorated with wartime graffiti. One, with a flying hat logo, had been home to "THE ILKLEY MOOR BOYS"; another, with a leggy blonde, bore the motto "LILLIE MARLENE – HERE WE COME."

Most of our trips, however, took us to churches, museums and mosques. In the Canadian Institute we were given tea and shown some of the recently discovered Dead Sea scrolls. On Christmas Eve we went to the late night service at the Church of the Nativity in Bethlehem, an occasion principally memorable for the elaborate regalia of the diplomatic and ecclesiastical representatives present, the single exception being the American Ambassador, who looked the more impressive by virtue of coming modestly attired in tuxedo and black tie. Real power, it seemed, could be exercised without recourse to fancy dress.

༄ ༄

Not wishing to be entirely tied to the Brauns and eager to see the Dead Sea, I determined to strike out on my own. The problem, as I quickly discovered, was that there was no easy way of getting there on account of its being dead and there being no villages in its vicinity or even roads leading in its direction. Nevertheless, from the Hostel's rather rudimentary map of the area, I worked out that if I got up early enough, caught the Jericho bus, and got off at the T junction where the road came down onto the plain I could walk from there across the desert to the Sea. Providing there was time enough I could then follow the coast northward to the mouth of the Jordan, follow the river upstream to the Allenby Bridge, and from there catch the bus back to Jerusalem. In theory it meant covering about 20 miles; in the event it turned out to be rather more.

At first all went according to plan. Again I was wearing my Oxford blazer and slacks. It was much hotter down in the valley than up on the ridge, but that was no problem. I took off my blazer, loosened my tie and trudged on.

The Dead Sea when I got to it looked much like any other large body of water except that all around the water's edge, where the waves lapped on the shore, there was a dirty crust of salt. Nevertheless, the name was well deserved, for although the waves sparkled everything around was devoid of life there being no reeds, shrubs or any other form of vegetation in sight, nothing in fact but sun-baked rock and sand.

Ahead, rippling in the heat, I could see buildings. Presently there was a loud explosion, a column of smoke and lots of men running around. Seeing me, a lieutenant and some soldiers drove over in a Jeep. Who was I? What was I doing there? Affecting geniality but plainly suspicious, he insisted I meet his Captain. Radio calls were made. No, no they would not dream of letting me go on until I had had a meal and met their Captain. Their Captain was a long time in coming. Eventually he arrived, asked me about myself, looked at my officer's pay book, the only identification I possessed, slapped me reassuringly on the shoulder, and invited me to lunch. It was some sort of lamb stew, which we settled down to eat sitting cross-legged, the Captain instructing me on how to eat with my fingers. The building, I gathered, had once been a salt factory belonging to Jews, abandoned after the 1948 War and now being used by the Arab Legion for practicing demolition.

By the time they let me go I was well behind schedule. To complicate matters I discovered that the Jordan, rather than simply emptying into the Dead Sea as the map had indicated, filtered in through a large swampy delta. This meant that I had to retrace my steps, head north into the desert and rejoin the river higher up. But there, too, there were problems, for above the delta the Jordan snakes between immense sand dunes(another feature not shown on the Hostel map), so that to follow its course required alternately scrambling up and glissading down great sandy slopes. By now it was almost dark. Finding I was making little progress, I struck back into the desert and resumed my walk northward across a plain dotted with black Bedouin encampments.

The first two I managed to get by unnoticed, but at the third the dogs got wind of me and started barking. Thereupon men came running out and surrounded me, shouting and waving their arms. As a gesture of goodwill I got out a packet of cigarettes and offered them around. Each took a cigarette and stood expectantly waiting for a light. I accordingly got out my matches and made a second round.

So there I was in my Oxford blazer, out in the desert surrounded by angry gesticulating men in robes and sandals. Then I heard a sound with which I was all too familiar. It was the sound of someone working the bolt of a Lee Enfield 303. Did they intend shooting me? Having established that no one spoke English, I had so far said virtually nothing. Now I became voluble. "Glub Pasha," I said. "Me friend of Glub Pasha. Arab Legion. Me English. Friend Arab Legion and Jordan."

A mule was brought, the man with the rifle slung it crosswise over his back, mounted, and with two other men close behind we set off. I reckoned they wouldn't want to shoot me right there with the women and children peeking out of their tents. They'd take me down to the river. But when we got to the river they did not stop. Gradually my spirits lifted.

When eventually the lights of Allenby Bridge came in sight the man on the mule dismounted, hid his rifle under a pile of stones, and led the way to the guardhouse, the other two still hovering at my elbows in case I tried making a run for it.

At the guardhouse the sergeant in charge didn't know what to make of me. How had I got there? I'd walked. Where was I living? In Jerusalem. I had walked from Jerusalem? No, I had come by bus. So I lived in Jerusalem. Well, not exactly, I'd come from Egypt. How had I come from Egypt? I'd flown. So I lived in Egypt? At the moment but I really came from England. How had I come from England? By ship. I had come to

Jerusalem by ship? That was not possible. And so it went. It was a rigmarole with which I became all too familiar over the next ten days

After a number of telephone calls a garbage truck was flagged down. Wedged between a lance corporal with a sten gun and a suspicious driver who insisted on piling his possessions in his lap, I was driven into Jericho.

The police station was full of heavily-armed men who stood around glowering. Suddenly into the room strode a slim young lieutenant with an intelligent face and broad smile. He spoke excellent English and very quickly understood what the sergeant had failed to grasp. Apparently satisfied that I was who I said I was he snapped his fingers and ordered coffee.

"So," he said, "you are going to Oxford. While you go to Oxford I go to Scotland Yard."

"You are going to Scotland Yard? Why?"

"I have been chosen to go on a course. I am to become a detective."

He began giving orders to those standing around, who propped their weapons against the wall or laid them on tables and, still laden down by their bandoliers of cartridges, began rummaging in drawers and filing cabinets.

"How do you like Jordan?"

"It has been very interesting."

"And I hope to find England also interesting. Perhaps we can meet. Oxford to London is not, I think, very far."

We were sitting sipping our coffee when one of his men appeared carrying a large and handsomely decorated volume that, judging by its cover, dated from around the turn of the century. After spending a little while leafing through the pages he gave a snort of triumph and flung it before me. The book was entitled *The Police Forces of the World* and the illustration to which he pointed showed what I first took to be a rather corpulent London Bobby dressed in an old-fashioned helmet and tunic of the sort of that I associated with the Railway Police. This, however, was not a Railway Policeman, for he was not standing in a station but on the edge of a desert with palm trees in the background. Being rather swarthy and moustachioed he didn't look very English either. The caption said "Police Force of Trans-Jordan."

"Look," the lieutenant said slapping the picture, "Scotland Yard, Arab Legion – same thing."

We exchanged addresses and shook hands. One of his men came with me out onto the main road and flagged down a car to take me back up the mountain to Jerusalem.

Had I behaved irresponsibly? All I had done was set out to visit two of the Holy Land's most frequently mentioned features: the Dead Sea and the River Jordan. All the same, I had not met any other tourists on my outing. It was plainly time I started behaving more like a conventional tourist. But that, as it turned out, would not save me from getting into even worse trouble.

℞℞

Although the Brauns had taken me to all the other major West Bank cities, I had so far seen nothing of Jericho – apart, that is, from the interior of its police station. So, once again, I took the bus down the corkscrew road onto the plain, the driver blasting away so loudly on the horn at every blind bend that I wondered if there was any chance of his hearing someone doing the same thing coming the other way. Jericho, as I soon discovered, is a dull town. Perhaps because it is prone to earth tremors there are few large buildings. I had been told there was a museum, but it was closed that day I was there. In fact I had pretty much made up my mind to catch the next bus back when, in the middle of a residential neighbourhood I came across what looked like a giant anthill over which, much like Durham coal pickers on a slag heap, people were swarming. As I got closer it dawned on me that they were women and had upper-class English voices.

"What are you all doing? " I shouted.

"We are from Cambridge," came the reply.

"Yes, but what are you all doing up there?"

"We're archaeologists. We're looking at the earthquake wall. Want to come up?"

It was no great height, a hundred and fifty feet at the most, yet it towered over everything else around. At the top they had cut a deep trench within which women with trowels and sieves could be seen working.

I was introduced to the leader of the expedition, Kathleen Kenyon, a name that meant nothing to me at the time.

"So," I said, "is this where they blew the trumpet and the wall fell down?"

"Oh, there were lots of walls. They kept falling down."

"Why didn't they just go elsewhere?"

"Well, you see, they didn't ever completely fall down. And the houses didn't completely fall down either."

"So they went on repairing them for thousands of years?"

"*Many* thousands of years. How many is one of the things we're trying to work out. "

They gave me tea and we chatted about Egypt, my expedition to the Dead Sea, and what they were hoping to find. I have since learned that Jericho is reckoned the most ancient of all cities and by good fortune I had managed to stumble onto the dig credited with having established that fact. That the world's first urban community arose on that barren plain would be hard to explain unless, as the brigadier had suggested, things back then had been very different from what they were now.

It was on the bus back that my troubles began. At the T junction where I had got off on my previous expedition a westernised-looking Arab woman got on the bus and sat opposite me. My watch having stopped owing to all the perspiration that had percolated inside it, I asked her the time. This got us into conversation. She was, it turned out, a doctor, in fact Jordan's only woman doctor, and the little group of buildings at the junction were her clinic, her patients being mostly Bedouin such as the ones I had encountered who came in off the desert. How had she become a doctor? Her family had sent her to a private school in Cairo where her best friend had been the niece of King Farouk, who had arranged for her to get into Cairo Medical School. But it was not an altogether happy story.

"You see, here in Jordan a woman is not trusted. We are still very backward. Jordan has very few doctors but they send me here to work in the Clinic. My superiors are not doctors, but they are men and that is what matters."

I told her about what I had been doing. She said that if I had come a few years before I would have been able to visit the museums and art galleries in the New City, now occupied by Israel. Was there any way, I asked, that I could get over there and back? It was not a serious enquiry. At night I had heard intermittent machine gun fire. A war of sorts was still going on.

As we approached Jerusalem she said she hoped I would be able to come to dinner and meet her husband. I replied that I'd be delighted to but I doubted I could manage it as my leave was theoretically over. I was simply waiting for a message to tell me when to report to Mafraq for the flight back to Egypt. It was probably already waiting for me back at the hostel.

"What a pity. But why don't you come now for a coffee and meet my mother?"

What could be more natural? That there might be any impropriety involved in her offering and my accepting such an invitation never crossed my mind. I was nineteen, barely out of school; she was older, a doctor, someone in a position of authority. All the same, when she introduced me to her mother I felt a slight twinge of unease. Although she was thoroughly Western, her mother, a toothless old crone, was not. The apartment was heavily shuttered and smelled of strange cooking. This was not Western; this was Arab.

Scarcely had I sat down than the telephone rang. What she was saying I could not, of course, understand but it sounded as though she was pleading with someone. Finally she hung up and brought the coffee.

"That was my husband. You saw the policeman, the one waving the traffic outside? He saw me bring you here and he telephoned my husband and he is coming here to meet you. Now I want you to do me favour. You know you say you would like to go to New City? He is a policeman [she had not told me that] and maybe he could help you. So when he comes you say that is why I invite you to come to the apartment."

I did not have to wait long. Bounding up the stairs he arrived red-faced and breathless. "Hello, I am very pleased to see you. What are you doing here?"

He was considerably older than his wife, moustachioed, overweight, with a major's insignia on his shoulders and wearing a Sam Browne belt over his uniform. She brought him a cup of coffee and along with her mother discreetly withdrew. I could see no point in embarrassing her, so I started off on my spiel about wondering if there was any way of getting to and from the New City.

"Empty you pockets. Here, on the table."

I emptied my pockets. They contained nothing but a wallet with some notes, loose cash, a handkerchief, and my pay book, which he leafed through dubiously.

"Where is your passport?"

"In Egypt."

"Why did you not come to this country the proper way?"

"Because nobody told me to. I didn't know how to. I just flew into Mafraq and caught the bus."

"How long you known my wife?"

"An hour. Look, I just met her on the bus."

"She ask you to come here?"

"Yes, you see we had been…"

"Why were you down around the Dead Sea last week?"

This was unexpected. He already knew about me. In fact it turned out, after he had had his men take me down to the police station and lock me in a cell, that they knew quite a lot about me. Why had I gone here? What had I been doing there? At least since my visit to the Dead Sea they must have had me tailed pretty much all the time. Perhaps it had been someone who had been following me and not the man on traffic duty who had phoned him.

They let me out around 10.00 pm. The couple at Christ Church Hostel were indignant. They would register a complaint. I told them it wouldn't be much use going to the police; this chap was Deputy Chief.

The next day, while I was having breakfast, a car containing three policemen arrived. One stayed behind to question the hostel couple, the other two took me back to the police station. From the Deputy Chief's line of questioning it seemed as he couldn't make up his mind if I was a Jewish spy or a rival for his wife's affections. Apart from her having invited me to her apartment, all he had to go on for the latter was the fact of my having started my Dead Sea walk from the vicinity of his wife's clinic. I could, of course, be both a spy *and* a rival. Neither was incompatible with my also being a serving British officer.

They called for me another couple of times. Sometimes he questioned me, sometimes he left it to one of his sergeants, not the one I'd met at the Allenby Bridge, but another one equally incapable of working out where I had come from by ship, plane, bus or on foot.

That was how things stood when the call finally came through for me to report to Mafraq. No one tried to stop me leaving Jerusalem. Whoever had been following me must either have given up or taken the morning off. They had not entirely lost interest however, for a few weeks later I got a card from the Christ Church Hostel couple saying policemen had kept coming back for me and asking where I had gone. Perhaps the Major was just making sure I had really left.

There is a tail to this story. Some ten years later, meeting a Jordanian at a party and having launched into telling him the story, he cut me short.

"Oh, the doctor woman! You heard about the murder?"

"Murder!"

"Yes. There was a famous trial."

It transpired that there were a lot of things that she had not told me, among them the fact that her husband had three other wives. It further appeared that lack of recognition by her superiors was only one of her many troubles, the principal one being that she was at odds with her husband over just about everything – her insistence on working, style of dress, social attitudes and her not having children. In short, she was challenging all the accepted norms regarding the way wives were expected to behave in Jordanian society. Because she did not behave like a proper wife the Major had divorced her, which I gather it is easy for a husband to do in an Islamic country. Thus, cast out she had gone to live at her clinic. For an attractive divorcee to live in a remote place in an Arab country was apt to lead to trouble, as in due course it did. In a fit of jealousy one of her laboratory assistants, with whom she was allegedly having an affair, had murdered another of her laboratory assistants with whom she was also allegedly having an affair. As the *femme fatale* in the case she was charged with being accessory to the crime. In the event, she was acquitted, unlike her supposed lover who was convicted and executed.

No doubt the whole thing confirmed those who had disapproved of her lifestyle in the correctness of their opinions. My informant did not know what had happened to her after the trial. This was before the 1967 war and the Israeli occupation of the West Bank. I live in hope of meeting someone who can tell me what did happen, both to her and her former husband. I would like to think, at least in her case, that the story ended happily with her settled in New York, London, or possibly Tel Aviv, at all events somewhere where her talents would be properly appreciated. Perhaps some day an Arab Ibsen will get around to telling her story.

Back in Fanara my Christmas mail was waiting. It included letters from school friends with news as to how they and others were faring. None of them appeared to be having anything like as interesting a time as I was. Robin, who had accompanied David and me to France, had emulated David by winning a scholarship to Balliol and was now at Mons training to become an artillery officer. Peter Spencer (he of the model trains) was also at Mons, in his case hoping for a commission in the Army Catering Corps. Others had failed to get through WOSB, including one Bede

School and two former RGS head boys, proof that the Army's choice of potential officer material was pretty arbitrary.

From Mother I gathered that Old Charlie was keeping them well supplied with rabbits, pigeons, hares and partridges. The Toobys down the road had acquired a television set and invited them around to watch the Coronation. Mother was unimpressed: "Of course we will go around, but I don't think we will be getting one. I am sure it would give me an awful headache." Father was keeping an eye on my bank account, which was in a healthy condition. There had been encounters with Polly, who said she had heard from me and claimed to have written back. "You know," Mother wrote, "she is a canny girl and one can't help but like her, but oh! Love, she was so crudely done up. Quite a few people had a good stare at her in passing." Father had also encountered her and had a long gossip. According to Mother, he "put his hand on her arm and said 'Well, Polly, I hope it will not be long before we see you again.' She put her hand on Father's arm, gave it a little squeeze, and said 'Don't worry, it won't.' When Father came in he told me the conversation and finished by saying 'what a likeable girl!'" That sounded like Polly.

Likeable girls, however, have a way of causing trouble, for there was also a letter from Robert. He did not mention Polly but casually let drop that everyone at the RGS thought David and me "silly adolescent intellectuals" and were sure Oxford had made a serious error in awarding me a scholarship. For good measure he added that he had bumped into Margaret and been instructed to tell me that she never wanted to set eyes on me again. These, he explained, were not his views; simply things he felt duty bound to pass on as indicative of what people were saying about me in my absence.

I had not been long back in Fanara when word came that I had been assigned troop escort duty on a ship about to dock at Mombasa. Major Cook had sailed from Suez some weeks earlier with a mixed complement of returning East African troops. I would be replacing him on the final leg of the voyage, which would take me to Mauritius, the Seychelles and back by way of Aden and the Red Sea. Evidently the memory of Mauritians having mutinied aboard a troopship during the war had persuaded those in authority that it would be prudent to have officers used to commanding Mauritians on hand to deal with any trouble that might arise.

What had happened on that earlier occasion I was never told, but calling it a mutiny may well have been an exaggeration. There is no denying, however, that colonial troops tended to be less well disciplined than our own. I had lately witnessed one so-called "mutiny," although "protest" might be a better term. It had arisen out of 2065 Seychellois Company's objecting to having a Mauritian Commanding Officer foisted on it. To register its objection it had refused to be dismissed after morning parade, not a wise move in Egypt. A guards regiment was duly brought in to surround the parade ground and, as the sun rose higher in the sky one by one the Seychellois collapsed and were carted off. By mid-afternoon it was all over. The Company was subsequently disbanded and the Mauritian officer found alternative employment. Someone, presumably our Colonel, had blundered. Still, un-threatening though they were, such incidents persuaded those in authority that colonial troops needed careful watching.

British troopships had sailed the Indian Ocean for the better part of two centuries. Back in 1953 no one expected the British Empire to collapse quite as suddenly as it did. In his wartime speeches Churchill had continually evoked the notion of our struggle as being for its preservation. The world in which I had grown up had been full of legends of trade and exploration, of privations endured and cocktails on the veranda. No other empire, so I had been led to believe, had spanned the globe in the way ours did or been so self-evidently beneficent in its effects. How else would our colonies and dominions have acquired their railways, hospitals and schools? It was what made Britain great and put us a notch or two above France, Germany and all the other European powers. In terms of population it even put us ahead of the United States. I had read and dreamed about it as a boy and now I was to encounter for the first time. Yet what the jottings in my diary and my letters home describe is not the magnificent creation I'd been brought up to believe in but an institution on the point of dissolution, destined within a few years to be little more than a memory.

Our plane was twin-propeller DC3, old, noisy, and unreliable. The first day we followed the Nile, stopping off for a couple of hours in Khartoum to refuel and tinker with the engines. It was while were standing in the searing heat of the runway, vultures circling overhead, our pilot working on the engine, that I had my first intimation that times were changing. A smart private plane landed, taxied over to where we stood and disgorged three smartly dressed American couples. The women, lightly clad, stood giving orders to their husbands who clambered about unpacking suitcases and fur coats. That done, the three strode off in the direction of the hangars, their heavy-laden husbands struggling along behind with the suitcases and fur coats. Who they were, where they were going, and why they had fur coats I have no idea. Groups of Sudanese stood poker-faced as the procession passed, and then fell about laughing.

The Sudan is enormous. We had hoped to make Juba by evening, but one of our two engines failed some 300 miles short requiring that we make an emergency landing at Malakal. The view from the landing strip might have been lifted straight out of one of my boyhood adventure books: flat topped trees, flocks of strange-shaped birds, and along the perimeter fence, silhouetted against the bronze haze behind which the sun was setting, rows of half-naked men armed with spears. Strangest of all was the silence. After the noise of the plane it was that more than anything that contributed to the sense of unreality. Perhaps the others felt the same, for we stood without speaking, gazing at the men with spears who gazed silently back at us. Then, in the distance, we heard the sound of an approaching Jeep driven, as it turned out by the British District Commissioner.

As I was the only officer in the party he took me to the local hotel from where he telephoned for a lorry to collect the rest. In the lounge a large fan turned very slowly. From the coating of dust that lay over everything it was evident that no one had stayed there for a very long time.

The Commissioner proved an energetic sort "You will be wanting a beer, eh? I know what British soldiers like. Used to be one myself. Can't get beer around here I'm afraid. Have to come with me."

It was a long drive along a rough track. By the time we got there – a ramshackle shanty by the roadside – it was almost dark. I had enough Egyptian money to pay for a couple of crates. On the way back the Commissioner drove furiously. Dark figures, the brightly-coloured blankets they carried over their shoulders briefly illuminated in our headlights, leaped out of our way. I gathered he would be leaving in a few weeks.

"Britain giving up you see; pulling out. Hell of a country. My house is down by the river, planted a little garden, and do you know what? Got up this morning; bloody hippopotamus rolling all over it." I was enchanted.

I asked him what would happen after he left.

"God knows."

Back at the hotel we drank beer and had a meal of sorts. As there was not enough hotel accommodation to go round I was given a bed in the Assistant District Commissioner's residence.

I woke at dawn and walked down to the river. Women were starting work in the fields. Here and there tall marabou storks stood about like sentinels. Tall men, emerging from the woods, walked along the river bank. I sat on the end of a wooden landing watching pelicans and ducks passing up and down the river. The shrubs along the river bank were full of tiny birds. From time to time kingfishers flashed past, some brightly coloured, others black and white. There were iridescent insects too and snails with shells as big as my fist. No hippos were to be seen at that time, but after a while I spotted a crocodile a hundred yards or so out. In spite of all that has happened there since – the tribal and religious wars and struggles over oil – I shall always think of the Southern Sudan as a Garden of Eden, a place where, as in Henri Rousseau's painting The Peaceable Kingdom, men and animals live in harmony.

At breakfast the pilot's announcement that he had been up all night and had fixed the engine drew a round of applause. Personally I wished we could have stayed for weeks.

From Malakal we flew to Entebbe and from there to Nairobi. I was keeping a journal, scribbling notes along the way of things that struck me. At Entebbe I noted "the picture-postcard view looking out over the blue waters of Lake Victoria with the green hills of Uganda as a backdrop"; in Nairobi "the anxious faces of the whites gathered in the lounge bar to hear a radio address by the Governor" calling for steadfastness in dealing with the Mau-Mau insurgency; on the commercial flight down to Mombasa "seeing Mount Kilimanjaro jutting up out of a sea of cloud, a sight so beautiful I could have wept"; also "a little Japanese businessman sitting next to me, who never looked up from his notebooks the whole time"; in Mombasa's Palace Hotel "the enticing of two prostitutes in sweaters and knickers who stole my hat and that I had to chase to get it back."

By the time I got to the dock the troopship had taken on its contingent of King's African Rifles and was ready to sail. I found myself sharing a cabin with Major Cook, who would be flying back to the Canal Zone from Mauritius. The routine was much as on the *Empire Trooper* except that, as I wrote in my journal, "the heat here is like a Turkish bath so the dirt peels off me in rolls." On the second day we acquired a skua that followed us all he way, roosting on the masthead overnight. Otherwise we "saw nothing of interest except numbers of flying fish. These are very tiny. They skim along a few inches from the surface and then plop back. To escape their enemies, I suppose."

We spent a week in Mauritius. One of the KAR officers and I went out on dates with two nurses we had met on board. I also sought out Sammy Achanah, who had been invalided out of the Army with diabetes. His house, a long bus ride up into the hills, took some finding. I stopped at a police station to enquire the way. They pointed it out, but insisted I not go there because he was away. They would telephone him.

"Is there nobody there?"

"Oh yes, his wife is there. But you must stay here. I will telephone the Captain."

"But why can't I go?"

"It would not be proper. You must stay here; the Captain will come."

Eventually Sammy arrived looking thinner than when I'd last seen him and not at all well. He introduced me to his wife, a tiny middle-aged Indian lady who cooked us a curry. The idea that she and I might have got up to any hanky-panky in his absence was preposterous. Why I wondered, do some societies make so much trouble for themselves by keeping their women locked up? Then, remembering Robert's letter, it occurred to me that societies that didn't keep their women locked up also made a lot of trouble for themselves too.

Embarking troops in both Mauritius and the Seychelles I leaned on the ship's rails watching couples being married on the dockside. Some seemed scarcely more than children. There they stood, totally confused, priests shuttling from couple to couple, the great ship towering over them and every now and then giving an impatient blast on its siren, young men heading for the gangplank forgetting to kiss their brides goodbye, being grabbed by relatives and taken back, shaking hands instead of kissing, being taken back again, and finally, having been shown what to do, clambering on board, wild-eyed, and being slapped on the back by a hearty sergeant and told "Ah, vous etes 'married man' maintenant." Meanwhile, deserted brides were being shoved into taxis. Others, more determined, still in their wedding dresses with their bouquets in their hands, stood waiting to see the ship depart, while a few, apparently not having thought what to do argued vociferously with their parents. To be married on the quay and see one's spouse of five minutes depart for three years might make sense to the extent that it would entitle them to a maintenance allowance but in emotional terms it made no sense at all.

The rest of the voyage proved unremarkable. Having always been hopeless at cards, I was surprised to find myself fairly consistently winning at poker. We had shooting competitions with the KAR, firing at gas-filled

175

balloons attached to floating bottles, at which I also did well. At Aden, where the insurgency had yet to begin, I spent an afternoon and evening on shore, buying a number of duty-free goods, including three shirts with well known labels that on first laundering shrank to the size of pocket handkerchiefs.

I had had a minor dose of dysentery on the last leg of the voyage, probably as a result of something I'd eaten in Mauritius. Back in the Zone it returned with a vengeance and landed me hospital gobbling 36 tablets of sulpha guanidine a day along with spoonfuls of a grey powder that looked and tasted like cement. I was in a ward with three other officers, all mental cases. One was a national serviceman, like me still in his teens, who had been put in charge of a lumber yard from which a large quantity of timber had gone missing. When and how it had disappeared he had no idea. In fact, he was not entirely sure it had ever been there, but his predecessor, also a national serviceman, had assured him it was and on that basis he had signed for it. As any deficiencies would supposedly have to be made good out of his subaltern's pay of a guinea a day, it was hard to see how – given that the estimated value of what was missing came to over £1,000 – he would ever manage to pay off what he owed. Faced with the prospect of a court martial and a future of perpetual indebtedness he had effectively ceased to function.

The other two were majors in the REME. One was obsessed with the notion that everyone was wasting water; the other with the thought that during the Coronation someone would assassinate the Queen. Although I talked to them they seemed impervious to reason. One day we were visited by a brigadier complete with swagger cane and red tabs who argued with the one anxious about the Queen but to no better effect. Finally, losing patience, he shouted "Get a grip on yourself! Good God man, you're a British officer!"

After he had gone the major shook his head and said "His shouting won't do any good. You know that coach the Queen travels in? It isn't bullet proof."

While I was recovering, word came through that I was to report for a month's training with the Inniskilling Dragoons, the purpose being to ensure that after demobilisation, when I become part of the Territorial Reserve, I would know at least something about armour. I travelled down with Malcolm Trevor, another Armoured Corps officer who, like me, had been serving with a Mauritian Guard company. The camp at Shalufa was enormous, its barbed-wire perimeter encompassing enough miles of desert to serve as a tank training ground. The buildings were widely dispersed too. The CO, a nice man with the air of a worried headmaster, interviewed us on arrival. The regiment, he explained, had lately served in Korea and suffered casualties. They had hoped to return to the UK but had wound up in Egypt instead. As much remained to be sorted out he would shortly be flying to London. However, he hoped we would enjoy our time with the 'Skins.' I could not have wished for a pleasanter introduction to what turned out to be the most appalling set of people I have ever met.

I can fully appreciate why, given all the regiment had gone through, it might not warm to having the likes of us palmed off on it. Lacking as we were in polo ponies and county connections we were not the sort of recruits that even at the best of times they would have welcomed into their Mess. Looked at from their standpoint, our arrival must have seemed like just one more humiliation. Yet even when these and other allowances are made I still find their sheer bloody-mindedness hard to credit. At mess that evening I shook hands with my squadron commander and his second in command, Captain Peter Martel. Peter, the son of a famous Second World War general, who had been assigned to look after me. A handsome figure in his cavalry blues he bore a distinct resemblance to Stewart Granger in the film version of *The Prisoner of Zenda* then showing up the road in Fanara. With no particular show of affability he asked me what I intended doing after I left the army. I told him I'd be going to Oxford. "Oh," he said. "On a scholarship, I suppose."

He did not ask me to sit with him at dinner or even enquire if I was comfortably settled. I thought sadly of Sammy's taking me to the Quartermaster's stores and offering me chocolates, boiled sweets and Christmas pudding.

But it was not until the following morning that the full extent of their awfulness became apparent. I breakfasted at 6.30 knowing that parade was in the tank park at 7.00 am. No one spoke to me. At 6.45 I became uneasy; the tank park was a mile away. At 6.50 I went around asking if anyone could give me a lift. They looked at me blankly. At 6.55, spotting

Martel and a couple of other officers getting into his Jaguar, I knocked on his window and asked if he could give me a lift. "I suppose so," he said. We drove in silence. As he was taking the others to the far side of the park, I got out at Squadron Office. "Don't slam the fucking door," he shouted after me.

And so it went. On subsequent mornings Malcolm and I got up very early, breakfasted alone, and set off down the road on foot before the rest had even reached the mess. If we left it late we would find ourselves practically running along the dusty track while contingents of our fellow officers roared past in their private cars.

In time we managed to lay on a 15 cwt to drive us down. We also discovered that we were not the only ones being cold shouldered. There were officers from the Service Corps and the Engineers in the Mess, unlike us key figures in the day to day functioning of the regiment, who were being similarly treated. The trouble with the Skins, we decided as we sat watching them strutting about in their Ruritanian uniforms, was that they lived in a world that made no allowance for the existence of the middle class. There was the working class, good solid chaps used to obeying orders; and then there were chaps like themselves, superior sorts, accustomed to issuing them. Their conceit knew no bounds. They had, so one of them told me, a sergeant in one of the squadrons who had resigned his commission in the Artillery in order to serve with them. "Wanted to serve with a decent outfit, you see." I wondered if theirs were the daughters whose pictures I had once admired on the frontispieces of *Field* and *Country Life* and if they were equally insufferable.

One night we were as usual sitting around feeling like stowaways on an ocean liner when an Irish captain in REME told a story that made us laugh. "Back in Ireland," he said, "it is a well known fact that in the days of King Billy when the 'Skillins' were formed there were three leprechauns, good leprechauns these were. One of them gave them their uniforms that are so handsome with the green trousers and all; and another made them rich so they could buy whatever they wanted; and a third gave them the confident manner of Protestant squires. But then there was a fourth leprechaun, a wicked leprechaun this one, and he made them all shits."

And yet, ghastly though they were, I desperately wanted to be accepted. Theirs was, or at all events had formerly been, a crack fighting regiment. They had fought at Waterloo and Balaklava; Tennyson had written a poem about them ("The Charge of the Heavy Brigade"); Captain Oates of Antarctic fame had been one of them; so, too, had Edmund Allenby after whom the Allenby Bridge was named. I had volunteered for the Armoured Corps, also for Korea, thinking I would do what they had just done. I was reminded nightly of what that had involved when a lieutenant with whom I shared a room and who had had the misfortune to step on a mine unstrapped his artificial leg and stood it, boot and all, it at the end of his bed. Shits they might be, but they had seen action, which was more than I had done.

My situation would not have been so bad if they had given me something useful to do. Nominally I was in charge of a troop of Centurion tanks. That would have been a fine thing had the tanks been available for driving around rather than lying partially dismembered in a vast hangar. As petrol was short and driving them around used an unconscionable amount, the Squadron spent most of its time on maintenance. Whether this served any useful purpose or was simply a way of keeping the troops occupied I have no way of knowing. I do know that Centurions had Merlin engines which were prone to breaking down in desert conditions. But, whatever the explanation, it was work of a kind that, on the basis of a three-day tank maintenance course at Mons (albeit repeated) I was totally unqualified to supervise.

"Well, sergeant," I said my first morning, "what's the project for today?"

The next morning I could hear them mimicking me as I approached, "Well, sergeant, what's the project for today?" so I had to invent a different form of words.

"Morning, sergeant, did you get everything finished yesterday?"

"Yes, Sir."

"So what are you doing now?"

"Draining the sump, Sir."

Oily faces in greasy caps peered out at me from under the vehicle's belly.

No one suggested I don overalls and join them, delighted though I'd have been to have done so. But cavalry officers did not crawl under tanks; they left that to REME officers and "trogs," namely other ranks. In fact, I'd have been willing to get down on my hands and knees and scrub out the regimental toilets simply for the sake of having something to do. Anything would have been better than standing around looking stupid. What I really longed for was proper training, for in spite of my abject performance at Mons I clung to the belief that I could still be an effective tank commander. Real war, I told myself, would be nothing like our staged manoeuvres on Salisbury Plain. In a real war I wouldn't have bothered with coded map references, nor would my driver have gone around in circles. I'd have told my tanks to head for the fucking wood on the right, which, if they'd any sense, was what they would have already been doing.

Military service, it is commonly said, consists of long periods of boredom interspersed with brief periods of intense action. Take away the latter and it pretty much sums up the experience of the British Army in Egypt. It was a particular problem for the cavalry. What could they do with rows and rows of tanks they weren't allowed to drive? If only they could have kept their horses! Horses would have needed grooming and exercising. Soldiers are not the only ones who experience long periods of inactivity. So, too, do firemen, but fire engines can be waxed and polished. A well-polished fire engine is a thing of beauty. In the case of tanks, however, there is nothing to polish. The difference between a clean tank and a dirty tank is practically indiscernible. Tanks just are ugly. The only thing you can do with a tank, other than drive it around and fire its guns, both extremely expensive and therefore discouraged, is to take it apart and put it together again. This keeps the troops occupied; the drawback is that when the tank is put together again it frequently doesn't work.

This was our experience the one time we set off on a serious exercise. It was an impressive sight in the early morning, the sun barely over the horizon, to see the monsters roar into life and go groaning and clanking towards the desert; or rather it would have been if so many of them had not failed to roar, expired with a gasp before they reached the gates or spluttered to a halt on the road outside. I had been relieved of my command, pretty much nominal anyway, as only one of my tanks was operational. Following in a truck I passed tank after tank, their crews, stripped to the waist and with their repair kits laid out beside them, anxiously peering beneath their engine canopies.

Whether we would have managed any better in a real emergency there is no way of knowing. There was a moment when it looked as if we might be put to the test. This was in mid-May 1953 when word came from the C-in-C Middle East that the Egyptian Army had moved its armour onto raised ground overlooking the Canal. Colonel Nasser, the principal architect of the military coup that overthrew Farouk, had lately displaced General Neguib and taken to giving speeches in which he vowed to run us out of the Middle East. An order duly arrived telling us to prepare to advance on Cairo.

On 13 May we laboured all day loading the tanks with ammunition and petrol for the 60-mile dash. Everyone was cock-a-hoop at the prospect of being able to write off all the equipment that, like the subaltern in the hospital, they had signed for when they took over from the 8th Tanks and had never actually seen, possibly because the 8th Tanks had never seen it either, and now could claim to have lost in battle. A spot of excitement, then, and the books wiped clean – a prospect to gladden any soldier's heart!

The plan was that the Royals in their scout cars would go first and the Inniskillings in their tanks would trundle along behind. Each officer in the Royals would carry with him a letter stating, "This is a peaceful occupation. If you do not fire on us we will not fire on you," which he was to present to any Egyptian officers he might encounter.

If, in spite of this, he were to be fired on, he was immediately to get back into his vehicle and radio Squadron using an agreed code word which, if my memory serves me correctly, was "Bingo." Squadron would then radio Regiment, which would radio Brigade, which would radio the C-in-C Middle East, who would then radio Winston Churchill in Downing Street. Then, if Churchill wished the occupation to continue, the word "Bongo" would be passed back down the line and the officer crouching in his scout car could consider himself authorised to return fire. At least in theory that was what was supposed to happen; what we were actually told was: "If the buggers fire at you, fire back at them."

What part Malcolm and I were to play in all this was never specified. Very sensibly we were not to be put in a position where we might start a Middle East war. For the time being we were to stay at Shalufa. Still, there was a chance we would eventually get to see the Pyramids!

Then it all just fizzled. What happened, nobody ever told us. Perhaps the Egyptians simply withdrew; or Churchill had second thoughts; or maybe the Americans pulled the rug out from under the whole enterprise as they were to do three years later. (That, of course, was after we had all left and Nasser had seized the Canal.) So back we went to the same old boring routines, unloading the shells we had loaded and tinkering with the engines. What I desperately wanted was for them to give me some troops I could actually command.

Having finally woken up to the nonsense of my hanging around the tank park supposedly in charge of work I was not equipped to supervise, the Regiment got rid of me for a week by sending me away on an explosives course.

Unlike the Arab Legion troops I had run into down at the Dead Sea, this did not mean actually blowing things up. All we ever detonated were detonators. Essentially it was a course in booby-trapping, for which purpose I discovered the army had a variety of vicious little devices to put under doors, chairs, doormats, bodies or anything else our enemies might move or step on and thereby blow themselves to pieces.

It was a ghoulish sort of warfare. Tank gunnery, as I had encountered it as an officer cadet and now with the Skins, was geometrical and abstract, a matter of straight lines (armour piercing), and parabolas (high explosive), directed at targets so far away as to be barely visible even through binoculars. Booby trapping was a different and altogether nastier kind of warfare requiring no bravery, only a degree of cunning. In a way it reminded me of catching rabbits. You set the trap, had a comfortable night's sleep, went about your daily business, and when you eventually went back, either that evening or several days later, there was a terrified creature with its leg in the steel jaws. In the case of booby traps, however, you probably did not go back and it was a human being who got his bones splintered. By way of illustrating its potential we were divided into teams that took turns booby trapping and clearing some derelict huts. The result was always the same.

Aware though we were that the huts were booby trapped and familiar though we became with the devices employed, the team that went in to do the clearing *always got blown up!* Of course, by the end of the week we could have coped with the traps we laid at the beginning, but by then we had learned how to booby trap booby traps, so the outcome was always the same.

ৎ৽ ৎ৽

Back in Shalufa no one asked me how I had got on. Once more I found myself hanging around the tank park with nothing to do. What I desperately wanted was for them to give me a body of men I could actually command. Then, quite unexpectedly, they did.

It was the night of the Queen's Coronation. For months the glossy magazines had been full of the celebrations planned to mark the inauguration of "A New Elizabethan Age." Jane Vane-Tempest-Stewart was to be one of the maids of honour. All over England there were to be fireworks, parades and street parties. As its contribution to the celebrations the Inniskillings planned a Grand Regimental Dinner. Not being an officer of the Regiment, I was not invited. My contribution would be to relieve someone who had been invited by taking over his night patrol.

It was a cloudless night, the arch of the Milky Way clearly visible overhead. There were six of us in two Daimler armoured cars, a corporal, four troopers, and me. Our orders were to drive up and down an oil pipeline and radio back every hour. In the course of our motoring we saw nothing except, momentarily caught in our spotlight, a pair of eyes that the men said belonged to a wolf. The moon rose around midnight to reveal a bleached-out landscape of rocks and sand dunes stretching into the distance as far as the eye could see with no human habitation or so much as a telegraph pole in sight. From time to time we would stop and chat.

"Is it true they are giving away free beer in London tonight sir?"

"Bet they're having a rare old time in Trafalgar Square."

"Wish I was there."

By 4.00am I'd been on the go for 22 hours but still felt wide awake. We were on a hilltop with a clear view in all directions. I could see that some of the men were dozing. Never had I felt more clear headed and in command of a situation. It was a glorious feeling. There I was, not yet twenty, in charge of a body of men engaged in guarding the lifelines of the Empire! "Why don't you all have a nap," I said, "I'll keep watch."

Looking out across that landscape it occurred to me that I might as well have been on the moon itself. There was, I remember reflecting, something strangely dream-like about the whole scene, as if what I was looking at was not the real world but a photo-negative impression of it, the boulders and other objects around us, even our armoured vehicles themselves, appearing less substantial than the shadows they cast.

I awoke with a start to find the landscape fully restored to its familiar daytime appearance and the sun already well above the horizon. The rest were still fast asleep. With a bit of luck they hadn't noticed that I'd slept. Anyone could have walked up and popped a hand grenade into each vehicle. And what about my radio reports? People were shot for such things. I deserved to be.

We motored back to camp to be confronted by a scene that might have been painted by Breughel. The Officers' Mess had been extensively smashed up. Slumbering bodies lay around. Terrorists could have walked in and massacred the lot.

My sin was never discovered. I'm told that Acker Bilk, the jazz musician, also a Canal Zone veteran, spent time shovelling sand in No 50 Correction Centre in Moascar for having fallen asleep much as I had done, except that my being an officer in charge of a patrol made my crime that much worse. Admittedly, up there on that barren hilltop, with nothing but sand for miles, it would have required a fair amount of resolution on the part of an enemy to have approached us. Still, I had put all our lives in danger. Perhaps I was not cut out to be a tank commander after all.

It was Peter Martel who broke the news that my secondment was ending: "I do not know," he said with what can only be described as a curl of the lip, "if you already know, but you are going back to wherever it is you came from at quarter past nine on Friday." And that was it. No handshakes, no invitations to drinks, no gift to remind me of my time with the regiment. No one said, "It's been a pleasure having you with us." Plainly it hadn't.

I bumped into Martel a couple of years later. It was in a train corridor and he was wearing a business suit. I asked him how things were at the Regiment. "Don't know old boy. You see I left. Working for Rootes Motors."

"How are things at Rootes Motors?"

"Oh, it's great fun; a piece of cake"

In the end, though, it would be the Unions that consumed that particular piece of cake.

My demobilisation came sooner than expected. Arriving at Stansted in the early morning we were met by a team of customs officers who spent the better part of two hours going through our baggage. What they were looking for they would not say. What they found were dozens of little gifts that the returning troops had bought for their families and girlfriends. Being an officer they assumed I must be in charge, so I was compelled to stand helplessly by as one after another the returning national servicemen fell into the same trap.

"Have you purchased any items abroad that you wish to declare?"

"No."

They would then rummage through the soldier's baggage. "I see you have a lady's watch here. You are aware that unless you have been abroad for more than two years you are obliged to pay duty on any imported watches or jewellery?

"I suppose so."

"So how long have you been abroad?"

"Two and a half years"

"You are National Service aren't you?"

"Yes."

"So you can't have been abroad for two years. I am afraid I must confiscate this watch, and charge you not only with having illegally attempted to smuggle into the country a lady's watch in contravention of Her Majesty's customs regulations, but also with having lied to a customs officer. Now, let me ask you again, have you anything to declare?"

As an officer I was not questioned nor was my baggage searched. That did nothing to lessen my indignation at the way some forty young men for no good reason had been made to spend the better part of two years bored out of their minds in a country where they were not welcome and on their return been humiliated, robbed and criminalised.

Tired, hungry, and extremely angry we mounted a bus and were driven into London.

7: WHY STUDY HISTORY? 1953-56

"DO YOU EVER feel like a brain on stilts?" The psychiatrist at the Warneford was eying the bunch of tests I had just completed.

"No, do many people?"

"Quite a few. They have worked hard to get here and don't want to let themselves and other people down."

"More here than at other places?"

"I'm afraid so. You see they are used to being top of the form, and then they get here and well…."

Feeling like a brain on stilts, I gathered, was one of the early signs of cracking up. Although I'd been in Oxford less than two days it was reassuring to find I hadn't begun to feel that way yet. Still, I'd look out for the signs.

The summons to attend the Warneford had been on the table in my room when I arrived. It explained that the Warneford was Oxford's principal psychiatric hospital and offered a variety of services to students. I should not hesitate to avail myself of them as and when the need arose. Meanwhile, it was eager to learn more about those of us who did not feel that need, at least not as yet. How, it seemed to be saying, was it to distinguish the balanced, or at all events functioning, from the unbalanced and dysfunctional? It hoped I would be willing to help in that regard and had made an appointment accordingly.

Thus, on a hot afternoon in early October 1953, I and a gaggle of other Magdalen freshmen, maps in hand, made our way through Oxford's leafy suburbs to the Warneford where we were given ink-blot tests, asked about our backgrounds and ambitions, photographed in the nude (front, back and sides), measured with callipers (to determine our bone-muscle-fat ratios), and questioned at length about our sexual experiences (regarding which I lied outrageously). I ought to feel grateful, the man with the callipers told me, for being a mesomorph as ectomorphs tended to be skinny and rather highly-strung while endomorphs went to the other extreme, being solid and a bit dim mentally, so one was apt to find more of them at red-brick universities. At least those were his findings to date. Finally, by way of homework, I was sent away to write a short story on the basis of a sketch showing a seated young man gazing out of the window of a barely furnished room.

I never wrote my story. It nagged me for weeks. This was Oxford science, cutting-edge stuff. Of course I could see what they were getting at: the young man was lonely, unhappy and at a loss for anything better to do than sit and look out of his window. That, however, was far from being my situation. Had they given me a sketch of a furiously busy young man I might have complied for, along with the summons to the Warneford, there had been numerous other summonses and invitations. Did I aspire to be an actor, climb mountains, enter politics, explore remote places, sail yachts, pilot light aircraft? Opportunities for fulfilling all of these ambitions were on hand. As the big thing at Magdalen at that time was rowing, the College having lately gone head of the river, I signed up for the Boat Club thinking that would be enough to be going on with. In the event it almost proved too much.

Magdalen is Oxford's most beautiful college, its richest too. Standing rather apart from the rest, its slender Tudor tower overlooking the River Cherwell, it has a distinctly regal appearance. No other college is so spacious and yet so private. Arriving there in October 1953 and seeing it in the warm glow of autumn made me wonder why I had ever thought I would prefer Balliol. Being a demy, or half-fellow, meant that I was on the college establishment and as such entitled to attend College feasts and wear a longer gown than those worn by mere commoners. Its main advantage, however, was that it allowed me to live in College for the whole of my three years. On an autumn morning, looking out over the deer park, the mist rising from the river and the sun just touching the dome of the Radcliffe Camera, it would have been hard to think of a scene that better epitomised Matthew Arnold's description of Oxford as "that sweet City with her dreaming spires."

Also newly arrived in Oxford were various acquaintances from the North East, including Alan Dumble, the bright boy from Barnes Infant School, and others from Mons and the Canal Zone that I'd run into more recently. My principal guide my first year, however, was Laurence Shurman, two years ahead of me at the RGS and now in his final year reading Law at Magdalen. He had been one of the crew that had gone head of the river and it was largely at his instigation that I, too, became a rower. Plainly he had come into his own at Oxford. David Boll on the other hand, appeared a less assured figure than formerly. His time at Balliol had worked out less well than he had hoped. He put it down to his having read History rather than English, but I suspected there was more to it than that. From the way he described them, his troubles sounded uncommonly like those dealt with by the Warneford.

✌ ✌

Up to the Great War and even beyond Magdalen had served largely as a finishing school for sons of the well-to do. Back in the eighteenth century Edward Gibbon had famously described Magdalen's Fellows as "decent easy men who supinely enjoyed the gifts of the founder," and something of that attitude had lingered on well into the twentieth. Although not architecturally quite as grandiose as Christ Church, its grounds are no less spacious. They are, moreover, better protected from public view, which was partly why the Prince of Wales, the future King Edward VIII, chose to enrol there. To say that he studied would be something of an exaggeration, but the same might equally well be said of a good proportion of his contemporaries. Nevertheless, in earlier times there had been many, Joseph Addison and Oscar Wilde among them, who had made names for themselves as undergraduates and gone on to become distinguished writers. None, however, has evoked Magdalen's glories as vividly as John Betjeman. Arriving in 1925 as a commoner and occupying rooms in New Buildings (1703) adjacent to those I would later occupy, he had set about launching himself on the world as an aesthete and socialite. Looking back after an interval of twenty years he recalls

"The wind among the elms, the echoing stairs,
The quarters, chimed across the quiet quad
From Magdalen tower and neighbouring turret-clocks
Gave eighteenth-century splendour to my state.

To him life was "luncheons, luncheons all the way."

Magdalen New Buildings

Had I been a well-heeled layabout I would doubtless have enjoyed Oxford more than I did. Being wealthy would certainly have made a difference, although I doubt I would have attended as many luncheons. By the 1950s living in the style of the 1920s was no longer an option, the war and rationing having put paid to that. No champagne breakfasts, therefore;

in fact no lavish meals in rooms at all. Toasted bread (held by a fork in front of the electric fire) and spread with peanut butter (un-rationed) was as much as most of us managed. Still, had I been wealthy I might have bought books, dined regularly at the George Hotel, dabbled in politics, explored remote places, sailed yachts, even piloted light aircraft. I'd certainly have preferred spending my vacations in the snows of the Himalayas or the jungles of Borneo to sitting, bored and penniless, in Sunderland.

Being a layabout, however, was no longer an option, at least not at Magdalen, something that Betjeman, ignominiously expelled without a degree, was among the first to discover. Rather unfairly he blamed C S Lewis, although in reality it was a fate he brought upon himself by not working and by failing examinations. All the same, he was correct in associating Lewis with a tightening up of academic standards. Like the two senior historians of my day, Bruce McFarlane and A J P Taylor, Lewis was one of a new generation of Fellows intent on improving the College's intellectual standing, a necessary task following the 40-year presidency (1885-1928) of that most notorious of Oxford social snobs, Sir Herbert Warren. Henceforward academic potential rather than the social status would be the criterion used for admission. Hitherto Balliol had been the clever college. Now Magdalen would out-Balliol Balliol. Out, therefore, went rejection letters to a lot of disappointed Etonians, and in came a lot of aspiring grammar school boys like me.

I doubt that anyone with a school record like mine (i.e. with no 'A's and several failures at O Level) would get into Magdalen these days. In retrospect it is plain that the college had taken a gamble. Two years in the army had in no way lessened my suspicion that it had, quite simply, made a mistake the concealing of which would necessitate my having to work extremely hard.

Not being part of the Great Oxford Myth, work seldom features in accounts of undergraduate life. Nor, as I quickly discovered, was it much talked about by undergraduates themselves. Effortless superiority is what Oxford admires. "I find I can get by perfectly well on an hour or so a day," I recall one of my seniors remarking. Whether he did as he said I much doubt. I was altogether too much in awe of my tutors to attempt anything of the sort. They were, it must be said, an exceptionally distinguished lot even by Oxford standards. (Three of the four have entries in the new *Dictionary of National Biography* and there may well be an entry for the fourth when his time comes.) Yet flattering though it was to be thought worthy of being individually tutored by men of such eminence it was also more than a little daunting, especially as I was invariably ill-prepared.

This last was not entirely my fault as essay topics were assigned on a weekly basis. Thus, arriving back in College from vacation we would find notices posted on the board in the Porter's Lodge summoning us to see the two tutors to whom we had been assigned for the forthcoming term. As we normally got back on the Friday and saw our tutors on the Saturday there was hardly time to catch one's breath before getting down to work on the first week's essays. Nevertheless, there would be friends back from vacation with tales to tell and other distractions, so it would probably be Monday morning before, if I were lucky, I got hold of books to tell me as much as I needed to know about, say, Henry II's relations with Thomas Becket. On Monday afternoon, however, there would be rowing and at 7.00 pm dinner in Hall. Thus it might well be at eight o' clock on Monday evening that, with a packet of cigarettes to hand and 14 hours to go that I would finally get down to writing my 1,200 words. As likely as not that would take me until 4.00 am, when I would set the alarm, sleep for three hours, have a hurried breakfast in Hall, add a few finishing touches to what I had written and, pleased that I'd put together a reasonably coherent account, hurry along for my tutorial. Being thoroughly exhausted, the rest of Tuesday, apart from rowing, would be a write off. Come Wednesday morning, however, my essay on the Dukes of Burgundy, about whom I knew and cared even less, would already be looming. And so it went. Others have written about how they found their time at Oxford a liberating experience. For me it was quite the opposite, as if the windows that had been opened up, first in the Sixthform and then in the army, had been slammed firmly shut. Mostly I blamed myself. Mine was not an efficient way of working, a fact I attribute largely to lack of confidence. All the same, writing 16 essays on as many unrelated topics in eight weeks is no small undertaking. So once the eight weeks were up it was a relief to get away, catch up on lost sleep, read some detective novels and forget the whole wretched business.

How others managed I do not know as all our tutorials were conducted on a one-to-one basis. Was 1200 words more than was expected? My tutors never said. I simply recited my piece and they responded by reciting theirs. Did others engage in the give-and-take discussions tutorials are supposed to encourage? If so, they never mentioned it. In fact they never mentioned history at all. History was something one did in private with one's tutors. Otherwise it was a bore.

So it was largely around this schedule of twice-weekly tutorials, afternoons on the river and late-night essay writing sessions that life revolved. Instead of the freedom and intellectual stimulation I had expected, I found myself following a strictly prescribed curriculum that in the course of the three years, allowing for some diversions into European, and in my case American history, took me through the history of England (410 to 1914) at the rate of approximately four essays a century.

It was a cocooned life. Many days, apart from walking to the boathouse by way of Rose Lane and Christ Church Meadow, I never left College. This was less constricting than it might have been given that Magdalen had its own fleet of punts and grounds extensive enough for half-mile strolls along the river. On summer evenings groups of us would punt up to the Fellows' Garden or play bowls on the lawn in front of New Buildings. Nevertheless, it was a life remarkably cut off from the outside world, the more so as I seldom bothered to read the papers the result being that such news as reached me came as often as not by word of mouth. The War in Korea was finally coming to a close; there had been disturbances around Carfax on Guy Fawkes' Night; the French had been defeated at Dien Ben Phu; sweets were to be taken off the ration; several undergraduates had been arrested and a number of policemen had lost their helmets; Britain was withdrawing its troops from the Canal Zone; Stalin's successors were jockeying for place; teams of night climbers had taken to attaching prams, bicycles and in one instance a whole car, to one or another of Oxford's airy pinnacles; two of Senator Joseph McCarthy's minions were scouring America's Embassy libraries in Europe in search of subversive literature; Oxford historians had reduced a visiting woman speaker to tears; Cohn and Schine were rumoured to be McCarthy's bum boys; Oxford Climbing club claimed that the night climbers came from Cambridge. All jumbled up as they were, one set of happenings seemed as remote as another. Of more immediate import was the ending of butter rationing which allowed us to dispense with the tiny jars and dishes in which we carried our weekly rations to Hall each morning.

One of the benefits of rowing, besides the exercise it afforded, was the forging of friendships. I took particularly to Magdalen's Americans, an impressive lot, the Rhodes Scholars especially. The world was their oyster. Being older and better funded than the rest of us they were also more confident. No currency restrictions affected their ability to travel abroad in vacations. Although we had managed to emerge on the winning side, they had been the war's real victors. Open, gregarious and optimistic, they brought a welcome breath of fresh air to the life of the college.

These qualities were on display when, early in my first term, Tom Boase, the President of Magdalen, invited a group of us to dinner in his lodgings. Tall, slim, white-haired and immaculately suited, he fitted his surroundings exquisitely. As we stood on his beautiful hearthrug with our glasses of sherry it was the Americans who weighed in with first impressions of England and tales of life back home. At dinner those of us in need of instruction were shown how to eat our artichokes. Helped by the sherry and wine the conversation was beginning to pick up as we tucked into our main course when an appalling thing happened. The President, who had embarked on some tale and was talking animatedly, *suddenly tipped his entire dinner into his lap!* We sat frozen as he slowly rose to his feet, allowing the mass to slide back onto his plate. Even the butler stood for a moment nonplussed before hurrying forward to clear up the mess. Meanwhile, dabbing himself with his napkin, Boase strode from the room only to reappear a minute later wearing a suit no less well pressed than the one before and, with a brief "Isn't life full of small tribulations," resume the tale he had been telling at the point he had left off. It was all done with such aplomb that we speculated afterwards as to whether he had staged it for our benefit.

In contrast to Boase's urbane charm, Bruce McFarlane, Magdalen's senior history tutor, faced life with grim determination. His speciality was the English aristocracy in the later Middle Ages. Although he had published relatively little it was a subject about which he was universally acknowledged to know more than anyone else. Stories abounded of visiting speakers who had had the temerity to venture into his territory and whose scalps he had taken. A big man, ponderous in manner, he walked with his head to one side, whether as a result of nervous tension or some physical infirmity I never discovered. In winter he wore a Spanish cloak and broad-brimmed hat. Once, clad in this outfit, he loomed up in front of me out of a snowstorm. I was returning from vacation and had a suitcase in each hand so that for a moment we stood confronting one another. The obvious thing would have been for me to remark on the weather. Instead I asked him if he had had a happy Christmas. Like all questions put to him it called for deliberation.

"I had," he said, "what you might call a family Christmas." He paused, so that I had supposed he had finished, but then he went on, "I stayed with an old friend from my undergraduate days." Again he paused. "I think that in future I will spend Christmases in College."

Thinking of those sombre bachelors up there on the High Table I found it hard to imagine them wearing funny hats and popping teasers in one another's faces.

I have every reason to feel to feel grateful to McFarlane, for I have little doubt that it was on the basis of his judgement that I had got into Magdalen. Yet, being a shy man and living as he did in a world far removed from mine, I found it difficult to warm to him in the way I would to other teachers. He talked of ecclesiastical archives and the discoveries he had made there. I have since visited cathedral archives and know them for the clean well-lighted places they are, but having little idea at that time of what they looked like I imagined him toiling away among rolls of dusty parchment like Mr. Casaubon in the gloomy vaults of Middlemarch. He had a cat, a Siamese, that would sit in his lap and that he would stroke during tutorials; also a vast collection of china cats, possibly given him by former students, that he used as book ends, flower vases, or simply to ornament his shelves, and had arranged in such a way that, having drunk a glass of sherry and in my state of exhaustion on account of having stayed up all night, they seemed to be swarming all over his room.

For one whose mind was plainly on higher things, the obligation of having to spend hours listening to hastily-prepared essays by the likes of me must have been a wearisome and thankless task, or so it would seem from a story lately told me by a former pupil. Like a number of my contemporaries, my informant had gone to work for Proctor and Gamble. Some years later, finding himself in Oxford, he had contacted Bruce, who had invited him to lunch and in the course of the meal had asked him to describe what exactly his job involved. He had accordingly launched into an account of how soap was manufactured, the ingredients that went into it, and how new products were developed and marketed. Feeling pretty pleased with the account he had given, he was greeted by a long silence, eventually broken by Bruce's observing, rather in the manner of one who has just listened to a painful personal confession: "It sounds to me very much as though you have become a commercial traveller."

Not everyone, it is fair to say, found McFarlane as daunting as I did. In spite of having published so little he possessed a devoted following of younger medievalists, one of whom, on hearing of his death reportedly exclaimed, "Why, it's like going off the gold standard." Thanks to their labours, three notable books were assembled out of the various drafts he left behind.

In contrast to McFarlane, A J P Taylor, Magdalen's modern history tutor, was very much at home in the modern world. He had never gone in much for archival research being rather a story-teller and man of opinion, as adept at turning out newspaper columns as works of scholarship. In fact most of what I remember of his tutorials relates to what he had said or was about to say in his newspaper pieces – Lady Chatterley and her gamekeeper, the sexual predilections of European statesmen, and the dispersal of the wealth of the British royal family thanks to the need to support its innumerable illegitimate offspring – none of which related in any way to my preparation for Finals, or, for that matter, to the essay I had just read. He also talked about marriage, sex (which was where Lady Chatterley came in), and why some academics got promoted and others did not (mainly, it appeared, to keep others out). In short he behaved in much the way one might have behaved oneself if one had lately been transformed from being a college tutor who did a little journalism into a media celebrity who did a little tutoring and was keen to get it over with as quickly as possible. Yet, wayward though he was as a tutor, there was no denying his brilliance as a lecturer. He would shuffle onto a platform, an unassuming figure in his baggy tweed suit and trademark bow tie, peer owlishly through his glasses, hesitate, and then entirely without notes keep an audience entranced with whatever story he had chosen to tell for exactly the time assigned. When television came along he took to doing the same in front of the cameras. As the nation's first television don he also appeared regularly on chat shows voicing controversial opinions of a kind peculiarly suited to rile his colleagues, such as airing the notion that academics should be promoted on the basis of their book sales. My last glimpse of him was as a member of a TV panel on the night of the first moon landing, an event he declared as being of absolutely no historical significance whatever. In his autobiography, *A Personal History*, he describes his politics as consisting of "extreme views weakly held." Appearing on political platforms he revelled in the adulation of audiences far larger than any Oxford could muster.

Reading his *A Personal History* made me aware of the extent to which his general reflections on life had mirrored his personal anxieties. I regretted in particular the times I had pressed him for his reminiscences of Dylan Thomas, knowing only that Thomas had been a frequent guest of the Taylors' back in the days when they lived at nearby Hollywell Ford, and having no inkling that he had contributed to the break up of Taylor's first marriage. Still less did I know that that AJP had paid him to stay away or that Thomas had responded by doing the rounds of the local pubs boasting of having acquired a new source of income. Taylor's response to my questions was always to tell me how he used to take Thomas to dine on high table where he would provoke the President, in those days Sir Henry Tizard, a former Whitehall Mandarin, by playing the role of poor little Welsh boy.

A Personal History is a bitter book, full of splenetic comments about the College and his former colleagues, characterising Tom Boase as "an art historian of no great distinction... who initiated nothing and presided happily over a gradual deterioration of both Magdalen's buildings and its academic standing," and McFarlane as a Communist homosexual, intellectually "not quite of the first rank and too involved with his pupils." Nevertheless, his account of his marital tribulations is honest and moving, not least his admitting to the fear that he was being laughed at on account of them – as may well have been the case. Although he did not tutor me until my final year, I first encountered him early in my second year when I moved to New Buildings. Usually we were in our pyjamas, either on the way to the toilet or getting shaved in one of the wash rooms on the top corridor. This prompted me to ask Karl Leyser, Magdalen's Dean of Students, if Taylor actually lived in College. "No," I was told, "but he keeps a bloody great brothel here." This was typical Karl. I doubt the story had any basis. I never bumped into any women wandering the corridors or staircases after hours as I surely would have done had the story been true.

A diminutive genie, Karl was full of such mischievous gossip. He was McFarlane's protégé and the College's other medievalist, but as lively and outgoing as his mentor was shy and ponderous. Dark-visaged, with glittering eyes, I doubt there ever was anyone as intelligent as Karl appeared. He had arrived in England as a German Jewish émigré shortly before the war and had been briefly interned on the Isle of Wight before being recruited into the army, eventually joining the Black Watch and rising to the rank of captain, an achievement in which he took inordinate pride with the result that he was still to be seen from time to time, an improbable figure in kilt and sporran, on his way to some social event. Word had it that as an undergraduate he had worked so hard that he had had no time for anything else and was now making up for it by combining his role as Dean of Students with that of Master of the Revels, presumably on the principle that if there was trouble brewing it was as well to know about it, although I do not recall that he was ever much of a restraining influence.

At the end of each term it was the College's practice to hold so-called "Collections." The name we were told derived from their having formerly been occasions when undergraduates tipped their tutors. I imagined the scene as being much as Gilray would have portrayed it, the humble tutor in clerical garb standing with hand outstretched, the wealthy young gentleman fishing in his waistcoat pocket for a gold guinea. We, however, were not wealthy young gentlemen nor were our tutors humble clerics, the boot now being firmly on the other foot. Had we been in any doubt as to the matter, the message was firmly drummed home at Collections, latterly transformed into occasions when tutors reported to the College President on our work and much jollity was had at our expense.

Wearing our caps and gowns we would assemble in front of the buttery from where, as our names were called, each in turn would walk the length of the echoing Hall to the High Table where the President, the Dean of Students, the Dean of Divinity and other senior members of the College, gathered together in their black robes like so many cormorants, waited eagerly for such titbits as might be thrown their way. Not ones for mincing their words, our tutors would pronounce their verdicts in voices loud enough to be heard by those awaiting their turn, some peeking around the oak doors, others merely standing with their ears cocked, preparing, as at some sporting event, to greet one on one's return with congratulatory slaps on the back or murmurs of commiseration. "Mr Temperley," A J P Taylor reported on one such occasion, "appears to be more interested in considering *why* he should study History than in actually studying it." This was an unfair swipe at me for a paper I had written for a group he had had me organise. Oscar Wilde, reprimanded by the College President on one such occasion showed more courage and presence of mind. Told that cutting tutorials was not a gentlemanly way to treat his tutor, he had shot back: "But, sir, Mr. Allen is not a gentleman," a comment for which he was promptly ordered out of Hall. Taylor's observation about me was mild, however, in comparison with what others got. One American Rhodes Scholar who had come to read Law under John Morris, a friend of his father's back in the days when *he* had been a Rhodes Scholar, was informed that he was, without question, the stupidest pupil Morris had ever tutored, a judgement that led to his being shipped off to the Warneford and eventually invalided back to the States.

Novels and reminiscences about life at Oxford make much of the rivalry between aesthetes and hearties, the former being represented as the sharper witted, as they had need to be given that the hearties were stronger and given to debagging them and throwing them in ponds. Betjeman describes hearties as "good college men who rowed in the college boat, ate in the college hall, and drank beer and shouted." Apart from the shouting this sounds rather like me. Magdalen still had its aesthetes, but none was ever debagged or thrown into a pond in my time. Perhaps this had something to do with our being a more varied lot than formerly, roughly one third coming from public school, one third from grammar school and the rest from overseas. Insofar as there was a dividing line it was not between aesthetes and hearties, or for that matter between the Left and Right, but between those who had been to public school and those who had not. Having been to an independent grammar school and being a rower I suppose I fell, socially speaking, somewhere between the two. In *Beyond the Fringe*, the famous stage review that began the satirical boom of the 1960s, it was a distinction both mocked and exploited. Most specifically it was spelled out in the scene in which Peter Cook and Jonathan Miller came in front of the curtains and confided that – as they presumed the audience had already noticed – they "came from good families" and had had the benefits of a Public School education, whereas the other two had "worked their way up from working class origins." The irony was that Cook (Radley College) and Miller (Westminster School) *had* been to public schools and that probably most in the audience *had* noticed. More to the point, it was Cook's public school arrogance that enabled him to treat Dudley Moore (Dagenham Grammar) as his comic side-kick.

Class distinctions were much discussed in the1950s, largely I suspect because the old demarcation lines were vanishing. There were, to be sure, still those who saw themselves as belonging to something called "Society," spoke with strangulated accents, put their sons into the military and sent their daughters to finishing schools. Debutants continued to be presented at Court right up to 1958. As an armoured corps officer cadet at Mons I had danced with some of them. But the whole ritual of girls "coming out," which is to say being brought in from the country, dressed up by their mothers' couturiers and shown around in the expectation of attracting suitable spouses, was beginning to seem ridiculous, not least to the young women themselves.

Still, the fact that there was a privileged group that went in for such rituals excited enough envy and curiosity to make Nancy Mitford's glossary of terms used by the upper classes ("U") and the lower orders ("non-U") a popular talking point. She had intended it as a tease and that was presumably how most people took it. All the same, it was useful to be told on good authority – Nancy being the eldest daughter of the 2nd Lord Redesdale – that "napkin" and "bike" were "U" and "serviette" and "cycle" "non-U." Whether these were real distinctions few were in a position to know, but that did not deter them from playing the game. What no one questioned was the assumption that it was better to be "U" than "non-U."

At Magdalen, where the spirit of Herbert Warren had yet to be fully exorcised, to have come from a grammar school was decidedly "non-U." Duffel coats and cavalry twills were "U," college blazers and worsted trousers decidedly "non-U." Doubtless similar distinctions existed elsewhere (although not, I'm told, in women's colleges). All the same, Magdalen was exceptional by virtue of having two junior common rooms. The one frequented by all and sundry was large, airy, nicely furnished, and well supplied with magazines and newspapers. Bond's Room, on the other hand, was small, shabby and dark. It was called Bond's Room because it was presided over by Bond, a Dickensian figure seated on a high stool with a large ledger in which he kept a record of who helped themselves to sherry before dinner and who took port, or possibly even something stronger, after. Yet, rickety den that it was, it was the College's bar and it was there that the smart set congregated. As a member of the Boat Club I occasionally went, although not often, mainly because I found its atmosphere uncongenial but also for reasons of economy.

Americans, observing all this from the outside, were bemused. It was a Rhodes Scholar who summed it up most shrewdly by quoting the old jingle about Boston "the land of the bean and the cod, where the Lowells speak only to Cabots and Cabots speak only to God." Not that we had any equivalents of Boston's Brahmins, although we did have a number of titled undergraduates. Who they spoke to it is hard to say as they spent little time in College, virtually never dined in Hall and seldom spoke to anyone although they were reputed to get on well with the college servants. One was Viscount Lumley, a fellow historian, whose family owed much of its wealth to its having at one time virtually monopolised the shipping of coal from Sunderland. I would have liked to find out whether he had ever set foot in the town and how much he knew about the source of his family's wealth. One term he had the McFarlane tutorial before mine, but we never spoke. The nearest we got was to nod to one another in an offhand sort of way when we passed on the stairs, rather as one patient leaving a doctor's consulting rooms might nod to another.

Looking back, I imagine the social divisions of the mid-1950s were an aberration for I cannot see the returning veterans who flooded in after the war having much truck with the public school versus grammar school distinctions of my day. Nor, for that matter, can I imagine that it continued into the age of Lennon and McCartney when for a time it became fashionable to play at being proletarian. Nevertheless, in 1954 it was a distinction taken sufficiently seriously to become the dominant issue in the election for the presidency of the Junior Common Room. It was a contest that, with the help of the overseas vote, the grammar school candidate, John Orton, duly won. Not willing to be put down so easily, however, the supporters of the losing candidate put an announcement in *The Times* recording the demise of "J C R S Martset, after long years of devoted service to Magdalen College, Oxford," which they gleefully displayed to Karl, who delighted them with an appropriate display of mock alarm.

Triumph though it was, Orton made the mistake of attempting to do what previous JCR presidents had done and hold court in Bond's Room where he was made to feel so unwelcome that he was reduced to begging those who had campaigned on his behalf to accompany him there. I remember seeing them sitting in a corner with their mugs of beer looking much as Malcolm Trevor and I must have looked in our corner of the Inniskilling's Mess. How long this went on I do not recall. By the time the next election came around it had all blown over with the result that a rather nice Wykehamist was elected.

Oxford has an odd effect on some people. From time to time I have met, mostly when travelling abroad, Oxonians who not only look back to their time there with nostalgia but have gone on looking, sounding, and even dressing in much the way they did back then. I doubt, though, whether there can have been many on whom it had quite the effect it did on Norton Smith. Norton had arrived hot-foot from New Orleans where he had been earning his living as a jazz musician. Not for him the Brooks Brothers' jackets and button-down shirts of the Ivy Leaguers. In his jeans and sweatshirt he was the all-American kid from down the block. Presumably there was more to him than appeared or Magdalen would not have accepted him. Still, it was as a banjo player, accompanied on the piano by Dudley Moore that he burst upon the Magdalen scene. However, the reason Norton is remembered and still talked about is not for his banjo playing but for the transformation he underwent as he acquired, first a three-piece tweed suit, then a bow tie, and in due course, suede shoes, a watch and chain, and finally, to cap it all, a posh English accent. His ambition was to get a First and remain in Oxford, but being over-eager he messed up his Finals by staying up all night revising. So instead of becoming a college fellow he went to teach Old English, first at Reading and then at Hull, where, he acquired an Elizabethan manor house, Portington Hall, thereby becoming Lord of the Manor of Portington and Eastrington. While at Hull he struck up a friendship with Philip Larkin, a fellow Jazz enthusiast, who remembers him as a "distinguished friend of mine, who once played banjo with the Dixieland Rhythm Kings and now edits fifteenth-century English verse." Years later, chancing to bump into him at a conference, I found him still recognisable, albeit now more portly, sporting a waxed moustache and with a hyphenated his name. I asked if he was still an American. He stiffened. "I'd be very grateful if you wouldn't mention it, old man. It was a long time ago." I later heard that he had moved to Dundee, bought another country house, and become a pillar of the local church in whose graveyard I'm told he now rests.

Dudley Moore, destined to become the most famous of my contemporaries, was not a conspicuous figure. Later, as one of the cast of *Beyond the Fringe*, he would help launch the satirical movement of the 1960s. Whether, in the early 1950s he was any more politically and socially alert than the rest of us I have no idea. He was an organ scholar and his principal interest then was music. So far as student politics were concerned the mid-fifties must have represented some sort of nadir for I doubt there has ever been a time when students were less political. Some, to be sure, made names for themselves at the Oxford Union, but that was careerism. There had been the war, which we had been lucky to survive, and then there had been socialism. But by the mid-fifties it seemed there were no good causes left, at least none worth marching for or even griping about. Wasn't Harold Macmillan telling us we had never had it so good? That the lack of causes was, in itself, something to gripe about appears to have occurred to no one until John Osborne made it the theme of *Look Back in Anger*, first staged the month I graduated. Soon there were lots of angry young men, although what they were angry about remained a puzzle, at least to me.

Unlike tutorials, which were college affairs, lectures were organised by subject faculties. Mostly I found them a waste of time, lecturers fulfilling their formal obligations to the University, sometimes by reading aloud drafts of forthcoming books, not infrequently to diminishing or even non-existent audiences. There were exceptions, AJP's early morning lectures on European foreign policy being perhaps the most notable. Another popular lecturer, an exceptionally handsome young man who lectured on the Barbarian Invasions, always seemed to have a disproportionate number of women in his audience. It was at one of his lectures that, a week or two into my first term, I met Jane Flambert.

Jane was reading History at St. Anne's. In contrast to my earlier girlfriends, she had a razor-sharp mind. Also, unlike me, she had invariably been top of her form in all her subjects. Once, so she told me, another girl had challenged her for that position, suffered a nervous breakdown, and left school. There was never any doubt, at least in my mind, as to which of us was the better equipped to cope with the Oxford History Syllabus.

Given the numerical preponderance of men it might be supposed that women would have had an enviable time at Oxford. Doubtless some did, but by all accounts their tutors were even fiercer than ours, never failing to remind those producing sloppy work that there were others, no less worthy, lining up to take their places. St. Anne's rules about men were even stricter than Magdalen's about women. Stories circulated about young women whose Oxford careers had been abruptly terminated on account of what would nowadays be regarded as minor indiscretions. The last thing women's colleges wanted was a rash of pregnancies.

Falling in love is a common enough experience, but to have done so within a month of arriving in Oxford, remained in that condition throughout my three years, and then gone on to marry its object was unusual and might not have happened had I not also fallen in love with Jane's family. They farmed down in Hampshire. She was the eldest of six, the bluestocking of the household. Esther, the next in line, was more socially inclined; the third, Helen, the sporty one, made a name for herself by becoming Britain's sky-diving champion. There were brothers too, also adopted children, for when her mother could no longer bear children of her own she began taking in other people's, cooking immense meals to feed this ever-growing brood. Mrs Flambert's family, the Eyre-Brooks, were more refined than the Flamberts (one had married a duke), but no less prolific. So besides brothers and sisters, actual and adopted, there were grandparents, uncles, aunts and innumerable cousins. One Eyre-Brook uncle had married a Flambert sister and farmed conveniently near to Oxford; another was a notable surgeon in Bristol. In short they were an immense clan spread across what, from my North East perspective, I regarded as England's heartland. This was the England of Thomas Hardy, of manor houses and country churches, of county fetes and hunt balls. Even more than the Lakes it impressed me as being what England *ought* to be

At the centre of it all, Squire of Littleton Manor, was Grandpa Flambert, a patriarchal figure. Out in the fields he wore a pith helmet with a kerchief stuffed under the brim to catch the sweat. Now almost blind and grown stiff in the joints he was usually to be found seated by the fire in the stone-flagged scullery, legs apart, grasping the shepherd's crook he used for hobbling about. There he would hold court, questioning visitors about their affairs and chuckling over the oddities of the modern world. More than anything, however, he enjoyed describing his own adventures and misadventures. His had been a hard life. Having lost both parents within months of his birth, his father in the famous Bath bridge collapse of 1877 and his mother as a result of a domestic accident not long after, his early years had been spent in a succession of Dickensian institutions where he had been ill-fed, bullied and frequently beaten.

Littleton

Turned out into the world at the age of 14 he had for a time been apprenticed to a cider maker, earning money on the side by trapping rabbits and scaring birds off crops. None of this, however, had prepared him for the major change in his circumstances which occurred when, at the age of 21 he had inherited the proceeds from the sale of the family farm, a sizeable sum left to him by his father's will. Eager to put it to good use, he had let himself be inveigled into investing in various unprofitable ventures, an experience from which he drew the lesson that when it came to business it was a case of every man for himself. As he would later recall,

> If you've got capital, once you let it loose, that is by starting a business, it's a job ever to get it back again. Farming is different. You've got a farm, you've got cattle, you can send them to market and get the money. You've got some corn; you can sell it and get the money. But you take on a business, a town business, you can lose a fortune very fast that way.

He had accordingly used what remained of his inheritance to buy Littleton. But farmers, as he soon discovered, could get into trouble too. Sheer physical endurance, combined with a measure of peasant cunning had got him through the hard inter-war years. Tradesmen, it was said, put up their prices when they saw him coming knowing he would expect them to knock off a penny or two. But now that success in farming depended on making large outlays on machinery and fertilisers such methods no longer sufficed with the result that most of his land was farmed by Jane's father, with whom he maintained a wary relationship.

Many found him hard to get along with. Grandma Flambert couldn't stand either his table manners or his snoring and had effectively banned him from her part of the house, so that while she ate in the dining room he ate in the kitchen. She had also chucked him out of her bed with the result that he had wandering hands and needed careful watching when young women were around. The household was run by an unmarried daughter, Dink, who also looked after the kitchen garden. Tiny, almost bird-like, she flitted about, filling the kitchen shelves with the jars of preserves, pickles and the corn dollies she sold at the village fete. "This is my daughter Dink," he would say on introducing her. "She's the runt of the family."

In short, he was an ogre who, out of respect for his age, position and decrepitude, had been granted licence to say whatever came into his head, the more outrageous the better, a role he happily hammed up for the benefit of London visitors. "So who's Nebuchadnezzar?" he would ask, peering at a bearded Jewish guest up for the weekend. Like some latter-day Homer, eyes closed, occasionally pausing to poke the fire, he would reminisce by the hour, laughing out loud and slapping his leg at the memory of some improbable turn of fortune. He had enjoyed meeting Americans in the war and would sometimes repeat tales they had told him. Mostly, though, he spoke of his own experience of starting out in life with few advantages and the various traps into which he and others had fallen. Now, his feet now firmly planted on his own broad acres, he could look the world in the face and laugh at its absurdities. And laugh he did as one recollection succeeded another. Visitors to whom he took a liking would be taken to the cellar to sample his cider. His was an Old Testament philosophy. Land, cattle, children and grandchildren were what mattered. By his account, the rise of the Flamberts was all his doing. Granny had simply borne his children. "Oh Lordy!" he would say,

> To think that it all started with one little boy! I had no one in the world when I started out. A poor orphan without a father or mother! But when I came of age and got my inheritance I bought cattle, good breeding stock. Mind you they are a hard lot those cattle dealers. Got to watch them – cheat you as soon as look at you. Then when the feller in the next farm got into trouble I bought some of his land, horses too. That was fifty years ago. Get Dink will show you the photograph, the one they had taken for my 80th birthday.

Dink having been sent for and the photograph produced there he could be seen seated next to Grandma under the Cypress on the Littleton lawn, a one-man population explosion surrounded by a vast array of children and grandchildren.

Thanks to Jane I began dividing my vacations between Hampshire and Sunderland. I took my 12-bore down, helping pay for their hospitality by keeping their deep freeze well stocked with game. Mr Flambert also had a .22 with which I became adept at potting pigeons and rabbits at longer range. When I first visited they lived in the small bungalow Jane's father had built when he broke with Grandpa. Later they bought Ridgeway, a handsome old rectory that reminded me of Hazel Bank and which, like it, had served latterly as a residence for land girls. The two farms combined covered some 500 acres of gently undulating limestone country on the edge of Salisbury Plain. Jane and I would spend our time going for walks, visiting neighbours and reading in the garden. I thought the Flamberts and Eyre-Brooks, numerous, amusing and hospitable as they were, the most splendid set of people I had ever met. Even their monster was a loveable monster.

❧ ❧

Looking back over what I have written I fear I have given Oxford less than its due. Whatever its defects, it was a world away from the degree factories of more recent times. Wasteful though individual tutoring was in terms of time and resources I got to know my tutors well. Had I read another subject, one that offered more scope for reflection, my experience would doubtless have been quite different. Nor is there any denying that working under pressure taught one to write.

Oxford also had its golden moments: playing croquet on the lawns in front of New Buildings on summer evenings, getting uproariously drunk on bump supper nights, eating out at the Restaurant Elizabeth, visits with Jane to Blenheim Palace, lazy days out of term spent punting on the river. I recall, too, the great shout that went up from the Iffley Road sports ground when Roger Bannister ran his four-minute mile. I was walking back to College from the boat house when I heard it and I swear it was one of the loudest shouts I ever heard. Others claimed to have heard it on the far side of the City. As an oarsman I failed to qualify for the first boat, but Magdalen's second eight was better than some colleges' first boats, several of which we succeeded in bumping in Eights Week. On such occasions Jane, and on occasion her family too, would come and watch.

There were also moments of excitement, like the time the Cherwell was in spate and a group of us took a punt up at the locks leading to Parson's Pleasure. We were enjoying ourselves pushing the punt into the weir and riding out on the force of the current when, pushing too far, the prow went under the cascade and in an instant the punt was filled and everyone except me was in the water. I'd saved myself by catching hold of the overhead walkway and hauling myself up to where I could see the punt, accompanied by its cushions and water boards, being swept, higgledy-piggledy, downstream. So running in pursuit I leaped in and began tossing such bits as I could onto the shore. After half a mile, having reached Magdalen Bridge and realising there was little I could do by way of rescuing the punt itself, I gave up. Tramping back, cursing the others for not helping, I encountered them coming around a bend in the path looking decidedly grey faced. It turned out that having been too busy saving themselves to see what I was doing and finding me gone they had concluded that I must be at the bottom of the whirlpool below the weir and had been diving in to find me. I shall never forget the look, first of incredulity and then of delight, on their faces at my sudden resurrection.

I remember, too, trips in Tom Coulson's Jaguar to pubs in Thame and Aston Clinton, and to restaurants as far away as the Hole in the Wall at Bath, from where, cigars in hand, we would stroll down to view the Roman Baths. Tom had been two years ahead of me at the RGS and so in the same year as David and Laurence, but it was only after they had gone down from Oxford that he and I struck up anything that can properly be called a friendship. Back in Newcastle I had always thought him an odd figure – a Geordie aesthete, intellectually precocious, brilliant at chess, and scornful of sports and, indeed, of the RGS in general. His speciality in those days had been Restoration comedy and his hero the decadent Earl of Rochester. Now a junior fellow at Merton with a "congratulatory" First in English and proud owner of a Jaguar, he far out-shone the rest of us. Yet in certain respects he had become even odder than before, for his consuming passion was now bull fighting. Long before it was fashionable, his rooms at Merton were plastered with bullfight posters. There were bullfighting newspapers and magazines too. Evidently there was little about bull fighting, right down to the finer points of matador dress, that that Tom did not know. Yet, pale and podgy though he was and the spinster-like way he fussed over serving tea, it would be hard to imagine a less Hemingwayesque figure. I mentioned having read *Death in the Afternoon* but he was dismissive. Hemingway was a poseur – talk to any Spanish bullfight correspondent.

Tom *had* talked to bullfight correspondents and in due course would become one himself. After I went down from Oxford word of his doings would reach me from time to time, mostly through David and Laurence. The Oxford fellowship he had been angling had not materialised. For a while he taught at St Andrews, then at Edinburgh and finally at Carleton University in Ottawa. Meanwhile he had married, divorced, quarrelled with colleagues, failed to find a publisher for his dissertation on Henry James, remarried, and was now, given his interests, in about as unlikely a place, or so it seemed to me, as well could be imagined. It was all very strange. Very occasionally our paths crossed. Our last encounter was in February 1976 in front of the Canadian Parliament buildings in Ottawa. It was bitterly cold and Tom, plainly unfit, had so much difficulty negotiating the snowdrifts that I found myself having to take him by the elbow. We lunched at a nearby restaurant. He said he rarely went out during the day or, indeed, at any other time if he could help it. His teaching was all at night. As he did not own a car, a taxi would pick him up and return him to his apartment after his class. The great thing about Canadian universities so far as he was concerned was that teaching lasted only half the year, so for the winter months he and his wife essentially hibernated until the arrivalk of spring when they would take a flight to Spain or Mexico and for six glorious months would tour the bull rings, mixing with bullfighters and supplying articles to the Mexican and Spanish press. He hoped soon to have earned enough so they would never have to set foot in Canada or Britain again.

Afterwards he took me back to his apartment to introduce me to his wife, a tiny Sicilian woman with whom he chatted in Italian while they made coffee. He died in the early 1980s and his wife shortly after. What they died of I do not know but plainly it was an odd life they led. Years later a friend sent me *Rita*, a closely-printed 445-page novel he had written under the pen name Maria Teresa Fernandez Ojeda. On its back cover was a picture of a bewigged Tom stylishly dressed in women's clothes standing on the balcony of what appeared to be a motel. The story, modelled on Joyce's *Ulysses*, describes what happens in the course of a single day to a couple living in a Canadian apartment much like Tom's. Its narrator is the eponymous Rita, also known as James, is both maidservant and husband. Mainly, though, it is about the excitement of dressing up in women's clothes. A note on the flyleaf says:

Maria Teresa Fernandez Ojeda is the pen name of a male transvestite. She is European and speaks Spanish. When away from transvestism, her passion is the Spanish *corrida* or bullfight. He is a university professor and has been happily married for many years. In addition to *corrida* and the practice of transvestism, the author is interested in languages, chess and cooking.

The friend who sent the book included a note reminding me that in addition to his passion for bull fighting "Tom knew a lot about cricket and was a useful spin bowler."

In 1956 Bulganin and Khrushchev, then on a tour of Britain, visited the College. The cold war was at its height so there was concern that nothing should happen to further worsen East-West relations. Apparently the Kaiser had visited Magdalen in 1913 and been much feted by the students, an episode that, according to Karl, had in some obscure way contributed to the outbreak of the Great War. Determined that there should be no repetition, he arranged that we be kept occupied by scheduling examinations to coincide with the visit.

It was a hot afternoon. We were busily scribbling away when, looking up, we saw the phalanx coming onto the lawn from the direction of Longwall and heading in our direction. Instantly we laid down our pens and swarmed outside. Leading the procession were B & K, looking as if they would have much preferred to be somewhere else. Behind them, fanned out like a huge peacock's tail, was a crowd of notables among whom I recognised Tom Boase and the Dean of Divinity. All had big smiles on their faces, presumably because this was for them a notable occasion and they felt flattered at finding themselves in such company. What surprised me was how tiny the Russians were, not only B & K but also Andrei Topolev, the aircraft designer, who was directly behind them. Compact, resolute and glowering, they made the exquisitely suited and extravagantly gesturing Tom Boase, presumably outlining the history of the college for their benefit, look an absurdly gangling figure.

What none of them had been prepared for was that we would suddenly appear where we did, right in front of the approaching throng, still less that Michael Korda would walk forward and put his hand on Bulganin's shoulder. The smiles on the faces of the phalanx behind gave way to expressions of alarm. Bulganin, totally unperturbed, reached up in the manner of one used to dealing with mischievous children, pinched Michael's cheek and waved him away. Michael stepped back, expressions relaxed, and the column swept by.

According to later newspaper reports B & K had not enjoyed their visit to Oxford. They were tired and running behind schedule. Before arriving at Magdalen they had been taken to New College, where, upon seeing Jacob Epstein's statue of Lazarus, Khrushchev was reportedly heard to say "a typical piece of Western decadence." Another version of the story has it that the remark was actually occasioned by the sight of Lord David Cecil, the foppish Professor of English Literature, who happened to be standing nearby.

✆ ✆

At the start of my final year two fears gripped me: one was that Finals would reveal how little history I had learned; the other that I would wind up either a business trainee like David, currently peddling detergent to grocers, or teaching games and general studies at some undistinguished private school. The fashion among the historians of my year was to apply to oil companies. I applied to Shell and BP. The Shell interview was a disaster. It went wrong from the first on account of my having let slip that after a year in the sands of Egypt I did not relish spending further years in the sands of the Persian Gulf. My BP interview, in contrast, was a roaring success; I warmed to them and they to me with the result that an offer of a traineeship duly arrived. At least I would not be unemployed.

But still there were Finals to be faced. A J P Taylor's jibe about my being more interested in *why* I was studying history than in actually studying it had hit the mark. The problem was that the history I had been studying seemed to me just a vast body of information to be memorised, the same old boring political history I'd studied at school. Then it had simply been the Tudors and Stuarts; now it was everything from 410AD to 1914. Perhaps they assumed we were all destined to become schoolteachers and needed a solid grounding in whatever our headmasters might require. To relieve the tedium and possibly make some sense of it all I had begun dabbling in historical philosophy, a subject not highly regarded by practicing historians and so not included in the Oxford History Syllabus. Still, it had caught my imagination and so I laboured over it.

That I was wasting my time in this way came to Taylor's notice quite by chance. He wrote a column for Beaverbrook's *Express* and to relax afterwards he liked to have students around. Would I, he wondered, like to organise an after-dinner discussion group to meet in his rooms? He would provide the wine and we would take turns giving papers, which could be on any topic that happened to interest us on the understanding that we would have the first hour and a half to ourselves and that would hold his peace until the Magdalen clock struck ten. These seminars – for that was essentially what they were – provided more intellectual stimulation than all the tutorials I took at Oxford put together. There was also, as it turned out, a pay off.

Here, then, was a platform for me air my views on the philosophy of history. What did we mean when we said something caused an event? Given that all events have multiple causes, why are some causes deemed more important than others? Is it because they are in some way out of the ordinary, or because they accord with our preconceived notions or interests? In short it was the kind of thing that seems old hat these days but was new and interesting back then. On this, as on other evenings, the moment of revelation came when the clock struck and Taylor intervened. Although he never actually said "Gather around children," he might as well have done, for there was never any doubt that his intellectual grasp of the problem in hand far exceeded ours. Although he did not dismiss what I had been saying as total nonsense, it was, in his view, of no conceivable practical use. The word "History" had two meanings. It was what happened, including what went through people's minds while it was happening, and nothing we might say or do subsequently could in any way alter that. However, written history was something else again, being just words on a page. The relationship between the two depended partly on such evidence as "History" in the first sense had left behind and partly on what questions historians might choose to ask of it. They could ask questions about events in the past in the same way as a surveyor might ask questions about a building. Some might be purely factual. In the case of a building, for example, a surveyor might ask, "How tall is it?" In that case there might be an agreed method for arriving at an answer. Many issues in history were similarly ascertainable. Other questions, however, necessarily involved matters of opinion – for example, how adequately did a building serve the purposes for which it was built? These were all perfectly valid questions.

The trick was to ask interesting questions of a kind that the available evidence allowed one to answer. History had many uses. Knowing about what happened in the past did not necessarily make one wise when it came to dealing with issues of the present, but it was unquestionably better than not knowing. I found this both shrewd and enlightening. The thrust of his argument, however, was that historians had serious work to do and so would be well advised to leave theoretical questions to philosophers.

It chanced that a couple of weeks later I spotted an announcement pinned on the notice board in the Porter's lodge offering a Yale Fellowship to be awarded on the basis of a competition for which entrants were required to submit essays on the topic "Why Study History?" It was the very thing I had worked on for months and on which I now had the benefit of Taylor's views. Just as one fortuitous set of circumstances had put Eric in front of the Edinburgh-to-London express, so an equally fortuitous set had now put me in the way of becoming a Yale Fellow. As at the RGS, my pursuing a maverick course had paid off. Once again I found myself flying by the seat of my pants, this time to the United States.

Jane and I got engaged on the eve of my departure. I bought her a blue zircon ring for £16.00, that being all I could afford. We had been together for three years at Oxford. I was setting off on an entirely new adventure. She was about to start training as a social worker. We would not see one another for a year. That was not quite as long as those couples I'd seen being married on the dockside in Mauritius and the Seychelles would be separated. Still, a year was a long time.

8: LAND OF PLENTY: 1956-60

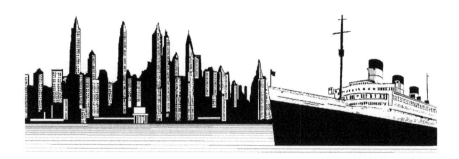

"HALF THE FUN IS GETTING THERE" the travel posters used to say. They don't say that any more, at least not about transatlantic air travel. No advertising firm would dream of trying it on. But in the days of the great Cunarders it was true. To cross the Atlantic as I did in the *Queen Elizabeth* was not only to travel in royal style but a holiday in itself, a period of five days with nothing to do, a time out of time.

Being a Fulbright, I travelled third class, which, in September 1956, meant travelling with a shipload of other young people a good proportion of whom were also Fulbrights, either Americans returning home or Europeans bound for American campuses. For many, perhaps most, it was the prelude to a wholly new adventure, perhaps even a new career. For those of us accustomed to the austerity of post-war Britain it also provided a foretaste of the plenty that awaited us on the other side.

This last was brought home to me at breakfast the first morning. At Southampton we had been hurried on board in the dark so it was not until I'd had a night's sleep and showered that I was properly able to take stock. Although the *Empire Trooper* had seemed large it was tiny as compared with the *Queen Elizabeth*. But it was the profusion of what was on offer at breakfast that astonished me most. At Magdalen it had been leathery toast, a cup of thin coffee, lukewarm bacon and a single egg. Here I was offered pineapple, watermelon, grapefruit, freshly-squeezed orange juice, croissants, porridge, a variety of cereals, omelettes, boiled eggs, eggs fried sunny-side-up, slices of bacon, slices of ham, sausages, pancakes with maple syrup and as many cups of coffee as I could drink. The dishes were heavy china, the napkins freshly ironed. And this was travelling Economy! What, I wondered, must breakfast be like in First?

I shared a table with Richard Selig and Mary O'Hara who had been married all of two days. Theirs had been a story-book romance. Richard, a Rhodes Scholar at Magdalen, had already made his mark as a poet. His first vacation he had made a pilgrimage to Dublin where, sitting in a pub, he had heard Mary's voice on the radio. He had immediately rung up the studio, arranged to meet her, taken her out to dinner, and in the course of the next couple of days persuaded her to try her luck on British television where she quickly made a name for herself as a harpist and singer of Irish ballads. Now she was on her way to the United States with every prospect of achieving even greater fame. The marriage of the American poet and the Irish folk singer had caught the imagination of the British press and public. I had travelled down to Southampton with them and helped carry Mary's three harps on board. Like me, she had never seen food in such profusion, so to impress her Richard undertook to demonstrate how Americans ate, pouring maple syrup over pancakes and stuffing them into his mouth one by one until she had to beg him to stop.

What made ocean travel preferable to air travel – even more than the sumptuousness of the meals – were the opportunities it offered for meeting people. I once asked the historian Denis Brogan how he had got to hob-nob with America's elite the way he had. As often as not, he said, it stemmed from contacts he made on the way over. By my time this was less easy on account of currency restrictions obliging us to travel Economy – a pretty accurate reflection of European-American relations at that time. As a result, the only way of getting to rub shoulders with American celebrities was by climbing over the rails into First. That, as I soon discovered, was not difficult. I could not eat in First, but no one seemed to mind my wandering around, listening to the palm court orchestra, browsing through the books in the library or simply savouring the grandeur of it all. Still, being an interloper made socialising difficult.

The topic of the moment was the impending Anglo-French invasion of Suez. Having no love for Egyptians and supposing Nasser's seizure of the Canal illegal I supported it. So, too, did a rather voluble Frenchman at our table, who turned out to be the newly-appointed Yale Professor of

French. Cecil Day-Lewis, whom Richard had got to know on account of his having lately been Professor of Poetry at Oxford took the other side. The recently-retired Vice-Chancellor of the University of Southampton refused to be drawn. He, too, had sat at our table that first morning with his nose buried in an enormous volume of Virgil's poems, something he said he had dreamed of doing throughout his dreary years of chairing university committees.

Mostly, though, I spent my time in the company of younger people. In spite of having just become engaged to Jane I took up with a pretty girl fresh out of sixth-form and now off to the States on a one-year English Speaking Union fellowship. We danced, went to shows and were apparently getting on swimmingly until around the third night at sea she disappeared and was later spotted in the shadow of one of the funnels in the embrace of Peter Heyworth, a former graduate student at Magdalen now on his way to join the University of Toronto's English Department.

The largest and certainly the noisiest group in Economy was a contingent of seventy Iowa girl pipers returning in triumph to the US having won the top award at that year's Scottish Bagpipe Festival. I'd scarcely encountered American women before, not many having found their way to Oxford, but here they were, using the same gestures and expressions as their male counterparts to the point of saying "Come on guys" even among themselves.

Deserted by my ESU schoolgirl, I asked one of them to dance. She, it turned out, was not a piper but a sword dancer, and plainly a very good dancer, although from the way she compressed her lips it was plain she preferred dancing with swords to dancing with me.

"You're very silent," I remarked after various attempts to engage her in conversation had failed.

"If there was anything to say," she said, "I'd say it."

Over the years word would reach me of those who shared that time out of time. Cecil Day Lewis became Poet Laureate. Peter Heyworth and the English Speaking Union schoolgirl kept in touch and eventually married. Mary O'Hara became even more of a celebrity in the United States than she had been in England. Within little more than a year, however, Richard was dead. Apparently they had already known that he had a form of leukaemia and that his days were numbered. After his death, Mary returned to England, spent 20 years in a nunnery, resumed her folk-singing career, wrote a book of memoirs and eventually remarried.

I saw her shortly after she returned to the stage looking much as she had all those years before.

For me, as for a good swathe of my contemporaries, a period of study in the United States was our version the eighteenth-century Grand Tour. Unlike the travellers of former times we were meritocrats rather than aristocrats. Now that the nexus of wealth and power had shifted westward it was the USA rather than the Continent that beckoned. Few of us were rich and even if we had been it would not have been of much use on account of the restrictions on taking money out of the country. So it was on the basis of American beneficence rather than at our own expense that boatloads of us headed westward – aspiring architects like Norman Foster and Richard Rogers (both Yale), novelists like Malcolm Bradbury and David Lodge (Yale and Berkeley respectively), politicians like Shirley Williams (Columbia), journalists like Godfrey Hodgson (U. Penn), and future television personalities like Bamber Gascoigne (Yale).

Now that crossing the Atlantic is such a commonplace experience it is hard to convey the thrill of visiting the United States in the 1950s. Rip Van Winkle slept for thirty years and awoke to find the world transformed. Far from falling asleep, we Europeans had spent thirty years tearing ourselves apart, but the effect was much the same. To arrive in America was to find oneself in a land where the future had already arrived, where doors opened as one approached, where there were automobiles as long as buses and buses as long as railway carriages; where cab drivers smoked cigars as big as Winston Churchill's; where there were supermarkets piled high with every conceivable kind of produce; where there were shoppers who made purchases in such bulk that they needed shopping carts to wheel them out to their family cars. There were also highways along which traffic flowed like water through a pipe, highways that looped around one another, rose up into the air, swooped over the tops of buildings, and without a single stop light bore one from the centre of cities, through industrial zones and suburbs, over rivers and finally out into the open countryside. As in the Washington Irving story, however, what most impressed the new arrival was not so much these marvels as the way they were taken for granted, so that when one expressed astonishment at sight of something one would immediately be told it was old-fashioned and would shortly be scrapped and replaced by an even newer version.

Of course England has all those things now, but it did not then. I recall being most forcibly struck by the contrast one night shortly after my arrival on finding myself lying awake in someone's house after a party and listening to the machines quietly switching themselves on and off, the central heating, the clothes washer, the clothes dryer, the deep freeze, the refrigerator, the dishwasher. This was the future and it worked.

No less vividly I remember the opposite experience of re-encountering England after having been away for three years. I was on a brief visit to gather research material for my dissertation and had taken a charter flight to Amsterdam by way of Reykjavik. In those days Icelandic Airlines still used propeller aircraft, so it was after some eighteen hours in the air and an overnight ferry crossing from the Hook of Holland that I arrived in Hull in the early morning to find the dock workers on strike, stunted figures in cloth caps huddled around a brazier and eyeing us as we struggled ashore with our suitcases. Here, then, was my native land – rain, cobbled streets, row upon row of tiny back-to-back cottages, smoky chimneys, iron railings, advertisements for Guinness, wooden railway carriages, glossy Bronco toilet paper – all just as it had been when I left. A few days later I took a bus over the Pennines to Liverpool and all the way there were peeling advertisements, smoke-blackened bricks, abandoned mills and on the faces of the people standing at the kerbside the same dreary look of resignation. Perhaps that was what the angry young men were angry about.

Of course there was poverty in America too. One only had to go down into the Italian and Portuguese sections of New Haven to see it. But what made it different, or at all events appear different, was the rapidity at which it was disappearing. There was nothing interesting about America's residual poverty. What was interesting, new, and exciting about the United States was not its poverty but its burgeoning wealth. Harness modern technology to the world's energy resources and there was apparently no limit to what could be achieved. Visit any American city – New York, Washington, or better still Houston or Dallas – and there one could see it happening before one's very eyes. For the first time in human history, or so it seemed, there was a nation with the capacity to eliminate poverty once and for all,.

This was not just my view but a belief reflected in the writings of serious-minded social thinkers of the time. My Yale dissertation supervisor was David M. Potter, author of one of the more sophisticated expressions of the optimism of the period: *People of Plenty: Abundance and the American*

Character. Having been the visiting Harmsworth Professor of American History at Oxford in 1947-48 he had experienced Britain's post-war austerity first hand and thereby persuaded that what distinguished Americans from Europeans was not, as Americans liked to think, their democracy or high principles but their unparalleled material abundance. It permeated their thinking and determined their actions in ways of which they were largely unaware, making them on the one hand optimistic and energetic and on the other wasteful of resources and ill-equipped to understand the problems of those less amply endowed.

Americans themselves had feared that once the fighting was over the economy would revert to the state it had been in the Depression; but nothing of the sort happened. Manufacturers simply switched from tanks and aircraft to producing cars and refrigerators. Taking these trends and extrapolating them into the future gave birth to a new profession, Futurology, whose exponents spent their time shuttling from think-tank to think-tank. According to them, the principal challenge facing the United States in the years ahead would not be creating wealth but disposing of it. Why the wealth would virtually create itself! Machines would build machines. Thanks to perpetual, incremental growth there was no limit to what could be achieved. Human beings would resemble the "lilies of the field, who toil not, neither do they spin." Bliss was it in that dawn to be alive and to be American was very heaven. Yet rather than cause for celebration there were those who found the prospect daunting, for how would Americans keep themselves occupied in a world of unlimited leisure? Play golf? Travel around in family helicopters? Establish space colonies? Fly to the stars?

The utopianism of the American 1950s contrasted sharply with the minimal aspirations of post-war – and by that time post-Suez – Britain. I was reminded of the difference by the regular arrival of letters from Her Majesty's Government addressed to Lieutenant Temperley (I had been promoted in absentia). They came in re-used brown envelopes so tiny that I was surprised the US Postal Service was able to handle them. Yet someone back in Britain had gone to no small trouble in their preparation, for they came, hand-addressed and held together with white sticky labels. And why had someone gone to all that trouble? In order to provide me with a postal order for three shillings and sixpence to be used solely for the maintenance of my uniform and equipment and for no other purpose whatever. Had I found a way of depositing these sums in a savings account they would, by the end of my four years, have paid for precisely two American haircuts.

છ્ય છ્ય

At Yale I followed the standard course for intending PhDs, which consisted of two years of seminars followed by two years of dissertation writing. Seminars, as I soon discovered, suited me much better than tutorials. In all those years of tutoring I had been so consistently out-gunned that I'd never once won an argument. Yet at my first Yale seminar I did exactly that. In the course of discussion someone said, "Wars never decide anything." It was so absurd a comment that I could hardly believe my ears. "What about the American Civil War?" I said. "It put paid to slavery and made the United States a nation state." It hadn't been difficult. I had merely stated the obvious. Even so, I left the seminar with a spring in my step that I'd never felt on leaving an Oxford tutorial.

YALE'S CONNECTICUT HALL

In fact I had left Oxford hating English History. There was just too much of it. It dribbled on for century after century to no good purpose. All those Henrys and Edwards and their bloody battles! There had always been a market revolution of some sort going on; someone was always reforming the exchequer; the middle class was always rising; the Commons were always making things difficult for the Lords, and both were forever at odds with the Monarchy. Whole careers were built on displaying evidence to prove that one monarch was more competent than another. The big issue in my day seemed to be whether the English Civil War had been caused by the gentry's rising or falling, although which it was actually doing seemed to depend on whose heads one counted. Who cared? I certainly didn't.

American History, in contrast, was fast-moving. Presidents came and went at shorter intervals than kings. It also seemed to have a direction, ideals too, though Americans did not always live up to them. Still, they were there and provided a base for measurement. Nor did one have to go nosing through household accounts to find out what the American Civil War was about. Great moral and political issues were at stake. Even at Oxford, where I took Slavery and Secession as my special subject, I had found American history stirred my emotions in ways that English history signally failed to do. Here was a nation, vibrant, expansive, yet committed to practices so patently at odds with its proclaimed principles that, as in some Greek tragedy, only a massive bloodletting could resolve the contradiction. To this day I cannot read Lincoln's Gettysburg Address aloud without my voice breaking.

As already indicated, the teacher with whom I had closest contact at Yale – and who, back in 1947, had introduced the Slavery and Secession option to Oxford – was David Potter. He had the subtlest mind of anyone I have ever met. *People of Plenty* was simply a diversion from his main field of interest, which was the antebellum period. Unlike others in that field, who tended to interpret the events of those years in the light of the war that followed, Potter pointed out that those living at the time viewed them quite differently. There had simply been too many cries of "Wolf!" Even after the states of the Deep South had declared that it was their intention to secede there was no way of knowing if they were serious, which explains the curious inertia of Lincoln and his party during the crucial four months leading up to the shelling of Fort Sumter.

Potter's ability to put himself into the position of people in the past and thus understand their mindset carried over into his teaching. However muddled or badly phrased a question he would quickly divine what it was in the questioner wanted to know. Being a southerner – he was from Georgia – he was always elaborately courteous to students. True, he carried this further than most, thanking students for papers that would have been given short shrift at Oxford. Nevertheless, in my four years at Yale, I never once encountered the kind of put-downs, or for that matter the academic backbiting, to which I had become accustomed there. It also struck me that Yale's historians took their teaching far more seriously.

In part this may be explained by the fact that they saw themselves as actively engaged in training the next generation of America's university teachers. Yet I saw enough of Yale's undergraduates, whose career intentions were, I suppose, much like those of my Oxford contemporaries, to persuade me that the programme there was far more flexible and innovative. Like the pre-1832 British electoral system, Oxford's way of reducing the teaching of history to an over-specialised, examination-driven grind was one that no person of rational mind would ever have invented.

Rather than having to memorise old things, the challenge at Yale was discovering new ones, so that instead of reading out weekly essays we wrote short dissertations. One, which became my first scholarly publication, concerned an 1838 contretemps involving Andrew Stevenson, the American Minister in London, and the Irish MP Daniel O'Connell who had accused him of being a "slave breeder." Stevenson had responded by challenging O'Connell to a duel. In the event no duel was fought, but the issues raised –Virginia's code of honour and practice of selling off its surplus slaves – kept newspaper readers on the two sides of the Atlantic entertained for months. Another paper was on the subject of Phrenology, inspired by my having chanced upon a large collection of early nineteenth-century treatises in the Sterling Library stacks. Phrenology, although eventually shown to be nonsense, had a big impact on thinking at the time. What particularly intrigued me was the way its advocates had shocked their religiously-minded contemporaries by advancing exactly the same arguments that I would use to shock my contemporaries at the RGS a century later.

I had been put onto the O'Connell-Stevenson piece by Samuel Flagg Bemis, at that time America's leading diplomatic historian, the winner of two Pulitzer prizes and author of the standard college textbook on the subject. His detractors referred to him as "Samuel Wave the Flag Bemis" on account of his allegedly uncritical approach to US foreign policy. This was unfair, for he was strongly opposed to US imperialism as represented by the acquisition of the Philippines and would doubtless have been even more critical of its latter-day exploits in the Middle East. He also had a mischievous sense of humour, once describing West Point to me as "The finest military academy – on the Hudson River." He had known Harold Temperley, whom he would refer to in seminar as "the Great Temperley," largely, I think as a way of pulling my leg. For part of one summer I actually lived in his house.

In spite of my affection for him he never ceased to remind me of the cartoon character Mr Magoo, being short sighted, having a harsh voice, and wearing old-fashioned button boots such as might have been worn by my grandfather. Like Mr Magoo he was also an erratic driver being in the habit of accelerating and then taking his foot off the pedal and letting the car coast for long distances, a practice that someone had told him saved petrol but that naturally attracted the attention of other motorists. Once, when a car that had been behind us honking and flashing its lights drew up alongside at an intersection, its occupants craning their necks too peer at him, he coolly observed them for some time before turning to me and remarking, as if genuinely surprised, "Funny thing – they look like quite nice people."

My first Christmas in North America I spent in Montreal with Jim and Edith Horton, the couple who had offered to take me in as a wartime evacuee and whose food parcels had helped keep us going through those long lean years. I travelled up on Christmas Eve through the bleakest winter landscape I'd ever seen. We had always thought of the Hortons as being our rich Canadian relatives, but although they lived in Westmount, supposedly the smartest section of town, their apartment was a modest two-bedroom affair. Jim had a deeply lined face and looked not at all well. Edith, in contrast, was bristling with energy.

Immediately on my arrival she made three announcements. First, I had been invited to have dinner that very night with Lorna Norman, a friend of theirs who had served with the Canadian forces and been a regular wartime visitor to Braeside. Second, being Canadians, when it came to the Queen's Christmas Address I should not expect them to stand to attention when the British National Anthem was played. Third, although Canada was a young country the Canadian dollar was worth more than any other money in the world, an observation that, as I eventually discovered, meant that the US dollar exchange rate had for once tilted in Canada's favour.

I hastened to assure her that as regards standing to attention she need not worry as I was a republican. This, I could see, rather took her aback, the more so when on further questioning it was revealed that rather than the conventional young Englishman she had expected she had been landed with something a whole lot worse, namely one who had fallen head over heels in love with the United States. Thus, almost before I had got my coat off everything began to go wrong. How badly they had gone wrong I did not find out until the following morning.

When I returned from Lorna's around midnight both Hortons were already in bed, so it was not until I got up the following morning that I was able to wish them a merry Christmas. My cheery greetings were not reciprocated, nor were the gifts I had brought opened.

"Aren't you going to see what I got you?" I asked hopefully. I was breakfasting on my own, they having already breakfasted.

"Well, it's a bit late now," Edith said, "you see, we gave our gifts last night"

"Oh, you should have said."

"You didn't ask. We always exchange presents and have our dinner on Christmas Eve."

It suddenly dawned on me that not only were there to be no presents; I was not going to get a Christmas dinner either.

"What," I tentatively asked, "are the plans for today?"

"Well," she said, "I'll be cleaning the flat as usual, so I'm afraid I'll have to ask you to step out for an hour or two. And by the way, we woke up in the night and there was an unpleasant smell in the flat, which we found was your pipe, so I put it out on the window sill."

She had seen me hunting around and said nothing, but there, sure enough, it was, encrusted in ice, it having snowed in the night and the run-off from the window pane frozen around it.

So that was to be my Christmas, driven from the apartment with nothing better to do than walk the town.

"Oh," she added, as I was getting ready to depart, "you'll need to wear galoshes. We Canadians always wear them. There's a pair of Jim's might fit you, but you had best get a pair of your own when the shops open."

Not many people were abroad that Christmas morning – a few fathers and sons trying out sledges and that was about it. When I got back to the apartment after an hour or two of fruitless wandering I was reprimanded for walking onto the carpet without taking off my galoshes. Towards evening, feeling in need of another smoke, I donned my winter gear, tramped around the block and returned, to once again be reprimanded for failing to take off my galoshes.

And so it went. After a couple of days of random wandering I discovered that the down-town Hudson's Bay Company store, contrary to what its name might suggest in the way of selling snow-shoes and huskies, was not only a perfectly ordinary department store but that it contained a model living room, considerably larger and more commodious than the Horton's, where I could spend the day reading and writing letters. Surprisingly, no one minded. They did not mind me smoking either. Had I been a bum who had wandered in from the street no doubt I'd have been thrown out, but, looking reasonably respectable and busily engaged in doing the sorts of things people did in sitting rooms, the shop walkers seemed pleased to see me and would nod and smile when I arrived.

Why Edith spent a full three hours every day cleaning that tiny flat remained a mystery until I discovered that she was obsessed with germs. She imagined them as lurking in every dark corner, swarming like ants, hiding under the sofa, infesting my handkerchief and escaping out of my trouser pocket. The only remedy was to root them out, pour disinfectants on them, gather them up in paper tissues and flush them down the toilet. At one hotel in Edinburgh, where they had stayed at during their Coronation tour, germs had been so omnipresent that they had felt obliged to use their spare underclothes to dry their hands and had spent the entire night sitting bolt upright in two chairs

Although he said nothing, I suspect all this was a great embarrassment to Jim. At the end of my stay he drove me to the station and as we parted muttered something about Edith being under a strain and slipped a parcel into my hand which turned out to contain several tins of the type of tobacco he had noticed I was smoking. I wrote a dutiful letter thanking them, but received no reply. In fact, I never heard from them again. My parents, however, received a letter saying they must find my brother a great consolation. Looking back, I realised I had had a lucky escape. I must be the only person in the world with cause to be grateful for the sinking of the *City of Benares*.

The great American universities differ from their British counterparts by virtue of being primarily great graduate schools. Most had started out as institutions for the training of either ministers or farmers. In the latter part of the nineteenth century, however, when serious scholarly research had become a requirement, they had reorganised themselves on the German rather than the British model, thereby acquiring properly-organised graduate schools with the result that thereafter an increasing, and in some cases the largest, proportion of their intake was at the graduate level.

Like most incoming foreign students, I spent my first year in Yale's Hall of Graduate Studies. There, as I quickly noticed, a number of my British contemporaries were eagerly acquiring crew cuts and American accents. As Yale was a notably Anglophile institution I felt less of a curiosity speaking with an English accent than I might have done at, say, a Midwest institution. In fact, to be English was, if anything, an asset.

Nevertheless, a number of encounters gave me a new perspective on my home country. One was with a local parent-teachers' association that had invited me to explain how the British educational system worked. Although I had experienced it, I had given it little thought, but impressed as I was by America's wealth I took that as my starting point. Being so much poorer than the US, I explained, Britain could not afford to keep its young people in full-time education for so long. We had, therefore, based our educational system on the principles adopted by Civil Service reformers a century earlier, namely, selection by competitive examination. The aim was to do away with inherited privilege by giving everyone an opportunity to prove themselves. In practice, however, it became rather like a game of musical chairs, the largest number of chairs being removed at age eleven, when around three-quarters were eliminated, others at age sixteen and so on. University education was free, but entry was limited to some seven per cent of the age group. That, however, was not the end of the matter, for degrees were divided into categories, Firsts, Seconds, and so on, and there were other even more stringent examinations, for example to get into the Foreign Office or win prize fellowships at All Souls. They should think of the British educational system as pyramid designed to ensure that the best brains came out on top.

"So what happens to the rest?

I could tell from the questioner's manner that he was the sort who probably did not think highly of striped-pants diplomats, still less of All Souls fellows.

"Well," I said, "they do thing more suited to their abilities, practical things like becoming carpenters, plumbers and engineers."

"So how does Britain train its engineers?"

It suddenly occurred to me that half the men in the audience were probably carpenters, plumbers and engineers, rightly proud of their accomplishments, and that it had never occurred to me to enquire as to how their English counterparts were trained.

I waffled on for a while about apprenticeships and, in the case of engineers, university courses, but with a growing sense that things had gone awry. At that point a hard-faced woman piped up and wanted to know whether it was the same with girls as with boys. Pretty much, I said, at least in theory, but a lot depended on who they married and that depended on how attractive they were.

It was a catastrophe, not because what I said was wrong – it was, in fact, an all too accurate description of how the British educational system worked – but on account my unthinking acceptance of the meritocratic assumptions on which it was based. I was told there would be a report of the meeting in the next day's *New Haven Courier* so I bought a copy, and, sure enough, there was a reference to it in the index but no evidence of it on the page indicated. Mercifully, someone had killed the story.

Encounters with expatriates could also prove revealing. One of the curiosities of living in North America is meeting what could be called professional expatriates. One such was Colonel Arnold Strode-Jackson, although in his case his appearing to trade on his Englishness may simply have been a reflection of the way people in his circle were used to speaking and behaving back in the 1920s. Always in a silk cravat with a matching silk handkerchief in his breast pocket, he had retained the disconcerting habit of adding an interrogative "what?" to the end of his sentences, as in "Jolly good party this, what?" Americans did not know whether to be impressed or burst out laughing. Yet, comic figure though he now appeared, he was a man of substantial achievement, having been awarded a gold medal at the 1912 Stockholm Olympics for winning the 1500 meters. Already something of a national hero, he had subsequently gone on to become one of Britain's most highly decorated soldiers in the Great War. In *Rommel: The Desert Fox*, Desmond Young, compares his soldierly qualities to Rommel's. In short, he was, or at all events had been, a real-life John Buchan hero.

Yet, by the time I encountered him, he was pretty much reduced to living on his wits. He had married an American heiress and for a time had attempted to run the lumber business she inherited, but the firm had collapsed and the money was now all gone. Tales of their penury abounded. A local farmer, calling to demand payment for his eggs, had reportedly been fobbed off with a glass of sherry and a copy of Arnold's privately-printed autobiography. My own encounters with him were mostly on the Connecticut cocktail party circuit. On being reminded that I had been to Magdalen he would talk wistfully of his friendship with the Prince of Wales rather as if he might turn out to be a mutual acquaintance. As the Roger Bannister of his day he looked back on the years before the Great

War as a Golden Age and would enquire if I shared his impression that the country had latterly gone to the dogs. So there he was, miraculously preserved like a fly in amber, and still cherishing memories of a long-vanished England. Now the high point of his year was when, kitted out in his Brasenose blazer and 1914-style Oxford bags, he went to the dockside every summer to be photographed by the *New York Times* greeting the arriving Oxford and Cambridge athletics teams.

My acquaintance with the Strode-Jacksons, like much else that happened to me during my four years at Yale, came about through my friendship with Mike and Lynn Kitzmiller. Mike, who was also starting out in graduate history programme, had led an adventurous life. Following his parents divorce he had run away and spent two years in the South Pacific working as a deckhand on yachts belonging to dodgy American businessmen. One had employed him to look after his mistress, Anna Chevalier, a Polynesian beauty whom someone had "discovered" and taken to Hollywood, an assignment that had led to Mike's being shot in the leg by one of Anna's former lovers. Returning to the US he had got into Yale on the basis of an IQ test and on graduation had gone to work on a newspaper. Now he was back, only temporarily as it proved, prior to going on to become a Democratic Party Mr Fixit on Capitol Hill and eventually Staff Director of the House Commerce and Energy Committee. Once again I had found a friend older and more experienced than I was. As it turned out I could not have found a guide better qualified to introduce me to the wonders of Connecticut society, Washington politics and Kentucky bourbon.

The reason for Mike's being back at Yale was his friendship with Joe Curtiss, a Yale professor and former head of wartime counter-intelligence in Turkey, a rich bachelor who lived in Killingworth, a few miles out of town, where he kept open house for Mike and other favoured students. It had been there that, lying awake at night I had listened to the machines switching themselves on and off.

Yale's Elizabethan Club

Mike and Joe were also instrumental in getting me elected to Yale's Elizabethan Club, so named because it held copies of the First Folios of Shakespeare and other rare publications of that period. The main advantage of belonging, however, was that it occupied agreeable premises close by the Sterling library, offering free teas, which included cucumber sandwiches, and, for those so disposed, an opportunity to play croquet on the lawn. There I met, among others, the author and journalist John Hersey. Normally I am tongue tied when confronted by authors whose books I have read. As it happened, I had read both *Hiroshima* and *A Bell for Adano*. However, our first meeting proved providential in that, having failed to catch his name and finding him sitting on his own, I held forth in a totally unabashed way about a story I had just come across in a nineteenth-century newspaper about a rescued African slave who kept running away from London and barbecuing sheep on Salisbury Plain. I said it would make a marvellous novel. He agreed, and would later tease me by asking how I was getting on with it. He was then working on *The*

War Lover, a story about American flyers in East Anglia, and would ask me questions about English usages.

So it was that eating cucumber sandwiches and playing croquet at the Elizabethan Club or lying sprawled on Joe Curtis's lawn drinking his bourbon while the fireflies flickering their lights on and off among the bushes Yale became for me what, back in more leisured times, Oxford had been for generations of young Englishmen.

ൟ ൟ

I met a number of other distinguished Americans during my four years. My oddest encounter was not at the Elizabethan Club but in one of the foyers on the second floor of Yale's Sterling Library. On entering the building I had noticed a number of photographers hanging around the main concourse but had failed to enquire what was happening. So there I was, laden down with books and waiting for the elevator, when suddenly the doors opened to reveal non other than former President Harry S Truman. I do not know which of us was the more nonplussed. He, apparently expecting a crowd of reporters and barrage of flash bulbs, had his hands clasped in a two-handed victory wave and was plainly disconcerted to find only me. The elevator was packed with dignitaries, so there was no question of my getting in. For what seemed an interminable time we stood looking at one another while people shuffled around and buttons were pressed until at last the doors slid shut and he was borne away.

Near the end of my first year I met Alistair Cooke, like Harry Truman a visiting Chubb Fellow. The big news story at the time was school integration. Might it be possible, I asked him, to get a summer job on a newspaper, preferably one in the South, so that I might get some insight into what was happening? My Yale fellowship would not even see me through the summer and with the prospect of Jane arriving in late August, I desperately needed money. He gave me the addresses of people I should write to in the South and suggested I try visiting the New York offices of the major British papers.

None of this bore fruit. Those at the desks of British papers listened politely, said they would be happy to receive anything I wrote but were not prepared to put any money up front. Nor, this being June 1957, the year of the Eisenhower recession, were there any jobs going in Connecticut for someone without a union card. So I jumped at the offer when Frank

Goodman, a Magdalen Rhodes Scholar friend now at Harvard Law School, offered to drive me down to Texas. There were always jobs going in Texas, he said, and along the way I might try calling on some of those whose names Alistair Cooke had given me. If nothing else, I'd at least see something of the South.

Rolling south down the Skyline Drive and Blue Ridge Parkway in the shimmering heat of early summer it was borne home to me that I was in the greatest country on earth. Apart from a couple of trips to New York and one to Washington I had not so far been outside of Connecticut. Now the whole continent was opening up in front of me a vast land basking in prosperity. Here were signposts pointing to places with legendary names – Lynchburg, Roanoke, Nashville, Chattanooga – roads that if you drove on far enough would take you all the way to the blue Pacific. At night the air was balmy and fireflies glimmered along the roadside. Never before, in the whole of history, or so it seemed to me, had a people enjoyed so many blessings.

Arriving in New Orleans, we were greeted by a marching band. In Bourbon Street we drank mint juleps and ate grilled catfish. The following morning, however, when I visited the *Times-Picayune* offices, I found that no one there had any recollection of having received my letter and that there were no jobs going. In Houston, a chaotic mixture of shacks and skyscrapers, the story was the same. Plainly Texas was booming. But in San Antonio, when we finally got there, the job situation was no better than in New Haven. I pored over the employment sections of the San Antonio papers. Apart from door-to-door selling, for which the demand appeared limitless, there was nothing at all. "We limit our salesmen to $3,000 a month for the first month" one ad said. It was for selling stove hoods. I rang for details. Frank's father, unimpressed, took me down to the local hardware store where hoods the same as the ones I'd be selling were on offer, fully installed, for $100 less than I'd be asking.

However, there was one ad for an entirely new enterprise offering "limitless opportunities for salesmen with initiative." We were invited to assemble at its office at 8.00am the following morning. The office turned out to be a single room off a long corridor, with a notice pinned to the door saying "First Memorial Park, San Antonio, Texas. Please Enter." All it contained by way of furniture was a filing cabinet, a table, and not enough collapsible chairs for the dozen or so potential salesmen who had turned up. We were addressed by Fred Felty, a big man in cowboy boots with that corn-fed look I had learned to associate with upper-crust Americans. He was real pleased we'd all turned up. If we had been wondering what it was all about, the aim was to provide San Antonio's "Nigras" with a proper modern cemetery. Frankly, what they had had up to now, all overgrown and vandalised, was a disgrace to the City. And why had it gotten like that? Because it lacked perpetual care and that was exactly what we would be providing. For the first time in San Antonio's history, blacks could have what whites had long enjoyed – a maintenance-efficient cemetery. Instead of headstones there would be brass plaques set flush with the ground so as to allow a lawn mower to pass over. He passed around pictures of what looked like a golf course surrounded by bits of statuary. But perpetual care did not come cheap. The message we would need to get across was that when people paid $200 – the bargain opening offer – they weren't buying just an itsy-bitsy piece of land; they'd be investing in a fund to pay for the ground being properly maintained. However far ahead they looked, there'd be someone out there mowing.

He then introduced Sam, who would lead our sales team, a salesman of long experience and legendary achievement newly arrived from Tennessee. Sam's appearance was not prepossessing; in fact his clothes rather looked as if they had been slept in, but, as he explained, the moment Mr Felty had phoned about this great project he'd dropped everything and come right on down. He had something of a hot-gospeller's delivery. The first thing we had to realise was that First Memorial had real earning potential. Something we'd need to get over to our customers was that we were offering them a great deal. Even if they had no cause to use it, a burial plot was a sound long-term investment. We'd be starting first thing in the morning, 8.00am sharp, when he'd give us our dossiers and assign us our districts. While we knocked on doors he'd be visiting the city's black ministers.

We then drove out to First Memorial. As I didn't have a car I drove with Sam. He apologised for having to take me in his old car, but his new car hadn't yet arrived. There had been some mix up with his luggage too, which was why he was still wearing the clothes he'd been wearing when he left Tennessee.

The cemetery, when we got there, looked much like all the other fields around, some of which contained cattle. But, as Sam pointed out, Dallas and Houston had once looked like that. It was the way all land looked before it was developed. I could see some of our party shaking their heads. As I lacked a car, he offered to pick me up next morning from the Goodman's.

So, for the next two weeks, for twelve or more hours a day, I plodded the pavements of San Antonio's black districts. Apart from Sam, I was First Memorial's only salesman. It struck me as odd that, since we were selling to blacks, we employed no black salesmen, but Sam said that blacks would be more likely to trust a white-run enterprise. Those on whose doors I knocked were courteous. Mostly those at home during the day were women. They would invite me in for coffee or cold drinks and listen while I showed them black-and-white pictures of old-fashioned graveyards gone to ruin and glossy colour prints of modern easily-maintained ones. However it would soon become evident that their interest centred on me rather than on what I was selling. They wanted to know about England, how blacks were regarded there, and how I came to be in Texas. When I left they would say things like, "It was real nice talking with you, but when I die I don't mind what happens; you can bury me out there at the bottom of the yard for all I care." Perhaps they saw that I was not a dedicated salesman. Some of those I called on were divorcees. One or two wondered if I couldn't, maybe, come back in the evening after the kids had gone to bed.

San Antonio, I discovered, had essentially two black districts: an old run-down section with rickety and unpainted houses and a smart new section with lawn sprinklers and double garages. Here blacks had cars, telephones, refrigerators, television sets and as often as not automatic washers too. My parents had never had a car, telephone, TV, or a refrigerator let alone an automatic washer. In spite of being disfranchised and otherwise discriminated against a good proportion of San Antonio's blacks were better off materially speaking than most British families that I knew. It quickly became evident, however, that there was no point in my plodding around these smarter districts whose residents were mostly either service folk from the nearby military bases or young, mobile and disinclined to make provision for anything as remote as death. So, it was on the older and more run-down sections of town that I concentrated.

Sometimes Sam ran me there, occasionally Mr Felty. Generally, though, I got about by bus or by walking. Texans, whether white or black, were not much given to walking. Often I was the only person on foot. Policemen in squad cars eyed me curiously. I ate in black bars and restaurants. Posters of a kind I'd not seen before showed happy African Americans drinking Budweisers, smoking king-sized filters and doing all the other things happy whites were shown doing on posters elsewhere. Waiters would ask me where I was from. Once or twice I was taken over to be introduced to customers who had been in England in the war and we would swap reminiscences of Liverpool or Portsmouth.

In time I got to know Sam and Mr Felty. Mr Felty came from an old San Antonio family that had evidently known better days. I recall his once shaking his head and saying, "If ma Daddy could see me now, sellin' burial lots to Nigras!" Sam's luggage never did arrive, neither did his new car. The problem, it turned out, had more to do with his wife than with the transportation company. Odd comments led me to suspect that First Memorial was not the only reason for his leaving Tennessee in a hurry.

At the end of two weeks I had not sold a single burial lot. My decision to quit was precipitated by the belated discovery that even if I had made a sale my 20% commission would have depended on the purchasers keeping up their monthly payments. Sam told me I was giving up a great career. "That accent of yours," he said, "real wows the 'Nigras.'"

Meanwhile, Frank having departed for Mexico on holiday, my presence in the Goodman household was becoming an embarrassment. When I told his father I'd quit he said he wasn't surprised. He'd been making enquiries and found someone who owned an automotive business in Fort Worth who would give me a job; he also had friends there who would put me up while I found somewhere more permanent. "This," he said, "will all be something to look back on."

His friends lived in one of Fort Worth's swankier suburbs. I took a taxi there from the bus station. Green-breasted lawns rose up from the road to where shade trees afforded glimpses of gravelled turnarounds and white-pillared porticoes. And there, as I struggled up the drive with my suitcase and haversack, as if to complete the picture, was a Doris Day look-alike, flanked by two little tow-headed boys. "Hey," she said, "you look like you need to go to the ice cream parlour." It was as if I had walked into a

Hollywood movie. Her car was a long convertible. We drove with the roof down and the radio playing. The ice creams were handed to us through a hatch. As we drove slowly back, licking our cornets the oldest little boy called out from the back, "Mummy, when I grow up, should I be a rich man?" Without a moment's hesitation she replied, as though it was the most obvious thing in the world, "That's the only kind of man to be, son." No one at Oxford had ever told me that, or at Yale either.

"That's the only kind of man to be, son"

My new employer, Maurice Rabinowicz, was plainly a rich man. Everything about him – his silk suits, alligator shoes, half-chewed cigar, and enormous automobile – proclaimed him a man of substance. He was also generous. As a prominent member of Fort Worth's Jewish community he had not only done Frank's father a favour by finding a job for me but he had also found jobs for a lot of other people, including a number of Jewish refugees from Europe. As he seldom visited the business I cannot claim to have known him well, but judging by the way it was run I could only assume that his views on racial matters were liberal. In deference to local sensibilities, the outside sales force was entirely white; internally, however, a meritocratic system operated, with blacks in a number of senior positions. Being Texas, this last may not have been as unusual as it would have been in, say, Mississippi or Alabama. All the same, United Auto's mix of red-necks, blacks, European migrants and Mexican Americans made it about as multicultural an enterprise as one would likely encounter anywhere in North America.

The Company employed around 30 people. Its being engaged in interstate commerce entitled me to the national minimum wage of one dollar an hour, rising to two dollars for overtime and three dollars for work on Sundays. Some weeks I managed to clock up 80 hours. Mostly I was employed unloading automotive parts arriving in freight cars from Detroit, sorting them out in the warehouse, reloading them onto trucks and despatching them to dealers in Amarillo, Lubbock and other far-off places. We worked stripped to the waist, our sweat dripping onto the cardboard boxes we handled. By mid-morning the tin roofs of the freight cars were hot enough to fry eggs.

Dallas-Fort Worth epitomised what was exciting about 1950s America. God was in his heaven; Eisenhower was in the White House, and Neiman Marcus, the super-store of the super-rich, only just down the road. Here was the consumer society in full flood: glitzy new shopping malls, aluminium-clad skyscrapers, stretch limousines, billboards advertising futuristic products. Mostly I only glimpsed it from the back of trucks, but it was plain that an awesome transformation was taking place. Once Texas had been cattle; now it was oil. The result was a curious mix of the rugged giving way to the citified – men in cowboy gear riding around in air-conditioned cars, Annie Oakleys in shopping plazas, newspaper stories of old-time cattle rustlers found in city flophouses, and everywhere, belting out in high decibel from radios and juke boxes, those jaunty electronic voices celebrating the simple virtues of Mid-America.

United Auto. Fort Worth, Texas

At United Auto the radio was always on. It came on when we threw the main switch in the morning and went off when the switch was thrown in the evening. Top of the Top Ten that summer were Pat Boone's *Love Letters in the Sand* and Frankie Lymon and the Teenagers' *Goody Goody*. Every hour the disc jockey would read out the lucky number on a dollar bill in circulation and spin a wheel to determine the size of the prize – anything between $100 and $1,000 – that awaited whoever got to the station with the lucky bill in the next two hours. Every hour we would check the bills in our billfolds (unavailingly – but that did not stop us living in hope). Between times we'd listen to the same doo-wop and rock 'n' roll numbers as they came around with the regularity of luggage on an airport carousel, interspersed at intervals by news items and ads. However, there was never any doubt as to the station's priorities. Whatever the news item – civil rights debates in Congress, power struggles in the Kremlin, Althea Gibson winning Wimbledon – the announcers' voices kept an even tone but would instantly assume a new urgency when they switched to ads for detergents, diapers or power steering. All summer long, in the warehouse, on the road, in the freight terminal, the same music, songs and huckstering voices would pursue us.

With Alaska's admission to statehood Texans could no longer boast of having the largest state, but that did not prevent them boasting of having the largest everything else. Behind their folksy informality there lurked the urgent need to keep the cash registers ringing and the assembly lines running. A much-heralded consumer breakthrough that year was striped toothpaste. Back in Britain we had barely got away from having our toothpaste come in round tins like boot polish. Americans, long accustomed to having theirs in tubes, were going one better by introducing a striped variety. There were ads for it everywhere, even serious articles explaining how it was done. These came to mind one Sunday morning as, strolling down a deserted railroad platform waiting for my work mates, I found myself facing two identical stainless steel drink fountains, one marked "white," the other "colored." These Americans, I thought, what will they dream up next? Coloured water! And so I pressed the button marked "colored."

Most of my work mates were "colored." Southern blacks, as I well knew, were a people burdened with a tragic history and still sorely oppressed, yet no group could have appeared less cowed than my workmates. What impressed me was rather their exuberance and good humour. They were also, I discovered, great raconteurs. I had long known that Jews were much given to telling funny stories about Jews. Our Jewish salesmen had a seemingly limitless fund of them. But what I had not been prepared for was to find that blacks had a similar fund of stories about blacks. In return, I told stories about stiff-upper-lip Englishmen, parsimonious Scotsmen and inebriate Irishmen. Whether it was the stories themselves, or, more probably, my accent, these went down better in Fort Worth than they had ever done elsewhere, so much so that when Maurice had an important visitor to entertain he would have me hauled sweating from some upper gallery to tell one.

Insofar as anyone at United Auto felt a victim it was probably Dan, my immediate boss. Although Jewish, Dan was bursting with racial animosity. He was also very stupid. The two were not unconnected. Much of his resentment of blacks, it was plain, stemmed from his not being up to his job. Supposedly he supervised our work, but mostly he lurked in a sort of cave that, like some beleaguered Neanderthal, he had built for himself out of cardboard boxes at one end of the warehouse and where, with the aid of a stub of pencil, he tried to figure out the loading schedules he'd been given. From time to time he would emerge to give instructions. When, yet again, these turned out to be wrong there would be ill-concealed merriment. His workforce, mostly black, regarded him as a standing joke. Worse still, it was usually Harry, the shipping clerk, a black whose status in the organisation was superior to his own, who detected the error, whereupon Dan would retire muttering to his lair. Obliged to work with blacks much cleverer than he, life was one long Calvary, made all the worse by my arrival. Early in our acquaintance he had made clear his view that people who attended Ivy League colleges were all perverts and pinkos. This was in response to some slighting remark I had made about the late Senator Joseph McCarthy. Once, as we passed in a corridor, he snarled, "Why don't you go back to England and take your nigger friends with you?"

Charlie, who was in overall charge of the warehouses, also made racist remarks, but never with any animosity. He would say things like, "I like my coffee the way I like my women, hot and black." One day as we were all sitting around over coffee the subject came up of a black who had been arrested up-state for some offence against a white woman, and there was much speculation among blacks and whites around the table as to whether he would be lynched. Shortly after, catching Charlie on his own, I asked what would happen if a white man raped a black woman.

"Hell," he said, "you can't rape a nigger!"

Yet Charlie and Harry, the black shipping clerk, not only worked amiably enough together all week, but met up at weekends at baseball games and so far as I could gather their wives were acquainted. In his case the racism was not visceral, as it was with Dan, but simply part of his red-neck braggadocio. A couple of times over the summer he flew out to Las Vegas and came back boasting about how much money he had lost. Losing money gambling in Las Vegas was apparently a macho thing to do. Easy come, easy go, that was Charlie's way.

The saddest member of the workforce was Saul, brought over from Czechoslovakia the previous year under a scheme organised through the local synagogue. He was small, tense, and looked undernourished. It was whispered that he had lost his family in the Holocaust. He was the latest of a succession of European immigrants, the others having been there long enough to adapt to Texan ways, acquire suits and get themselves absorbed into the sales force. They talked, mostly in a humorous way, about their experiences in German camps and afterwards in American camps awaiting transportation to the States. Saul spoke hardly at all and seemed to resent friendly approaches. He would sit over coffee, an anxious look on his face. As a workmate he proved difficult. We'd be in the warehouse sorting out a new delivery and suddenly he'd begin shouting and hurling cartons at me. Eventually I discovered the reason – he couldn't read. The labels made no sense to him. My discovery made our relationship all the more difficult, for he now feared that I would give him away and have him sacked, although I doubt that that would have happened.

When I left United Auto to go back up North they presented me with a handsome cowhide briefcase that I was to continue using for many years. There had been a whip-around and people had contributed generously. They all assembled in the front office beneath the girlie calendars and racks of sun glasses. Maurice made a speech, saying that what I was getting was made of good Texas cowhide, and his pretty blonde secretary made the presentation.

That evening, a hundred miles or so north of Dallas, my bus passed through the town of Commerce. I knew it was Commerce because the bus had to pass under a sort of heraldic arch inscribed, "WELCOME TO COMMERCE: THE BLACKEST SOIL, THE WHITEST PEOPLE." Yet there was not a white person in sight, the road beyond being lined with rickety houses where elderly blacks could be seen sitting on their front porches while barefoot children played in their dusty yards. I remember thinking what a fitting finale it would have made for the sort of account I had envisaged writing when I had toured the offices of the London papers. That was what the South was supposed to be like. Doubtless many parts of it were, but as a summation of my actual experiences, it simply wouldn't do. Too much was going on. Real life just wasn't that stylised.

⚬⚬

Jane's ship was a day late getting into New York. I had booked into the Hotel Martinique at the junction of 49 West 32ⁿᵈ Street and Broadway where I spent my time flipping over memory cards in German and English. It was what I had spent every spare moment doing back in Texas, and now with Jane's imminent arrival I was growing panicky. Like Latin at Oxford, Yale's German requirement threatened to overturn my whole applecart. Fail German and I'd find myself pumping oil in the Persian Gulf.

The Martinique would later achieve notoriety on account of its being at the centre of the Seventies scandals arising out of the enormous profits unscrupulous landlords were making by housing the homeless at the state's expense. *The New Yorker* ran a whole series of articles on it. By then it had fallen into total decrepitude with sewage running down the walls, and muggers roaming the corridors. In the Fifties, however, it was not the homeless but visiting Fulbright scholars that it housed, incoming liners being littered with brochures advertising its low rates and convenient location. At that time it was being renovated from the ground floor upwards, a process that by 1957 had reached the 10ᵗʰ floor, the floors above that being those offered at cut rates to visiting foreign academics. As those already renovated were particularly favoured by prostitutes and their clients it gave newly-arrived visitors a distinctly skewed impression of the United States.

Jane, who had put on weight, arrived looking even handsomer than I remembered. I, on the other hand, was skin and bone as a result of the exercise I'd been getting in Texas and of not having eaten properly in my desperate effort to save enough to pay for her visit. What Jane made of the combination of me and the Martinique I do not know; probably she was too excited and flustered to take it all in. Even staying at the Martinique, however, was more than we could well afford. However, Jane had an Eyre Brook cousin in Pittsburgh, so after a few days spent sightseeing in New York we took the bus there

Over the year I had got to thinking of Yale as a rather superior version of Oxford, or rather as being what Oxford might have been had it been richer and put its house in order. Often I was tempted to think the same about the United States vis-à-vis Britain. Then I would remember McCarthyism, Jim Crow laws and all its other oddities, not least its religiosity. I doubt Jane's relatives were especially religious but they said grace before meals and were regular church goers. Our first Sunday, however, I was invited along to "Sunday School." Unlike British Sunday schools these were gatherings of the congregation held in the absence of the minister, men meeting in one room, women in another. So here was a cross section of the Baptist middle class of that part of Pittsburgh – garage owners, bank managers – in fact the American counterparts my parents and the people they knew, meeting to air their views on religious matters. Because there were so many different sects I had supposed they had strict views on theological issues, that presumably being why they had split apart. But here, it transpired, anything went. One church member had a bee in his bonnet about UFOs. They were a genial group, prepared to give him a hearing, although I gathered they had heard it all before. Others chipped in with comments about other mysterious things the government was concealing. Whether they put their belief in these stories much on a par with their belief in Christ and the resurrection or, indeed, whether they had any views on Christ and the resurrection I have no way of knowing as the subject never came up. Yet these were men with real jobs, responsible citizens, far more capable than I was at fixing a car engine or a leaky pipe – the modern equivalents, it might be thought, of Mark Twain's Connecticut Yankee at the Court of King Arthur – and yet who, unlike Twain's hero, were prepared to give credence to all manner of flapdoodle dreamed up by our modern Merlins.

Back in Connecticut I introduced Jane to the Kitzmillers. Although we were engaged, I had given no thought to the notion of our getting married – not because I was opposed to the idea but because it appeared totally impractical. She had the wrong sort of visa and was only half way through her almoner's course; I could barely support myself on my Yale Fellowship and was still at least three years short of getting a PhD. But Jane and Mike got talking and gradually it began to seem less impractical than I had assumed. Connecticut needed social workers; Jane could work and train at the same time; there would be money left over to help supplement my Fellowship; cheap temporary accommodation was to be had in the form of City property awaiting demolition. Jane had even brought a dress that would perfectly well serve as a wedding dress – in fact it was hard to see what other use she had supposed it might serve.

We were married in the University's Chapel. Mike, who had pretty much arranged it all, was my best man. Jane's mother and aunt came over to help with the organisation; her cousin from Pittsburgh gave her away; Frank Goodman and other Oxford friends came down from Harvard for the celebration; I made a speech which people thought funny. In view of all the obstacles that had to be cleared out of the way and the breathless haste with which it was organised it all went off surprisingly smoothly.

ᔆᔆ ᔆᔆ

Thanks to Jane's cooking I also began to appear less skeletal. I managed to get through my German examination at my second attempt, mainly I suspect because, having already invested so much in me Yale could hardly bring itself to throw me out. I also got through my history oral examination, again at a second attempt, having failed disastrously the first time around on account of not having had the sort of high-school and college background in American history that Yale history graduates would normally have had. My Yale PhD dissertation, on the other hand, I completed in two years flat. By Yale standards this was something of a record, but I was driven on by the fear that if I did not complete it in that time I never would. With my Fellowship about to end and in the knowledge that Jane and I would then be expelled from the country, there simply was no alternative.

Most of the writing was done in a private office in a rather seedy block in down-town New Haven, rented on my behalf by J. Holladay Philbin for whom I was simultaneously ghost-writing a book. It was a job I had inherited from Hector Kinloch, another Brit, who had just completed his PhD. He had inherited it from another yet another Brit. In fact it helped a succession of Brits through their final years at Yale. My predecessors' work, as I quickly discovered, was not entirely up to scratch, as I have no doubt my successors would later conclude about mine. So far as I could see the whole thing was a huge white elephant, but as Holladay was immensely rich I felt few qualms.

Being rich, you could almost say, was Holladay's profession. Large, affable, now in his late 60s, he had drifted through life without apparently doing much except enjoy himself. His wife, the former Helen Pratt, was even richer. Their principal address was 1088 Park Avenue, New York, but they also had homes in Sarasota and Martha's Vineyard. Being rich and idle would probably have caused neither any unease had not Helen's sister been married to Christian Herter, until recently Governor of Massachusetts and lately appointed US Secretary of State. For one sister to be married to a man who had never done anything and another to a high-achiever had given rise to family pressures that had led poor Holladay (Yale, Class of 1913) to ask one of his former professors if there was a project he could undertake that might afford him at least the appearance of being occupied and at the same time enable him to leave behind some sort of scholarly monument. The result is *Parliamentary Representation, 1832, England and Wales* (privately printed, New Haven, 1965), a surprisingly useful handbook that describes the state of England's parliamentary boroughs before and after the Great Reform Bill.

So it was that on the third floor of an office block mainly occupied by realtors, bail bondsmen and debt collectors that I spent the academic year 1959-60 labouring over my two projects. From time to time Holladay motored up from New York to see how things were going. He also had a Major Thomas Ingram, whom he once brought over so we could better coordinate our efforts, assembling material for him in England.

He himself did virtually no work on the project, although he was always meaning to. Once, in a fit of good intentions, he invited Jane and me up to Martha's Vineyard to spend the weekend "really getting things into shape." The invitation was modestly worded, implying that as Martha's Vineyard was merely his summer place and we would therefore have to rough it a bit. This proved to be far from the case. What we found was not the typical New England family residence we had anticipated but a mansion with two so-called "cottages" attached. We got the smaller. Nevertheless, with its umpteen bedrooms, elaborately-equipped kitchen and well-stocked cocktail cabinet it was large enough to have accommodated a large family in comfort.

In the mansion itself, where we had dinner the first night, we were waited on by a butler and maidservants. Famous film stars, so the Philbins told us, had houses nearby. The next morning, when Jane and I took a stroll, we wondered if we had misunderstood, for there was no nearby establishment half as grand as theirs.

I had arrived for the dinner with an armful of files. This, as immediately became apparent, was not in keeping with the nature of the occasion. Before I had even had time to apologise, however, Holliday had started in with his own apology. Since inviting us various pressing engagements had arisen. He would come over first thing in the morning and we could discuss it all then, but he was afraid they would prevent us having quite as much time together as he had planned. He knew I must feel disappointed having worked so hard and trekked all that way but that was just the way it was. In fact I was not in the least disappointed, having arrived feeling guilty at how little I had to show for what he had paid me, it being rather a relief to discover that I was not going to be subjected to the probing investigation I had anticipated.

The reason for his elaborate apology became clear the next morning when it emerged that the pressing engagements to which he alluded involved golf and fishing. Having got me out there, it transpired, I was the last person in the world he wanted to see. But what was he to do with me? He offered to lend us a car so we could see the island. I explained that neither of us had a licence. Very well then, he would lay on a car and a driver to take us on a guided tour. He would also arrange for a succession of meals to be laid on at various stopping places.

Martha's Vineyard is not a large island and in winter there was not a lot to see apart from deserted summer homes and acres of moored boats. Most of our tour, therefore, was spent eating and drinking while our driver, who seemed an uncommunicative sort, sat in the car outside. It was only on the way back, after we had polished off the final lobster and bottle of Chardonnay that I asked him what he did when he wasn't driving people around.

"As a matter of fact, sir, I'm the Deputy Chief of Police here on Martha's Vineyard. Today's my day off but Mr. Philbin is an old friend and I'm always happy to do him a favour."

This set bells ringing. There had been a lot on the news lately about Colonel Abel, the only genuine Russian spy ever to have been infiltrated into the United States and who had allegedly gained entry thanks to having been landing from a submarine somewhere on the New England coast.

"This may sound like a stupid question," I said, "but is looking out for Communists one of the things you do."

"Not a stupid question at all, sir. In fact it's mostly what I do?"

This took me aback. "Really," I said, "what sort of people are they?"

"New Yorkers, writers mostly; they come up here for the summer."

"Yes, but what do they actually do?"

"Well, I'll give you an idea. The other day I'm walking down the street and there's one of these guys, waves over, friendly as can be. The next day, there's the same guy; takes no notice. That's the sort of people they are; you never know where you are with them."

"Yes, but what do they actually *do*?"

"OK, I'll give you another example. We have this PTA meeting, you know parents and teachers. Know what these guys do? Ask for a recount of the votes. That's the sort of people they are; always out to make trouble."

"Right, they're difficult people, but do you think they are actually in touch with the Soviet Union?"

"I don't know about that sir, but they are in touch with the mainland."

I've often wondered if he was the same Deputy Chief of Police who made such a hash of things a few years later when Teddy Kennedy and Mary Jo Kopechne drove off the bridge at Chappaquiddick.

 confidence confidence

With my PhD almost complete and my Fellowship ending, the prospect of unemployment loomed. There were plenty of university jobs I might have got in the United States, but my visa prevented me from taking them. I applied for a post at the newly-established University of the West Indies. A professor from the University of London, who happened to be passing through New Haven, interviewed me for the post. Sam Bemis, on a trip to Jamaica, also put in a word on my behalf, but nothing happened. Tired of waiting, I telephoned.

I had assumed that Jamaica being on the same longitude would be on Eastern Standard Time, but although it was 10.00am in New Haven, when I finally got through to A P Thornton, the Chairman of the UWI History Department, he was still in bed. I asked when I might expect to hear about the job.

"Hard to say, you see I'm off to Toronto."

"Have you any idea when a decision will be made?"

"Can't say, old boy. Do you know Toronto at all?"

"I'm afraid not. But what is happening in Kingston?"

"It's a very strong department they have there at Toronto…"

The cost of all this was terrifying. I had been told the Miami-Kingston link was by radio rather than cable and it certainly sounded that way. In fact, it sounded as though I could hear the waves surging as his voice, rising and falling, became fainter and fainter "…frightfully pleased about it…packing up in the next …." until the roaring of the waves drowned it out entirely.

And that was the last I ever heard from the University of the West Indies.

Meanwhile, unbeknown to me, others had been working on my behalf, in particular Bill Gaines, a shadowy power broker with Yale and US Government connections, whom I would later run into lurking in the background at various conferences. It turned out that Alan Conway, who taught American History at the University of Wales, Aberystwyth, would be away for a year and a substitute was needed. Would I be interested? Indeed I would. In due course a long handwritten letter arrived from Reginald Treharne, the Chairman of the Aberystwyth History Department, offering me the post and explaining the duties involved. Apart from a visit to the fairground at Llandudno I had never visited Wales. Uncertain as to whether the US Post Office would even know where Wales was I addressed my letter of acceptance to "Aberystwyth, Wales, England," in spite of which it was agreed that I would teach at Aberystwyth for a year in return for an annual salary of £800.

So back to England I went, as did the other Yale Fulbrights who had travelled out in the mid-Fifties, Bamber Gascoigne to become a University Challenge quiz master, Norman Foster and Richard Rogers to transform the skylines of London and other world cities, others to take up academic posts, pursue careers in politics and otherwise influence the development of modern Britain. But for my visa problems I would happily have stayed. Malcolm Bradbury, with whom I was destined to have a close working relationship extending over some 40 years, had no such problems. He had a post in Yale's English Department and an immigrant's visa. I told him he was mad to give them up for an assistant lectureship in the extra-mural department of the University of Hull, but he was about to be married and Elizabeth, his fiancé, did not much care for the idea of living in the United States.

My journey back was very different from my journey out. I was now a married man with a job and an academic career in prospect. The salary offered was less than princely but at least I had got a foot on the academic ladder. It was better than becoming a Canadian lumber jack, a desperate expedient that had crossed my mind as being preferable to school teaching. As it turned out I need not have worried, for although the Aberystwyth post was the only one in American history that came up that year, the vast expansion in British university education – and in American Studies in particular – that came in the 1960s meant that for a time there would be more jobs than candidates

But what principally made the return trip different was that I had not finished my PhD dissertation and unless I did so within a week I would have to pay a full year's Graduate School fees. How I would manage to do that out of Aberystwyth's £800 was hard to see.

The Kitzmillers drove us down from New Canaan. There was a crisis at the dockside when we found the car boot containing not only our luggage but our travel documents would not open. It was a hired car and we could not get the key to work. Technical assistance was summoned, there was talk of calling in wreckers, then suddenly, magically, the key worked, the boot opened and we were hurried on board just as the gang planks were being raised. It was one of those archetypal experiences that, along with examination failure, still haunts my dreams.

I had left multiple copies of my dissertation back at New Haven, all neatly typed and ready for binding, so only the conclusion and bibliography remained to be written. In normal circumstances they could have been done in a couple of sittings; in my state of exhaustion they took the whole voyage and more besides. All day long and far into the night I sat in the lounge moving words around. Towards midnight the card players would make their noisy exit. Canoodling couples would wander in off the upper deck and continue canoodling. Then they, too, would take themselves off and men would appear with mops and buckets, and still I went on moving words around.

I mailed the final pages from London. In due course a letter arrived saying that my dissertation had been read and accepted. Never again would I have to sit an examination. No one would ever discover how little I actually knew.

EPILOGUE

AND AFTERWARDS? Well, although often sorely tempted to move back across the Atlantic I stayed in England and pursued an academic career, which is to say I lectured, wrote books, attended conferences, edited a learned journal, even served as chairman of a national association. Whether another career would have suited me as well or better it is impossible to say. Looking back over what I have written suggests I was not cut out to be a vehicle mechanic, a tank commander or a door-to-door salesman. However it also reminds me of how little would have been required for things to have turned out quite differently. The train that killed Eric could just as easily have killed me. Any number of lesser events – a failed Latin examination, a girl found in my bed – could equally well have sent me ricocheting off in quite another direction. That contrary to what I feared and very likely deserved none of them did so astonished me at the time and seems scarcely less astonishing now.

Writing an account of one's own life, as I have latterly discovered, is a very different proposition from writing about the lives of others. There is, of course, the need to resist the temptation of blowing one's own trumpet and paying off old scores. The principal difference, however, is the fact of starting out knowing, or at all events believing one knows, what went on inside the head of the person whose life one is describing. This has obvious advantages as compared with having to rely on the written record or what can be deduced on the basis of people's actions. The disadvantage is that is that what one remembers may not be what actually happened. Of course there are still facts that need to be checked, and to the best of my ability I have done that. Friends have helped too, although sometimes their memories have proven as fallible as my own. Letters and diaries, of which I have over the years managed to amass a large collection, have been useful to the extent that they have reminded me of people's names and of where I was and what I was doing at particular times. Most, in fact, deal with bread-and-butter matters, although here and there are passages I have found worth quoting. I have deliberately spared both myself and my readers my adolescent soul-searchings, partly out of embarrassment but also in the hope that my drawings, quite a few of which I do include, are more indicative of my feelings at the time.

Representing what goes on in the minds of very young children is more of a problem. They, if my memory serves me right, live in a very strange world and in this account I have tried to convey something of that strangeness without going as far as James Joyce does at the beginning of *Portrait of the Artist* and writing in baby language. But how *does* one convey in joined-up sentences what goes on in the minds of those who do not have joined-up thoughts? Did I really think that babies were sold in Woolworth's? It was what my mother told me. Did I really think that the dead calf that I watched coming out of a cow's backside had been eaten by the cow? I had heard of animals eating their young. On the basis of what I knew and had been told the conclusions I came to appeared perfectly logical. Adults are quite capable of believing incompatible things, so it's hardly surprising that children are too. I'm willing to admit, however, that later memories do get substituted for earlier ones and not infrequently people come to believe things that never happened at all. By his later years Kit Carson, the famous Indian fighter, had read so many dime novels in which he featured as a character that when historians came to interview him about what he had actually done they found that he could not distinguish fact from fiction. I hope I have not been guilty of anything so egregious.

A more insidious danger is that memories, particularly those that make good anecdotes, tend to grow, acquiring in the course of repetition details that were not part of the original experience. I have tried to guard myself against that, although, memory being the malleable thing it is, I cannot swear that I have always succeeded. On the other hand, I freely admit that in taking a wry look at myself and the world in which I grew up I may have done an injustice to any number of people, not giving them full credit for their achievements and making them appear more absurd than they actually were. I can only say in defence that when I describe people it is generally speaking by way of indicating how they appeared to me at the time, that is to say to a distinctly fallible witness aged somewhere between 3 and 27 rather than how they appear to me now. How St Peter and the *Oxford Dictionary of National Biography* view them is something else again.

It is also the case that people who impress one when one is young tend to impress one less as one grows older. This applies particularly to the relationship between sons and fathers. If, on this account, I appear to have done a disservice to some I beg forgiveness. When it comes to autobiography, honest reporting and objectivity do not readily go together.

In the process of writing I have accumulated a great many debts, not least to all those friends, acquaintances, and total strangers whom I have plagued with questions about their memories of events that occurred 50 or more years ago. I am particularly grateful, however, to Jane, Tom Arie, Correlli Barnett, David Boll, Bev and Joyce Carss, Gillian Frayn, David Lodge, Bennett Maxwell, Esther O'Callahan, Laurence and Mary Shurman, Ann and Anthony Thwaite and my brother Alan for reading earlier drafts of what I had written, correcting me on points of detail and for advising me on matters of presentation. My wife, Kitty, who has been much involved from first to last, has borne it all with characteristic fortitude.

∾ ∾

I lately revisited some of the places I have mentioned, partly to refresh my memory, partly to see how much they have changed. Having lived through the most remarkable period of economic growth ever recorded, I ought not to have been surprised to find most looking more prosperous than I remembered. All the same, on returning to the North East I had expected to find large expanses of industrial dereliction and was agreeably surprised to find that that was not the case. It was heavy industry that made the North East distinctive. Now all that has gone, and along with it the flat-capped crowds that flocked to football matches, the mums leaning over the fence with their hair in curlers, the old men with hacking coughs sitting on park benches, the raggy boys in their older brothers' left offs, the shoeless toddlers playing in the street. Gone, too, are the trams, slag heaps and pit ponies. It is still the case that Sunderland is a place that few would go out of their way to visit, but its people look much like people elsewhere. They are certainly taller and healthier than their parents and grandparents. Even Silksworth, once the epitome of dreariness and deprivation, has taken on a new life. I'd imagined the old miners' cottages would have been bulldozed away years ago, but not a bit of it. There they still are, standing where they always stood, but spruced-up and pebble-dashed, with satellite dishes on their chimneys and cars parked outside. Up the road, where the colliery dominated the skyline, is the New Silksworth Sports, Recreation and Ski Centre, the slag heap having been turned into a plastic ski slope where locals can practice their slaloms before heading off to Norway or Austria.

Across the river, Monkwearmouth Colliery has been transformed into the improbably named Stadium of Light, home to Sunderland's football team. Close by, where there used to be shipyards, there is a bird-walk with notices identifying the different species. There are fish in the river too, and anglers along its banks. Gone are the cobbled streets that formerly clustered around St Peter's Church, now standing on a green hilltop overlooking the river much as it must have done before the Viking invasions.

Elsewhere in the North East the story was much the same. My old school looks more like a college than the old-fashioned establishment I remember. Usworth aerodrome, from which our gallant Hurricanes flew off to combat the Luftwaffe, is now a Nissan car factory, allegedly the most efficient in the country. The change that would probably have most astonished J B Priestley is the transformation of Gateshead from the dead-end town he visited into a major metropolitan centre complete with hotels offering a range of conference facilities and even a concert hall.

At its MetroCentre, said to be the largest out-of-town shopping complex in Europe, I picked up a copy of *Geordies*, a collection of essays arising out of a conference sponsored by the University of Newcastle and published by Northumbria University Press. As might be expected, there are those who lament the passing of the old ways. A former shipyard worker is quoted as saying that, ill-paid though he had been, he had got a degree of satisfaction from building a ship that he would never get from flipping hamburgers. Much of the essay writers' spleen is directed at the way the region's boosters are attempting to expunge the memory of its industrial past by going back to the Middle Ages, calling County Durham "The Land of the Prince Bishops" and reinventing "Northumbria."

The critics have a point. All the same, I came away impressed by the transformation that had occurred. Priestley described the North East as a "hideous muddle, where industry had had a dirty black meal and had done no washing up." The region needed re-inventing, and to a large extent the washing up has now been done. My sympathies, therefore, are on the side of the boosters, and although I can't say I'm aesthetically moved by Antony

Gormley's Angel of the North (referred to locally as the Gateshead flasher), it gives the region something it had previously lacked by way of a recognisable symbol. And if parts of Gateshead do now look like Dallas, it is hardly a matter for regret. The Dallas I visited back in the 1950s was certainly a more exciting place than the old Gateshead.

I doubt, though, that I would find the Dallas of today as exhilarating as the one I visited. Then it exhibited the brash extravagance later captured by the television series of the same name. To a world not yet fully recovered from the ravages of war it offered a tantalising vision of future growth and prosperity. As an impressionable new arrival in the United States I was persuaded, as also were many Americans, that not only was exponential economic growth something genuinely new but that it would simply go on for ever. Today this looks like a pipe dream. Unforeseen back in the 1950s was the way the excess wealth created would go preponderantly to the rich or the heavy price that would have to be paid in the form of environmental degradation. Of course most Americans are now far richer than they were during Eisenhower's presidency and much that appeared breathtakingly new then appears quite old-fashioned now. All the same, travelling by Amtrak through what was formerly America's industrial heartland; the sight of abandoned factories and derelict warehouses bears witness to the fact that the United States has ceased to be the role model it once appeared. No longer does it stand head and shoulders above other countries in terms of per capita income. Indeed, with regard to health care, life expectancy, the incidence of crime and other indicators of social progress it lags behind many other developed nations.

Nevertheless, for most Americans as for those living in the developed world generally, the changes of the past 50 years have mainly been for the better. The Europe into which I was born was spinning out of control. It is now not only far more politically stable but also much more prosperous. We know more too. My parents, and even more my grandparents, would be astonished by the things that we in the West now take for granted, like having our food flown in from distant places and having ready access to knowledge through the World Wide Web. Nor is it just a question of being better fed and having easier access to knowledge. We also tend to live longer and to encounter the disabilities of old age later. In this respect at least an unprecedented change *does* seem to have occurred. A western child born today, so we are told, stands a 50-50 chance of living to be 100.

I doubt the century just begun will prove any less eventful than the one lately past. So far at any rate there is no sign of any slowing down. Today the fear is no longer of our being conquered and enslaved or of our being engulfed in a nuclear holocaust, as for a time seemed all too likely. Rather it is that on account of the rate at which we are depleting the world's resources we will leave behind a world much poorer than the one we inherited.

But whatever the future, for children one thing at least will remain the same, namely their experience of waking up and finding themselves in a world of which they have no knowledge, a society of whose social norms they are unaware and whose language they do not as yet speak. In these pages I have sought to convey a sense of the excitement and wonder I felt exploring the mid-twentieth century world into which I happened to have been born. I have dedicated this book to my grandchildren. I hope that they and their contemporaries will feel the same sense of excitement and wonder exploring their worlds that I did exploring mine.

THE END

Lightning Source UK Ltd.
Milton Keynes UK
UKHW010659200820
368544UK00001B/25